Also available

*Compensation to Palestinian Refugees and
the Search for Palestinian–Israeli Peace*
Edited by Rex Brynen and Roula El-Rifai

The Palestinian Refugee Problem

The Search for a Resolution

Edited by
Rex Brynen and Roula El-Rifai

www.plutobooks.com

First published 2014 by Pluto Press
345 Archway Road, London N6 5AA

www.plutobooks.com

Distributed in the United States of America exclusively by
Palgrave Macmillan, a division of St. Martin's Press LLC,
175 Fifth Avenue, New York, NY 10010

British Library Cataloguing in Publication Data
A catalogue record for this book is available from the British Library

ISBN   978 0 7453 3344 1   Hardback
ISBN   978 0 7453 3338 0   Paperback
ISBN   978 1 8496 4819 6   PDF eBook
ISBN   978 1 8496 4821 9   Kindle eBook
ISBN   978 1 8496 4820 2   EPUB eBook

Library of Congress Cataloging in Publication Data applied for

10 9 8 7 6 5 4 3 2 1

Typeset from disk by Stanford DTP Services, Northampton, England
Text design by Melanie Patrick
Simultaneously printed digitally by CPI Antony Rowe, Chippenham, UK and
Edwards Bros in the United States of America

Contents

List of Figures

List of Tables

List of Annexes

Preface

This book is the third in a series on the Palestinian refugee issue, the result of two decades of engagement by the International Development Research Centre (IDRC) and others on thinking about solutions to the Palestinian refugee problem in the broader context of the Middle East peace process. The first volume, *Palestinian Refugees: Challenges of Repatriation and Development* (I.B. Tauris, 2007), and the second, *Compensation to Palestinian Refugees and the Search for Palestinian–Israeli Peace* (Pluto Press, 2013), both also edited by Rex Brynen and Roula El-Rifai, examined in detail the concepts of repatriation to a Palestinian state and compensation to refugees, both of which need to be addressed to allow for a resolution of the refugee problem.

This book provides a discussion of all key aspects of a solution to the Palestinian refugee problem, presenting a menu of policy options with a stakeholder cost-benefit analysis, rather than a blueprint for a solution. This is a typical approach for IDRC, which as a research donor, strives to promote evidence-based analysis which can influence policy processes. Thus, it is hoped that the knowledge presented in this book will be helpful to scholars and policymakers and will feed into the Palestinian–Israeli negotiations, now and in the future.

IDRC began its involvement on the refugee issue in 1992 through a programme of research called the 'Expert and Advisory Services Fund' (EASF), managed since 1999 by Roula El-Rifai. EASF aimed to support thinking about solutions to the refugee problem through knowledge development and support to policy networks on the refugee file. EASF supported Canada's role as Gavel of the Refugee Working Group as part of the multilateral track of the negotiations. The programme was funded by the Canadian International Development Agency (CIDA) and IDRC, in collaboration with Canada's Department of Foreign Affairs, Trade and Development (DFATD).

Over the years, the EASF contribution to the refugee issue through support to research and policy debates has been substantial. Thematically, EASF has supported activities on the issues of repatriation to a Palestinian state, compensation and reparations to

Palestinian refugees, public opinion, as well as host country issues. The EASF programme has also supported the work of the Palestinian Authority and the Government of Lebanon aimed at coordinating research and policy work on the refugee issue and learning from the experience and expertise of others.

In the last few years, EASF has focused its efforts on Lebanon, aiming to capitalize on a political opening to improve the situation of Palestinians in that country through work with the Government of Lebanon, the Prime Minister's Office and Palestinian NGOs. In addition, IDRC focused recently on the issue of implementation mechanisms for a refugee agreement and the detailed thinking about what needs to be done, when and by whom to pave the way for a smooth and sustainable implementation of an agreement. This book discusses these issues.

Through the EASF, IDRC convened three major international conferences on the Palestinian refugee issue, two stocktaking conferences on Palestinian refugee research in 2003 and 2007, and one on the issue of compensation in 1999. These conferences were part of what came to be dubbed the 'Ottawa Process', which consisted of informal discussions and meetings between Palestinians, Israelis, host country officials and Palestinian refugees, to support research and promote policy debates on solutions.

In coordination with DFADT, EASF and its partners participated in briefings to regional governments and the broader international community on the state of knowledge on the technical aspects of a refugee solution.

With IDRC support, the Palestinian Refugee ResearchNet (PRRN) was also established. In addition to its continuing regular email newsletter on the refugee issue, PRRN hosts a website (www.prrn.org) which provided a comprehensive, substantive and unique repository of knowledge on refugee research and policy work, including IDRC-supported work. More recently, it has maintained a blog (htpp://prrnblog.wordpress.com) which provides analysis and offers a forum for debate on this issue.

As mentioned, this book builds on the extensive experience of IDRC and that of others. In addition to many individuals, experts and scholars, including the authors of the chapters in this book, IDRC has worked closely over the years with many institutions and NGOs and governments, which has helped make the state of knowledge on the refugee issue what it is today. It is impossible to mention all, but we will mention a few. IDRC worked closely with Chatham House, which has managed a programme on the regional aspect of the refugee issue since 1996. Fafo, the Norwegian social science research institute, helped to develop and continues to develop important data on Palestinian refugees and their living conditions. The World Bank was instrumental in developing economic analysis as part of a solution, and Israel's Economic Cooperation Foundation developed thinking on the costing out of a solution. The Palestinian Negotiations Support Unit (NSU) participated in many Palestinian refugee activities and EASF and its partners benefited greatly from the NSU expert staff feedback on much of our work. EASF also benefited greatly from the expertise of staff of the International Organization for Migration on such issues as claims mechanisms and implementation mechanisms for peace agreements.

At the time of publication of this book, the editors are pessimistic about the current 'Middle East Peace Process'. We are also well aware of the deteriorating situation of Palestinian refugees in the region, especially those affected by the ongoing civil war in Syria. However, through this book, the editors hope to ensure that much of the knowledge generated over the years about solutions to the refugee problem, through IDRC and many others, will be preserved and thus available to stakeholders when and if they need it. Regardless of the framework that might be adopted for any future peace, it is our belief that without attention to the refugee problem, there will be no end to this conflict. We hope this book represents a modest contribution to thinking about and designing workable solutions.

Acknowledgements

This book would not have been possible without the support of many individuals and institutions. Thanks go to the International Development Research Centre (IDRC) for funding the publication and for funding the work of the EASF programme. The opinions expressed in this volume are those of the editors and the authors and not necessarily those of IDRC. We would like to express our thanks to CIDA for its financial support to EASF from 1992–2008. We are grateful to DFATD and to all the Canadian Gavels of the Refugee Working Group and Coordinators of the Middle East Peace Process at DFATD, for their general support to EASF activities. Special thanks go to DFATD's Global Peace and Security Fund, which supported IDRC activities on the refugee issue in 2011–2012, including the work which contributed to this publication.

Roula El-Rifai would like to thank Allan Thompson and Laith Rifai-Thompson for their support of her work on this file over the years. Rex Brynen would also like to thank the Social Science and Humanities Research Council of Canada, the United States Institute for Peace and McGill University for their support of his research in this area. The co-editors certainly thank all the contributors to this volume as well as the participants in EASF-funded activities. These include a great number of current and former officials in Palestine, Israel, the Arab world, Canada and the international community, who through their participation and encouragement of various initiatives on the refugee issue, contributed a great deal to enriching knowledge on this issue. We owe an equal debt to those in the academic and NGO research communities whose contributions on this issue have been invaluable.

Thanks go to Megan Bradley and Mark Mattner for their editorial assistance. We are also grateful to Pluto Press for having been so encouraging and very patient throughout the production process.

It is possible when talking about complex technical issues, as in this book, to forget that what we are really dealing with is people's lives and their hopes for a peaceful, safe and secure future. In this spirit, we would like to acknowledge Palestinian refugees themselves, who have suffered for far too long in the Palestinian–Israeli conflict. We hope that the knowledge contained in this volume holds out the prospect of moving closer to finally resolving their plight.

1

Research, Policy and Negotiations and Resolving the Palestinian Refugee Problem

Rex Brynen and Roula El-Rifai

F our core assumptions about the Palestinian refugee issue
underpin much of what this book is about. First, as editors, we
believe that the refugee issue will not somehow go away. The
forced displacement and continued involuntary exile of the Palestinian
people is a core element of Palestinian identity, a source of continuing
injustice and a key component of the Israeli–Palestinian conflict.
Achievement of a just and lasting Israeli–Palestinian peace will require
that the issue be resolved. Second, we hold the view that if peace is
ever to be achieved in the coming decades, it will be achieved through
negotiations and will likely be based on some version of a two-state
paradigm. Third, we consider that negotiations are facilitated by
making policy-relevant research and analysis available to all of the key
stakeholders, so as to inform the positions which they adopt and the
choices that they make. Fourth – and closely related to the third point –
we would also suggest that the sustainability of an agreement is likely
to be enhanced if it is based on solid principles, good data, productive
understanding, adequate resources and appropriate mechanisms. The
key purpose of this volume, therefore, is to advance the prospects for
an eventual resolution of the Israeli–Palestinian conflict by offering a

thorough analysis of the various issues and challenges that any future negotiations on the refugee issue will face.

That being said, there are a great many things that this volume does *not* assume. We certainly do not assume that successful permanent status negotiations are likely to happen any time soon. On the contrary, we tend to be rather pessimistic on that score, given a combination of Palestinian political divisions, a hardening of Israeli positions, rapidly-changing conditions on the ground, an uncertain regional environment and faltering diplomatic leadership from the international community.

We also do not assume that the negotiating frameworks and approaches that have been adopted in the past will necessarily be those that will be used in the future. Local, regional and even international circumstances are constantly changing. Achieving peace through a single agreement that resolves all permanent status issues may no longer be feasible, although partial, interim and transitional deals would contain (as the early Oslo era demonstrated) dangers all of their own. The two-state paradigm might itself even need to undergo some reconceptualization, especially as continued Israeli occupation and settlement of the Palestinian territories creates new obstacles to peace.

Despite this, we believe that the concept of a 'one-state' solution would pose great challenges. If the two sides have been unable thus far to settle their differences on the basis of political separation, it is hard to imagine how some form of unification would be easier – especially given the fundamental attachment of the overwhelming majority of Israeli Jews to preserving Israel as a Jewish state and the commitment of most Palestinians to achieving a sovereign Palestinian state in the West Bank and Gaza. We also believe it is unlikely that the future of the Palestinian territories can be resolved through some sort of political condominium with Jordan, as some right-wing Israeli commentators have suggested. Permanent occupation within a system that continues to deny Palestinians basic political rights is also not viable in the long term,[1] but for the time being, it seems to be tolerated by Israelis and the international community alike.

Indeed, it is the tragic combination outlined above – a refugee issue that will continue to be of importance, coupled with an uncertain political future in which diplomatic prospects seem dim – that gives rise to the contents and approach of this volume. In the chapters that follow, expert contributors have been asked to address each of the major aspects of the refugee issue. The topics covered include designing appropriate implementation mechanisms; the future role of the United Nations Relief and Works Agency (UNRWA) in implementing an agreement; questions of return, repatriation and residency; the attitudes of host countries; refugee compensation/ reparations; the question of claims by Jewish refugees; absorption and development; moral acknowledgement and other 'intangibles'; managing refugee expectations; and end of claims. Contributors are not offering one single diagnosis or set of recommendations. Rather, they explore the interests and concerns of all sides, synthesize earlier and ongoing research, and suggest a broad menu of possible policy options. Our hope is to provide analysis that will be of lasting value, flexible enough to remain relevant despite future changes of actors, circumstances and negotiating frameworks.

Research and Negotiations on the Refugee Issue, 1991–2012

The value of offering an overview and synthesis of key policy issues and policy-relevant research is heightened by the particular way in which the work of scholars and non-governmental institutions on the refugee issue has – and has not – affected negotiating processes in the past.

Prior to the start of the peace process in the early 1990s, research on resolution of the refugee issue was rather limited.[2] The various political sensitivities and taboos associated with the issue also limited the ways in which it was addressed. The historical narratives of the two sides stood in stark opposition to each other. Palestinian refugee advocates emphasized rights, grievances and historical injustices, but tended to pay much less attention to questions of negotiation approaches, trade-offs and mechanisms. Few Israeli scholars addressed the refugee issue at all, although the work of Israeli revisionist historians did begin to cast new light on the degree of forced displacement that had taken place from 1947–49.[3] Very few Israeli policymakers gave the issue much thought – it was, in many ways, the issue they hoped would go away.

This situation began to slowly change during the mid-1990s, in part because of the onset of the Middle East Peace Process itself at Madrid in 1991 and the research interest this attracted.[4] Some work was also encouraged, both officially and unofficially, through the Refugee Working Group (RWG) of the multilateral component of that peace process. In its 1995 'vision paper' for the Group, the Canadian Gavel of the RWG called upon the international community to support more policy research on the issue that would 'aim at providing the kind of mutually-accepted, objective and policy-relevant data required to inform negotiating processes, underwrite political decisions and define solutions, support the implementation of existing agreements, and facilitate the conclusion of future understandings.' It also called for efforts to 'promote additional mechanisms for encouraging dialogue, identifying, developing and testing options, and generating political scenarios' that would harness the energies and insights of 'civil societies of the region, the NGO, media and academic communities.' The paper suggested that 'Such energetic activity in support of the peace process – and the various models, scenarios, initiatives and formulations that it has generated – should be encouraged, circulated, and, where useful and appropriate, built upon.'[5] Although the Refugee Working Group would slowly wind down its activities in the latter half of the 1990s, Canadian engagement on the refugee issue would continue for more than a decade thereafter.

With the support of the RWG, Norway, and other governments, the Norwegian social science research institution Fafo began work in the 1990s on an ambitious series of studies on refugee living conditions and related issues, work that has continued up until the present day.[6] Through the International Development Research Centre (IDRC), Canada supported the 'Ottawa process', a broad array of unofficial conferences, workshops, and informal, track-two discussions between Israelis and Palestinians to encourage research and support negotiations.[7] IDRC also supported a variety of research projects undertaken by Israeli, Palestinian, Arab and international scholars, and NGOs. This period also saw the establishment, also with IDRC support, of the Palestinian Refugee ResearchNet (PRRN), an internet-based project that features a website, blog and daily email newsletter on refugee research and policy.[8]

With support from IDRC, the UK, the European Union and other donors, Chatham House also launched an extended series of meetings on the regional dimensions of the refugee issue.[9] This 'Minster Lovell

Process' (named after the small Oxfordshire village where many of the meetings took place) facilitated off-the-record Palestinian–Arab dialogue on a series of sensitive refugee-related issues, often with the participation of both scholars and a small number of international diplomats.

Starting in 1999 (and extending through until 2003), the World Bank undertook almost a dozen major studies that examined various economic dimensions of the refugee issue, with particular attention to the costs of refugee camp improvements, and the costs and policy modalities of refugee repatriation. These studies – undertaken with full cooperation from Jordan and the Palestinian Authority, and with tacit approval from Israel – were never formally published, but findings were shared with the major parties. Some summary information on some of the key findings was also published elsewhere.[10]

Within Israel a small but growing number of academics began to work on policy-relevant aspects of the refugee issue. The Economic Cooperation Foundation (some of whose senior members had been involved in the 1993 Oslo negotiations that led to the establishment of the Palestinian Authority) played a critical role, especially when Yossi Beilin and others took up positions with the Labor-led government of Prime Minister Ehud Barak (1999–2001).[11] On the Palestinian side, international donors helped to finance the establishment of the Negotiations Support Unit (NSU) to strengthen Palestinian policy analysis capacities, including those related to the refugee issue.[12] Refugee advocacy groups – most notably the BADIL Resource Center for Palestinian Residency and Refugee Rights, established in 1998 – produced detailed analyses of refugee conditions and legal assessments of their rights, and lobbied Palestinian negotiators to pursue a rights-based approach in negotiations.[13]

Such efforts dramatically increased the quality and quantity of available research on refugees. Considerable work was done (albeit, often at the last minute) in the run-up to the Camp David negotiations in July 2000. At Camp David itself, however, the negotiators rarely got beyond opening declaratory positions and clashing narratives on the refugee issue.[14] Indeed, Palestinian negotiator Akram Hanieh would later call the refugee committee 'the greatest failure of the summit.'[15]

Far more detailed and substantial negotiations – including the exchange of detailed drafts, as well as an Israeli 'non-paper' that attempted to develop a compromise position – took place at the Taba negotiations in January 2001.[16] Those permanent status negotiations failed, however, amid the violence of the Second Intifada, the collapse of the Barak government, and the February 2001 election of Ariel Sharon as Prime Minister of Israel. How much progress was achieved at Taba is contested. Some Israeli commentators have suggested that the Israeli refugee negotiating team had been too willing to make compromises, and that their positions did not fully enjoy government support. Similarly, some Palestinians also criticized their side for being too flexible. In an unofficial meeting held in Europe later that same year, the former refugee negotiators on both sides expressed the view that they had made real progress, and that (in the broader context of a peace agreement) agreement on the refugee issue was also possible.[17] Several elements from the Taba negotiations (and, indeed, several of the negotiators from Taba) were key in the development of the Geneva Accord, a 2003 document in which Israeli and Palestinian academics, activists, and current and former officials offered a model of a possible peace agreement, including a detailed section and annex on refugees.[18] In March 2002, the 22 member states of the Arab League endorsed the 'Arab Peace Initiative' at a meeting in Beirut, Lebanon sponsored by King Abdullah of Saudi Arabia. The initiative called for the withdrawal of Israel from Palestinian territories occupied since June 1967 and the establishment of an independent Palestinian state with East Jerusalem as its capital, 'in return for the establishment of normal relations in the context of a comprehensive peace with Israel.'[19] Although contested by Israel, the initiative formally affirmed for the first time the regional nature of a resolution to the Palestinian–Israeli conflict, including the Palestinian refugee issue.

During the next several years of the Sharon government no permanent status talks were held between Israelis and the Palestinians. However, ongoing projects by academics, think-tanks, NGOs and others did offer some continued analytical momentum on the issue. IDRC supported research on a range of topics, including the challenges of refugee repatriation;[20] the situation of Palestinian refugees in host countries,[21] with a recent focus on Lebanon, including support to the Lebanese–Palestinian Dialogue Committee in the Prime Minister's Office;[22] and property restitution and compensation with a recent focus on learning from experiences, practices and lessons learned from other reparation processes to inform the design of an appropriate implementation mechanism for solutions provided in a peace agreement on the Palestinian refugee issue.[23] Other notable policy-relevant work included that done by the Aix Group on the costs of a refugee agreement,[24] various projects at the University of Exeter,[25] the continued 'Minster Lovell Process' organized by Chatham House, and research and analysis by the Palestinian Negotiations Support Unit, Fafo, BADIL and others.[26]

Permanent status negotiations were only rejoined after Ehud Olmert became prime minister in Israel, with the so-called 'Annapolis round' of talks in 2007–08. While there were conceptual discussions on the refugees (largely revolving around possible numbers that might return, and discussion on some issues of modalities and mechanisms), this did not reach the level of detail that had been achieved at Taba.[27] Moreover, positions had hardened in the intervening years, with Olmert prepared to accept the return of only 5,000 refugees compared to the much larger numbers mooted by Israeli negotiators in 2001.[28] At Taba, the Israeli side had suggested 25,000 persons over three years, or 40,000 over five, with refugee return to be resolved over a 15-year period. This seemed to suggest a minimum of 25,000–40,000 persons, with the possibility of more on a generous reading.

In 2009, the political context shifted again as a new Israeli government under Prime Minister Benjamin Netanyahu assumed office. Since then, the Israeli government has placed greater emphasis on the counter-claims of Jews who were forcibly displaced from Arab countries, or to cast doubt on whether Palestinians have a legitimate claim to refugee status at all.[29] On the Palestinian side, continued political divisions and pessimism regarding negotiations provide little incentive to talk about the issue or signal any sort of future flexibility. More broadly, many doubt whether there remains any 'peace process' at all.[30] Despite this, in August 2013 the US government succeeded in once more coaxing the parties back to the negotiating table – although with what effect remains to be seen.

Linking Research, Negotiations, and Policy

While the surge in research on Palestinian refugees since the 1990s has undoubtedly been a good thing, it does not automatically follow that research on the issue automatically has influence on policy or negotiations. On the contrary, serious disconnects have often characterized the relationship between the two.

This disconnect was highlighted in June 2008, when Chatham House held three days of simulated refugee negotiations involving academics and (current and former) officials from Israel, Palestine, the Arab world and the international community. Among other things, the exercise showed the extent to which negotiators could become enveloped within a 'negotiation bubble' that could act as a barrier to outside ideas and feedback; underscored the technical complexity of implementing a refugee deal, and the policy analysis work that still needed to be done on this; and pointed to the need to engage both refugees and experts more effectively.[31]

One key problem has been that of simple *communication*: scholars do not necessarily interact with policymakers on the issue, and vice versa. Immersed in the pressure of day-to-day events, policymakers might have little time to develop a broad expertise on the topic. Scholars, by contrast, may not be well informed on the details of political and diplomatic developments, especially when these have not been covered in any detail in the regular media. They also tend to assume that policy debates and negotiations are won through well-crafted arguments, and hence pay too little attention to questions of diplomatic strategy, political context or modalities. Informal workshops under Chatham House-type rules of non-attribution can help bridge this gap and create informal networks that often continue once the meeting is over. Palestinian Refugee ResearchNet was also established to try to bridge this gap, with its associated FOFOGNET email list reaching more than three hundred researchers, diplomats, aid officials, NGOs and journalists each day.[32]

A second, more sporadic problem has been that of *political sensitivity*. In the past, the principal parties as well as others have sometimes discouraged research work that does not appear to be aligned with their negotiating positions. This problem has usually become more severe whenever permanent status talks have approached, with second-track or policy analysis being discouraged on the grounds that it might interfere with the sensitive negotiations. Because of this, the international community itself failed to even have serious discussions about how it might support the refugee dimension of any breakthrough in the peace process until December 2000, almost a decade after the peace process had begun in Madrid in 1991.[33]

A third challenge has been that of *knowledge-management*, or what is sometimes termed the 'shelf-life' of relevant policy analysis. Within the Israeli government there has rarely been any locus of responsibility or knowledge on the refugee issue, and few with any expertise in it. While at times (notably in 2000–01) policymakers reached out to scholars and think-tanks, at other times negotiations moved forward on a surprisingly narrow knowledge-base, further aggravated by personnel changes when governments change. The Palestinians, by contrast, have had a degree of institutional memory embedded within the NSU, as well as by the political continuity of many senior negotiators. While this continuity undoubtedly contributed positively to the amount of expertise available on the issue, it could also have the effect of senior negotiators relying on their own personal knowledge rather than adequately reaching back to others (from within the NSU, the PLO Department of Refugee Affairs, the Ministry of Planning and elsewhere) for relevant information and insights. In the case of the international community, regular personnel rotations and the passage of time has meant that policy-relevant knowledge or negotiations experience which might have been available at one time could be forgotten several years later. In the case of the World Bank's voluminous research on the possible costs and approaches to refugee repatriation, for example, none was ever formally published – and, a decade later, it was doubtful whether any of the World Bank staff working on Palestine knew of the content of this body of research, or even of its existence.

The linkage between negotiations, policy and research has also been shaped by the *nature of the negotiations themselves*. These have tended to be dominated, understandably, by those with political experience and/or legal expertise. By contrast, the social, economic and technical aspects of a refugee agreement (and its eventual implementation) have tended to be under-represented, both in terms of personnel and analysis. This is a particularly costly shortcoming, given that a finely-balanced political compromise could well unravel if it is not practical on the ground.

All of these problems have been compounded by the on-again, off-again nature of negotiations too. The result is a somewhat bipolar tendency to shift from periods of sudden interest in refugees – with a tendency to reinvent the wheel every time rather than build on past knowledge about solutions – to extended periods of considering the topic rather marginal to current concerns.

Finally, there is the problem of *synthesis*. With much now written on the refugee issue from so many different perspectives, it can be difficult for policymakers to pick out what might be most valuable for them. This book is one such attempt at synthesizing policy research for research and policy audiences alike.

Final Words

We believe that the analyses offered in this volume will not be the last word on the many political, technical and other complexities that surround the refugee issue. Its publication cannot fully resolve the disconnects between research, policy and negotiations, nor can it account for the passage of time and events on the ground that have the potential to change the frameworks and lens through which we view solutions. More importantly, all the knowledge generated through this volume and others cannot substitute for political will, an essential ingredient for any resolution of the Palestinian–Israeli conflict.

However, this volume is a modest contribution to thinking about workable solutions for the Palestinian refugee problem. It represents an attempt to ensure that this thinking is in the public domain, that knowledge generated will not be lost to the vagaries of the peace process and lack of institutional memory and will one day be beneficial to both scholars and policymakers alike. We hope that our contributions – together with the efforts of many others in the research community – represent a positive step towards thinking that solutions are in the realm of the possible, even to seemingly intractable problems such as that of the Palestinian refugees.

Notes

1. For a critical discussion of these issues, see Asher Susser, *Israel, Jordan and Palestine: The Two-State Imperative* (Waltham MA: Brandeis University Press, 2012).
2. A notable exception was the work on the documentation and valuation of refugee properties, including the work of the United Nations Conciliation Commission for Palestine in the 1950s and 1960s, as well as research by

researchers such as Yusuf Sayigh, Sami Hadawi, Atif Kubursi and Salman Abu Sitta. For a comprehensive overview, see Michael Fischbach, *Records of Dispossession: Palestinian Refugee Property and the Arab–Israeli Conflict* (New York: Columbia University Press, 2003).

3. Benny Morris, *The Birth of the Palestinian Refugee Problem, 1947–49* (Cambridge: Cambridge University Press, 1987); Benny Morris, *The Birth of the Palestinian Refugee Problem Revisited* (Cambridge: Cambridge University Press, 2004); Ilan Pappe, *The Ethnic Cleansing of Palestine* (Oxford: Oneworld Publications, 2006).

4. For examples of work spurred by the start of the Middle East Peace Process, see Don Peretz, *Palestinian Refugees and the Middle East Peace Process* (Washington DC: United States Institute of Peace Press, 1993); Shlomo Gazit, *The Palestinian Refugee Problem* (Tel Aviv: Jaffee Center for Strategic Studies, 1995); Salim Tamari, *Palestinian Refugee Negotiations: From Madrid to Oslo II* (Washington DC: Institute for Palestine Studies, 1996); Elia Zurek, Palestinian Refugees and the Peace Process (Washington DC: Institute for Palestine Studies, 1996); Donna Arzt, *Refugees Into Citizens: Palestinians and the End of the Arab–Israeli Conflict* (New York: Council on Foreign Relations, 1997).

5. Department of Foreign Affairs and International Trade (Canada), 'A Vision of the New Middle East: A Perspective from the Refugee Working Group', draft 6, Ottawa, 1995. Available online via Palestinian Refugee ResearchNet at: http://prrn.mcgill.ca/research/documents/DFAIT-vision6.pdf.

6. An overview of some (but by no means all) of Fafo's work can be found at: www.fafo.no/ais/middeast/palestinianrefugees/index.htm

7. For a detailed account of this, see Rex Brynen, Eileen Alma, Joel Peters, Roula el-Rifai and Jill Tansley. 'The "Ottawa Process": An Examination of Canada's Track Two Involvement in the Palestinian Refugee Issue', paper presented to the IDRC Stocktaking II Conference on Palestinian Refugee Research, Ottawa, 17–20 June 2003. Available online at: http://network. idrc.ca/uploads/user-S/10576789140Session_3_BRYNEN_OTTAWA_PROCESS_PAPER.doc

8. See Palestinian Refugee ResearchNet at: http://www.prrn.org

9. For details of the Minster Lovell Process, see the Chatham House website at: www.chathamhouse.org/research/middle-east/current-projects/minster-lovell-process

10. See, in particular, the chapters by Rex Brynen, Nick Krafft, Ann Elwan and Rachelle Alterman in Rex Brynen and Roula El-Rifai (eds), *Palestinian Refugees: Challenges of Repatriation and Development* (London: I.B. Tauris, 2007).

11. Beilin served as Deputy Foreign Minister (1992–95) and then as Minister of Justice (1999–2001), and headed the refugee negotiating team at the Taba negotiations in January 2001. Other members of ECF also served on the negotiating teams, or in advisory roles. See Yossi Beilin, *Touching Peace: From the Oslo Accord to a Final Agreement* (London: Weidenfeld & Nicolson, 1999); and Yossi Beilin, *The Path to Geneva: The Quest for a Permanent Agreement, 1996–2004* (New York: RDV Books, 2004).

12. The sort of work done by the NSU became public in January 2011 when some 1,684 memoranda, reports and other files were leaked to the television station Al Jazeera. The documents themselves can be found online at: www. aljazeera.com/palestinepapers/, while analysis of those related to refugees in particular can be found at the Palestinian Refugee ResearchNet blog at: http://prrnblog.wordpress.com/category/palestine-papers/

13. See the BADIL website at: www.badil.org

14. See Dennis Ross, *The Missing Peace: The Inside Story of the Fight for Middle East Peace* (New York: Farrar, Straus and Giroux, 2004). See also Clayton Swisher, *The Truth About Camp David: the Untold Story of the Collapse of the Middle East Peace Process* (New York: Nation Books, 2004); Gilead Sher, *The Israeli–Palestinian Peace Negotiations, 1999–2001: Within Reach* (London: Routledge, 2006); Robert Malley and Hussein Agha, 'Camp David: The Tragedy of Errors', *The New York Review of Books*, 9 August 2001; and Jeremy Pressman, 'Visions in Collision: What Happened at Camp David and Taba?' *International Security* 28, 2 (Fall 2003).

15. Akram Hanieh, 'The Camp David Papers', *Journal of Palestine Studies* 30, 2 (Winter 2011), p. 82.

16. For the text of negotiating positions presented by the two sides at Taba, see Rex Brynen, *The Past as Prelude? Negotiating the Palestinian Refugee Issue* (London: Chatham House, June 2008), online at: www.chathamhouse.org/publications/papers/view/108831

17. Specifically, they agreed that 'The failure to fully resolve the refugee issue was a product of time constraints rather than inability to make progress.' and that 'At Taba we proved it can be done, the refugee issue is not an obstacle to a comprehensive agreement.' From summary points of the meeting (taken by one of the authors), July 2001.

18. For the text of the Accord, see the Geneva Initiative website at: www. geneva-accord.org. For discussion of the refugee component of the document, see Rex Brynen, 'The Geneva Accord and the Palestinian Refugee Issue', paper prepared for a meeting of the No Name Group, 29 February 2004, online at: http://prrn.mcgill.ca/research/papers/geneva_refugees_2.pdf; and Menachim Klein, *A Possible Peace Between Israel and Palestine: An Insider's Account of the Geneva Initiative* (New York: Columbia University Press, 2007).

19. For the full text of the API, go to: www.al-bab.com/arab/docs/league/peace02.htm

20. See Michael Dumper (ed.), *Palestinian Refugee Repatriation: Global Perspectives* (London: Routledge, 2006); and Brynen and el-Rifai (eds), *Palestinian Refugees: The Challenges of Repatriation and Development* (2007).

21. See Souheil El-Natour and Dalal Yassine, *The Legal Status of Palestine Refugees in Lebanon and the Demands of Adjustment* (Beirut: Human Development Center, 2007); Oroub El-Abed, *Unprotected: Palestinian in Egypt Since 1948* (Washington DC: Institute for Palestine Studies, 2009); and Souheil El-Natour, *Palestinians and the Amendments of the Labour Law and Social Security* (October 2010) and *Impact on Palestinian Refugees of the Amendment to the 2001 Lebanese Property Law* (March 2012).

22. Rex Brynen, *Building a Better Relationship: Palestinian Refugees, Lebanon and the Role of the International Community*, (June 2009) online at: www.mcgill.ca/files/icames/BuildingABetterRelationship.pdf

23. See International Organization for Migration, *Property Restitution and Compensation: Practices and Experiences of Claims Programmes* (Geneva: International Organization for Migration, 2008), online at: www.iom.int/jahia/webdav/site/myjahiasite/shared/shared/mainsite/published_docs/books/Property_Restitution_and_Compensation.pdf; and Rex Brynen and Roula el-Rifai (eds), *Compensation to Palestinian Refugees and the Search for Palestinian–Israeli Peace* (London: Pluto Press, 2012); Also, see Heike Niebergall and Norbert Wühler (IOM), Development of Three 'Technical Options Papers on Aspects of a Just and Comprehensive Solution for Palestinian Refugees', on the subjects of *Inheritance Regimes, Organizational Structures, and Legal Closure*, November 2012, prepared for IDRC.

24. Arie Arnon and Saeb Bamya (eds), *Economic Dimensions of a Two-State Agreement Between Israel and Palestine* (Marseille: Aix Group, 2007). For this and other works, see the Aix Group website at: www.aixgroup.org

25. See Michael Dumper, *The Future for Palestinian Refugees: Toward Equity and Peace* (Boulder: Lynne Rienner Publishers, 2007).

26. Among studies with particular policy relevance, see Robert Bowker, *Palestinian Refugees: Mythology, Identity, and the Search for Peace* (Boulder: Lynne Rienner, 2003); and Shahira Samy, *Reparations to Palestinian Refugees: A Comparative Perspective* (London: Routledge, 2010).

27. For a highly critical account of the refugee discussions by the then senior NSU advisor on the issue, see Ziyad Clot, *Il n'y aura pas d'Etat palestinien: Journal d'un négociateur en Palestine* (Paris: Max Milo, 2010). See also the various leaked documents of the PLO's Negotiations Support Unit published by the Al Jazeera Transparency Unit, a summary of which can be found on the Palestinian Refugee ResearchNet blog at: http://prrnblog.wordpress.com/category/palestine-papers/

28. Negotiation Support Unit, 'Summary of Ehud Olmert's "Package" Offer to Mahmoud Abbas – August 31, 2008', from 'Palestine Papers', Al Jazeera Transparency Unit, online at: www.ajtransparency.com/en/projects/thepalestinepapers/20121821046718794.html

29. See, for example, the account of the 'First MFA conference on Jewish refugees from Arab countries' by Israel's Deputy Foreign Minister Danny Ayalon on his blog (3 April 2012) at: www.dannyayalon.com/News/439/, as well as Ayalon's YouTube video about Palestinian refugees (4 December 2011) at: www.youtube.com/watch?v=g_3A6_qSBBQ

30. International Crisis Group, *The Emperor Has No Clothes: Palestinians and the End of the Peace Process*, Middle East Report No. 122, 7 May 2012, online at: www.crisisgroup.org/en/regions/middle-east-north-africa/israel-palestine/122-the-emperor-has-no-clothes-palestinians-and-the-end-of-the-peace-process.aspx

31. Chatham House, *The Regional Dimension of the Palestinian Refugee Issue: Simulation Exercise Report*, 23–25 June 2008, online at: www.chathamhouse.org/sites/default/files/public/Research/Middle%20East/12092_prsimulation0608.pdf

32. FOFOGNET (The Friends of the Friends of the Gavel Network) was originally established to support Canadian efforts within the framework of the Refugee Working Group, at: http://prrn.mcgill.ca/uptodate/uptodate_fofognet.htm

33. Because of the sensitivities involved, the first 'No-Name Group' was disguised as an academic seminar, although official participants took part. Meetings continued at irregular times through until 2007.

2

Implementation Mechanism: Policy Choices and Implementation Issues

Heike Niebergall and Norbert Wühler[1]

The Role of the Implementation Mechanism

Acomprehensive resolution of the Israeli–Palestinian conflict will require a just and durable solution to the Palestinian refugee issue. Such a solution will have to address the question of residency for Palestinian refugees as well as the restitution of and compensation for losses suffered by them as a result of their displacement. No matter whether the peace agreement setting out the key parameters of such a solution will stay at a general level or whether it will go into detail, the implementation of the agreed-upon solution will require significant and sustained organizational and operational efforts. The preparatory work and the earlier negotiating positions of the parties, as well as so-called 'second track' and policy research projects, have put forward implementation models of varying complexity. These models have differed in the organizational structures they proposed, the memberships they foresaw and the functions they anticipated for the various bodies. They have, however, all proceeded from the premise that the implementation of the solution to the Palestinian refugee issue will require a mechanism that will be

15

supported by a dedicated organizational structure ('Implementation Mechanism' – IM).

The purpose of this paper is to identify the issues that will present themselves when designing, negotiating and establishing an IM for the solutions provided for in a peace agreement. The key questions that are addressed and the options that are presented in this chapter relate to how the IM will be established and what its organizational structure will be; how its bodies will be composed and what the terms of reference of these bodies will be; what rules and procedures these bodies will operate by; how the various functions of the IM will be coordinated; and how the IM will interact with outside stakeholders.

The paper summarizes the previously stated positions of the Parties and the perspectives of the other stakeholders on the implementation of an agreement. It examines the different policy issues raised and it analyses the implications as well as the costs and benefits of various options. Drawing on experiences from other mechanisms, the paper also sets out the issues and questions that designers and managers of an IM are likely to face, while still being conscious of the unique circumstances and challenges surrounding an IM for the resolution of the Palestinian refugee issue. The paper does not attempt to propose a blueprint for an IM, but rather explores the different options and describes what their likely implications will be. It does so for the mechanisms that are needed for the refugees' residency options, as well as for the anticipated restitution and compensation claims programme.

Mindful of the political realities and the likely need for compromises between and within the various parts of an overall comprehensive Peace Agreement, this paper also discusses which of the components of the IM could be prepared prior to such an Agreement, which should be regulated in the Agreement itself, and which would better be left for subsequent implementation by the mechanism. The important questions in this context are how to take into account the attitudes and interests of the host countries and how to link the preparatory work by sponsors and international organizations with respect to the IM with the negotiations of the Parties.

To be able to discuss the issues surrounding the organization and administration of an IM, this paper makes assumptions about certain key policy choices. While these assumptions draw on the previous work of the Parties and on other preparatory work, they are merely made for the purpose of this discussion and are not intended to reflect any anticipated positions or agreements of the Parties or others. The assumptions include the following:

- Residency options for Palestinian refugees will include: (i) return to Israel; (ii) repatriation to the new Palestinian state; (iii) integration in host countries; and (iv) resettlement in third countries;
- Compensation will be provided for properties which refugees lost when they were displaced and that will not be restituted;
- All refugees will receive a fixed per capita payment because of their displacement;
- Palestinian refugees will be given a choice regarding the residency options that the IM offers. Exercising this choice, however, will be subject to certain constraints. Within these constraints, the choice of the refugees needs to be maximized as much as possible;
- The IM will implement the restitution and compensation claims parts whereas its role in the implementation of the residency options will be primarily that of facilitation and coordination;
- Compensation/indemnification of host countries for the costs that they have incurred in hosting Palestinian refugees will not be dealt with by the IM (see Chapter 5 by Roula El-Rifai and Nadim Shehadi, *An Offer They Can Refuse: Host Countries and the Palestinian Refugee Issue*). Any possible compensation for the losses of former Jewish refugees from Arab countries will not be dealt with by the IM (see Chapter 7 by Michael Fischbach, *Addressing Jewish Claims in the Context of a Palestinian–Israeli Agreement*).

Aspects relating to the implementation of an agreement on the refugee issue are also addressed in other papers in this volume, particularly those on Return, Repatriation, Residency and Resettlement (Chapter 4); Refugee Compensation (Chapter 6); Refugee Absorption and Development (Chapter 8); and Host Countries (Chapter 5). The emphasis of this paper, however, is on the organization and administration of implementation rather than on policy and substantive choices.

This paper does not discuss the political issues in connection with a potential role for the IM in the restitution of property. The extent to which there will be restitution of property rights as opposed to compensation is an issue on which the Parties will need to agree. In negotiations so far, Palestinians have demanded restitution of property rights, while Israel has rejected that option. Whatever the political outcome will be, for the purposes of this paper it should be noted that restitution and compensation processes require almost identical organizational structures and administrative procedures and thus both of these components will be dealt with in this paper.

Implementation Issues in Palestinian Refugee Negotiations

The Parties have in prior negotiations and in their preparatory work dealt to a varying degree with the organizational structures for the implementation of both the residency options and the restitution and compensation parts of a Peace Agreement.[2] Of particular interest for the discussions on implementation are the positions put forward during the Taba negotiations in January 2001, i.e. the Palestinian Position on Refugees of 22 January 2001, Israel's Private Response to the Palestinian Refugee Paper (draft 2) of 22 January 2001, and the Joint Refugee Mechanism Paper (draft 2) of 25 January 2001.[3]

The structures proposed for the implementation have tended to be rather complex, often comprising a number of different bodies with large international memberships and specific technical functions. On the question of how much operational detail the Peace Agreement should contain, Israel generally leaned towards leaving operational details to the implementation stage. The Palestinian side favoured more elaborate provisions in the Peace Agreement, in an effort to minimize the risk of delays in the elaboration of the details and the need for post-Peace Agreement concessions at the subsequent implementation stage. The Joint Refugee Mechanism Paper (draft 2) at Taba detailed a number of specific technical functions for the proposed Repatriation and Compensation Commissions as well as for the Fund and the Secretariat.

The Parties' positions in prior negotiations and in their preparatory work regarding particular issues of implementation is outlined and discussed in more detail in the following sections, in particular in the section dedicated to the Organization of the IM and the Functions of its Bodies.

Main Features and Challenges of the Implementation Mechanism

An IM playing a meaningful and efficient part in the implementation of the residency options listed above and of the restitution and compensation components will need organs to take on or coordinate the following functions: policy guidance; prioritization and sequencing of residency options, restitution and compensation benefits; information for refugees about their options and assistance for refugees to obtain the benefits of their choice; determination or confirmation of refugee status; ensuring the availability of the residency options; establishment of a claims mechanism for the compensation part; and collection and management of the necessary funds.

The IM will face a number of challenges in the performance of these functions, which will likely include the following:

- The Peace Agreement may leave important policy issues for the IM to decide;
- The structures and procedures that the Peace Agreement will provide for the IM might reflect difficult political compromises. They may thus be sub-optimal from a technical standpoint and this may pose additional challenges at the implementation stage;
- The IM will have to address numerous and complex technical and operational issues simultaneously, with many stakeholders involved both inside and outside the IM. It therefore needs to create a flexible organization that can adapt to new and changing requirements;
- Quick results will be expected, and are desirable to avoid disappointment and backlash among Palestinians. On the other hand, the setting up of the IM will take some time. There is thus a need to identify fast-track activities and deliver quick-impact benefits;
- Initial outreach and managing expectations throughout will be crucial;
- What the IM will be able to deliver will depend to a significant degree on the level and manner of funding it will receive;

- The restitution and compensation claims part of the IM should be completed as quickly as possible. The residency parts need a long-term approach that aims at sustainability of the refugees' choice.

Establishment of the Implementation Mechanism

A solution for the Palestinian refugee issue will be one of the key components of a comprehensive Peace Agreement. As discussed above, this Agreement is also expected to contain at least the basic structure and functions of the mechanism to implement such a solution. While an agreement between the Parties will therefore be the first step in establishing the IM, it is very difficult to predict how much detail the actual Peace Agreement itself will contain in this respect, and how much will be left to its subsequent implementation. Possible approaches to this question and their implications will be examined in this section.

Question 1: What international endorsement should the IM receive?

An important question that arises at the early stage of the establishment of the IM is what international 'endorsement' the IM should receive.[4] A conference of 'sponsors' setting out their substantive commitments? Or 'only' a pledging conference announcing financial contributions? A UN Security Council resolution? What can be done prior to the Peace Agreement to align the international 'endorsement' with the IM? Such endorsement would relate to political support, financial contributions and participation and assistance in implementation. In principle, all stakeholders should seek as much international support for the IM as possible to enhance the chances of its implementation.

A conference of 'sponsors', including host countries and international organizations, could provide such support and would also provide a way to set out their anticipated commitments with respect to the IM beyond financial contributions. Such a conference would have to be concluded as close to the Peace Agreement as possible, but in any event prior to the commencement of the IM's operations. Given the scope and magnitude of the substantive commitments required for the functioning of the IM from actors other than the Parties, a pledging conference only announcing financial commitments would constitute a much weaker international endorsement.

Any solution of the Palestinian refugee issue will need significant support from political 'sponsors', donors, host countries and other implementing partners (both individual states and international organizations). Therefore, the alignment of the expectations and commitments of these stakeholders with those of the Parties will be crucial. In this respect, the communication and management of expectations prior to a Peace Agreement will be especially important.

A UN Security Council resolution following the conclusion of a Peace Agreement would add legitimacy to the agreement and to the IM. It would also provide an opportunity for the Council to bring closure to its previous pronouncements on the refugee issue. It is unlikely that the Council would 'take a fresh look' at the provisions of the Peace Agreement and the undertakings at the international conference, given the expected involvement of key Council members in both processes.

Question 2: Will the IM be a stand-alone mechanism, or should it be partly-embedded in an existing international organization, such as, the UN?

As with practically all the research and preparatory work, the Parties have in all their negotiation positions advocated for considerable international involvement in the IM. Both have proposed an international commission and an International Fund, and they have invited the participation of a variety of stakeholders in them. From the Israeli draft of the Framework Agreement on Permanent Status[5] to the Palestinian Position on Refugees at Taba,[6] Israel's Private Response to the Palestinian Refugee Paper of 22 January 2001 at Taba[7] and the Joint Refugee Mechanism Paper (draft 2) at Taba,[8] international organizations, in addition to other stakeholders, have been called upon to be members of the various commissions proposed.

Similarly, the references to the International Fund that the Parties have proposed for the IM have all included a call for the World Bank to participate. The Palestinian Position on Refugees at Taba foresaw a Steering Committee for the Fund composed of Palestine, the United States, the World Bank, EU, donor countries and possibly others, and it called upon the World Bank and the United Nations to be the 'Joint-secretariat for the Fund'.[9] The Joint Refugee Mechanism Paper (draft 2) at Taba contained almost identical language, with the addition that the Fund Secretariat was to be based at the World Bank.

Except for the last reference to a Fund Secretariat based at the World Bank, the substantial international memberships envisaged by the Parties would not necessarily lead to an 'embedding' of the IM in an international organization, but rather require international participation in the highest body of an otherwise stand-alone IM. While such participation would add political support and legitimacy to the IM, the extent to which the Parties' positions foresee it, could make such a body potentially unwieldy and slow down its operation and decision-making.

On the other hand, an IM that would be truly embedded in an organization such as the UN or the World Bank could draw on the administrative structures, procedures and the reputation of that organization. This approach was chosen, for instance, for the United Nations Compensation Commission (UNCC), which was established as a sub-organ of the UN Security Council to deal with the large numbers of claims arising out of the Iraqi invasion and occupation of Kuwait in 1990/91.[10] On the one hand, embedding it in the existing structures of an organization would shorten the start-up time for the IM, would save costs and add transparency. On the other hand, the IM would be bound by the organization's rules and procedures, which could be perceived as restricting the IM's flexibility. An embedding would also have the potential of exposing the IM too much to the politics of that particular organization.

An option that has been discussed by some is to activate and capacitate the UN Conciliation Commission for Palestine (UNCCP) for a role in the implementation of the refugee part of the Peace Agreement. While this may seem somewhat attractive for the restitution and compensation claims part, given the UNCCP's earlier work in this area, the Parties have so far not indicated that this is something they might consider.

Based on the great similarity of the Parties' positions in this respect, it is assumed that the Peace Agreement will foresee an IM that will in principle be stand-alone, with calls for significant international membership in the IM's highest body and possibly closer involvement of the World Bank in its Fund. Short of embedding the IM as a whole, a practical way to make use of the expertise and experience of relevant staff from international organizations (and possibly national admin- istrations) could be the seconding or loan of such staff to the IM. An embedding of just the restitution and compensation claims part of the IM in the UN is not advisable given the linkages of this part to the rest of the IM and its Fund, and the additional coordination challenges this would create. In any event, any embedding foreseen by the Parties would have to be discussed and agreed upon with the respective organization prior to the Peace Agreement, be it the UN, the World Bank or another.

For the efficient and effective performance of its functions, the IM will, however, have to have extensive cooperation and coordination with international organizations such as UNRWA, UNHCR and IOM to the extent that they will play a role in the realization of the refugees' residency options, and with other organizations to the extent that they may be involved in the wider rehabilitation and development work that is carried out in support of the refugees' exercise of their residency options.

Question 3: How much detail of the structure and operations of the IM should be regulated in the Peace Agreement and a 'sponsors' conference, and how much of this should be left for the IM to elaborate?

This is a question which is both technical and highly political at the same time and the answer to which depends on many variables. The main benefits of a comprehensive regulation of the IM in its constituting documents are clarity about its structures, the predictability of the process and the ability to respond early to expectations. In contrast, the key advantage of setting out only the main policies and principles in the constituting documents is the flexibility that this leaves for an IM to deal with new challenges and to adapt to the changing needs that are bound to arise during implementation.

As mentioned above, Israel has leaned more towards leaving the details to the elaboration of the IM. The 2001 Israeli draft of the Framework Agreement on Permanent Status, for instance, foresaw an International Fund to be established and supervised by an international commission and the World Bank. For property claims, it provided that

'[T]he modalities, criteria, timeline, and procedures of the registration of claims, their verification and pro-rata evaluation shall be drawn up as appropriate by agreement upon the establishment of the Fund and within its framework'.[11] Along these lines, Israel's Private Response to Palestinian Refugee Paper of 22 January 2001 at Taba also provided that 'Programs of a compensatory nature... shall be managed according to a definitive and complete register of property claims to be compiled by an appropriate arm of the International Commission and Fund'. With respect to the International Commission, it only stipulated that its 'mandate, structure and mode of operation' should be detailed in the agreement.[12] An exception is the Joint Refugee Mechanism Paper (draft 2) at Taba, which contains the only Israeli position with considerable details on the structure and operations of the IM.[13]

In an effort to lay down as many details as possible, the Palestinian side has favoured more elaborate provisions. The Palestinian Position on Refugees at Taba lists, for instance, seven specific functions of the proposed Repatriation Commission. It foresees that the Commission may open offices in other locations, shall establish a mechanism for the resolution of interpretative disputes, and shall establish a mechanism for appeal. With respect to the proposed Compensation Commission, it contains provisions on evidence, on the valuation of lost property, and on mechanisms to deal with interpretative disputes and appeals. The Joint Refugee Mechanism Paper (draft 2) at Taba contains provisions on such details of the IM as the valuation of material and non-material losses to be compensated, prioritization of benefits, time limits for claims, voting rules, questions of evidence, and functions of the Fund and the Secretariat.

Even if it was advisable or desirable for the resolution of the Palestinian refugee issue to deal with as many points as possible in the Peace Agreement, in the reality of the negotiations, where the refugee issue is only one of several key areas, it will not be easy to agree up-front on the many details that the IM will have to consider.

This could in the end have its own benefits. A very detailed framework – especially if it were less than optimal for the task – could make the operation of the IM challenging and its adaptation to changing needs cumbersome. Experience shows that leaving more details for elaboration by the IM is preferable in complex situations where it is impossible to anticipate all the scenarios and requirements, and where there is a particular need for a flexible mechanism that can adapt to unforeseen and changing requirements. The basis for the complex and massive operation of the UNCC, for example, was one sentence in a resolution of the UN Security Council. This was subsequently elaborated in a report by the UN Secretary General and general policy guidance from the Commission's Governing Council. More detailed policy and eligibility criteria were then developed through dedicated decision-making panels, which in turn were supported by the preparatory work of a large and highly specialized Secretariat.

However, there is another linkage that negotiators of an agreement are often not aware of, but which the reality of the subsequent implementation has borne out a number of times. The fewer details an agreement contains and the more the elaboration of the mechanism is left to an IM itself, the more important the composition of the IM's bodies and the selection and appointment of their members become, as the selection and appointment of members represent one way of maintaining some influence over the IM and the quality and efficiency of its operations. This is particularly relevant for the policy organ which will be called upon to give continuous guidance on substantive eligibility criteria, principles of procedure and, if necessary, prioritizations. In the case of claims programmes, this is of course also relevant for the decision-making bodies. Also crucial for large and complex programmes, albeit less visible from the outside, is the support that the Secretariat provides for all aspects of an IM and consequently the role that the head of the Secretariat plays in this respect. The more detail is left for implementation, the more significant the role of the Secretariat and its head is, and therefore the more important the latter's selection and appointment becomes.

The interrelationship between the questions regarding the level of (continuing) international involvement, the level of detail regulated in the constituting instruments and the composition and appointment of the implementing bodies requires that these issues are considered together as parameters rather than in isolation. These parameters and the importance that they are each given by the creators of the IM will determine the model that is ultimately chosen.

Organization of the Implementation Mechanism and Functions of Its Bodies

Given the multiplicity and complexity of the functions that the IM will have to fulfil, an equal multitude of options and variations is conceivable for its organizational structure. Different models have been used in the practice of national and international claims programmes and for the organization of large-scale return, resettlement and rehabilitation efforts. Lessons can be learned from their experiences, and a number of their features and challenges can inform the design of the IM. However, there are an equal number of features and challenges that are unique to the situation of the Palestinian refugees and that require specific solutions, and no mechanism has been established to date that has had to combine such a variety of functions as are anticipated for this IM. It is therefore not surprising that the organizational structures proposed for the IM by the Parties in their negotiation positions and discussed in 'second track' and other policy research work, have typically been complex, often comprising a number of different bodies with specific technical functions.

The Palestinian approach towards the specifics of the IM's organizational structure developed from a proposal for two commissions (one for repatriation and one for compensation) and an International Fund with a steering committee, to an elaborate set-up including an international commission with a board of directors, three technical committees (one for status determination; one for return, repatriation and relocation; and one for compensation and restitution) and an International Fund with a dedicated Secretariat.

The Reparation Commission foreseen in the Palestinian Position on Refugees at Taba, for instance, a large body composed of representatives of ten states and international organizations (including the Parties), was to have operational functions such as verification of refugee status, processing of applications, repatriation of and assistance to and protection of returning refugees. Similarly, the Compensation Commission under this proposal was composed of representatives from the Parties, the United States, the EU, the United Nations, the World Bank and donor countries. This Commission was to evaluate the Palestinian material and non-material losses, administer and adjudicate claims of real property by refugees, disburse the compensation payments and 'send a specialized technical team to evaluate the current value of the property for which compensation is due'.[14] The structure of the planned International Fund was equally elaborate. Priorities and policies were to be set by a Steering Committee composed of Palestine, the United States, the World Bank, EU, donor countries, and possibly others, and the World Bank and the United Nations were supposed to be the Joint-secretariat for the Fund.

The core structure proposed by Israel for the IM has also been an international commission and a fund. The Commission in the draft of the Framework Agreement on Permanent Status had an even larger international membership, and the Fund was to be established by that Commission and the World Bank. This Commission, on the other hand, was only to serve as the political umbrella of the IM, while the draft proposed a Registration Committee of the Fund for the technical task of the verification and evaluation of the refugees' property claims. The roles of the Commission and the Fund were expanded in Israel's Private Response to Palestinian Refugee Paper of 22 January 2001 at Taba which provided that these two bodies should have 'full and exclusive responsibility for the implementation of the resolution of the refugee problem in all its aspects, including the gathering and verification of claims ....'[15] The technical work on the property claims, however, was assigned to 'an appropriate arm of the International Commission and Fund'[16] without detailing any further the nature of such an arm.

The Joint Refugee Mechanism Paper (draft 2) at Taba then contained the most complex and stratified organizational structure designed by the Parties to date. This time it was spelled out that the Commission, again with similar international membership of states and international organizations, would be governed by a Board composed of representatives of the member states. The Board was conceived as the highest authority in the Commission, making policy decisions, implementing priorities, drawing up the procedures governing the work of the Commission and overseeing the conduct of the various arms of the Commission. At the same time, it was the Board that would valuate the Palestinian material and non-material losses, and for that purpose send the same specialized technical team to valuate the property for which compensation is due that was already foreseen in the original Palestinian position at Taba. Another more technical task for the

Board would be to seek immigration quotas from third countries so as to implement the resettlement options for Palestinian refugees.[17]

The Commission was to establish three technical committees: a Status-determination Committee; a Return, Repatriation and Relocation Committee; and a Compensation and Restitution Committee. The paper set out the respective functions and procedures of these Committees in more detail than prior negotiation documents had, including those for dispute resolution and appeals processes. The provisions for the International Fund were again similar to those contained in the original Palestinian Position at Taba, with the additional bracketed provision that the Fund should 'ask the World Bank to establish multilateral funding instruments to ensure that each aspect of this Agreement on refugees requiring financial assistance has corresponding instruments available to donors wishing to make use of multilateral mechanisms'.[18] Finally, the Fund was to audit and monitor the Commission to ensure efficiency and transparency.

In particular, the Palestinian views of how the IM should be organized thus seemed in general to be characterized by an approach that favours elaborate structures with dedicated bodies for each of the different activities. In the negotiation positions, these appeared as rather cumulative enumerations of relatively large bodies with multiple, especially international, memberships and specific functions. While such an elaborate and multi-layered international structure might guarantee outside support for the IM and would seem to provide it with (more than) sufficient organizational capacity for its various functions, it would at the same time carry the risk of making the mechanism cumbersome and slow. Furthermore, it would pose a significant challenge for the efficiency of its operations and for the coordination between its various bodies and with outside actors, whose cooperation will be needed in particular for the implementation of the residency options.

The following diagram depicts the basic general structure of an IM that would allow it to fulfil the functions and address the challenges outlined above. The bodies listed are intended to represent the main functions anticipated for the IM rather than its specific contours. Other structures are conceivable and feasible. The diagram reflects the key functionalities contained in most of the preparatory work and in past negotiations of the Parties. It streamlines these designs, however, taking into account experiences from and lessons learned by other mechanisms. Details are discussed in the following sections of the paper.

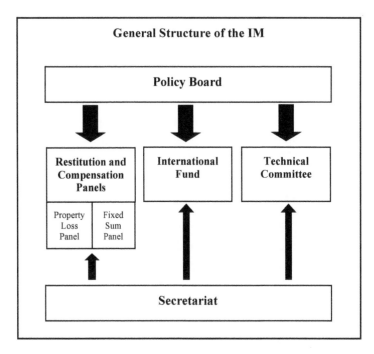

Figure 2.1   General Structure of the Implementation Mechanism

The structure depicted in the diagram is one that attempts to streamline a necessarily complex organization. It reflects the key assumption that the restitution and compensation part will be under the direct responsibility of the IM, whereas most of the activities in support of the refugees' residency choices will be performed by other organizations and agencies whose work the IM would only facilitate and coordinate through a technical committee.

The more 'traditional' components of the IM's area of activities with respect to restitution and compensation would thus be a policy board; a fund; the decision-making functions consisting of various panels to decide on restitution and/or compensation for refugees; and an executive secretariat with regional offices. The IM's facility to coordinate return, repatriation, resettlement, and integration and development will be a more complex second area which, although also under the general guidance of the Policy Board, will require greater procedural flexibility and capacity for continuous adaptation to developing needs. The various components of the IM will now be examined in more detail.

Policy Setting

The highest body of the IM as set out in the diagram is a Policy Board. Policy guidance is a key function in any complex reparations claims programme. For the solution of the Palestinian refugee issue, however, it could gain additional relevance should important policy choices not be made in the Peace Agreement but if they are left to elaboration by the IM. Other responsibilities of the Policy Board should encompass the representation of the IM at the highest political level, the approving of the IM's overall budget, the setting of priorities and ensuring progress of the IM's work, quality control of the technical work of the IM and resolving any disputes between the various components of the IM.

Question 4: Who shall be represented on the Policy Board?

Because of its significance for the successful operation and overall legitimacy of the IM, the composition of the Policy Board, the process by which its members are selected, and the way its voting rights are organized will be very important. Considerations of inclusiveness, political buy-in, ownership, the possibility of monitoring the use of financial contributions and so on will have to be weighed against, among other things, hesitations to share responsibility, and the willingness and the capacity to commit time and resources. The Parties have generally advocated wide representation of international stakeholders, with few variations on some specific members. The benefits of such a wide representation should outweigh its risks, as long as the Policy Board's rules prevent any members from blocking its work and their representatives act in accordance with their responsibilities.

A successful example of an inclusive model is the Board of Trustees of the German Foundation 'Remembrance, Responsibility and Future',[19] the policy body that supervised both an international compensation programme involving seven international partner organizations, which resolved 2.4 million claims and paid almost €4.5 billion, as well as humanitarian assistance programmes in 16 countries. This Board has 27 members, representing practically all the participants in the initial international negotiations that had led to the creation of the Foundation, as well as the main contributors to and implementers of the various components of the programmes. Notwithstanding its large membership, this Board has worked efficiently and has never held up the operations of the Foundation. Often, the Board takes its decisions with unanimity, but its rules foresee a majority vote to ensure that its operation cannot be blocked by a minority of its members.

The Fund

In addition to the funds for the payment of the refugee compensation, donors might also use the Fund to channel contributions for the implementation of the residency options. In any event, the combined financial amounts that the IM will have to manage will be substantial and will require significant institutional capacity and professional expertise. There is general agreement that an international financial facility will be needed for the IM. Both Parties have in all their negotiation documents proposed the establishment of an international fund to manage the financial affairs of the IM. The exact proposals have varied over time, but a common feature has been that the World Bank, possibly together with the UN, should play the leading role in the management of such a fund.

Questions relating to the activities and operations of such a fund have previously been addressed in the World Bank Papers,[20] and it is assumed that World Bank and/or other expertise will continue to be available in this respect. The following section therefore only deals with Fund issues that affect the organization and administration of the IM, i.e. the place of the Fund within the IM structure and its relationship with the IM's other bodies.

Question 5: Should the Fund be set up within the IM, or should structures and facilities existing within the World Bank and/or the UN be used to perform Fund activities for the IM?

Both Parties foresee a central role for the World Bank in the management of the Fund. Proposals have ranged from the complete

31

embedding of the Fund in the Bank to calls on the World Bank and the UN to perform (sometimes jointly) the function of the Secretariat for the Fund.

The establishment of the Fund within the World Bank (and/or the UN) would have a number of advantages. Its operation would be governed by existing rules and procedures that are tried and tested and that would guarantee transparency, accountability and good financial practice. Both organizations have experience with the establishment and management of special multi-donor trust funds. It would seem more efficient and less complicated, however, to use one or the other of the organizations rather than having them manage the Fund jointly.

The main challenge in a scenario where the Fund is outsourced would be the coordination of the activities of a Fund outside the IM with the work of the rest of the IM. The IM differs from a 'normal' multi-donor trust fund situation, in that it is supposed to manage and/or coordinate a multitude of activities that include more than just rehabilitation and development projects. Duplication and the need for additional layers of coordination with a Fund outside the IM should be avoided. It would therefore seem preferable to keep the Fund as such as part of the IM structure, but to bring into that Fund the World Bank's capacity and expertise by inviting it to become the Secretariat of the Fund, or at least by seconding or loaning Bank staff to that Fund. The details of such an insourcing would be worked out by the IM and the Bank once the arrangement was agreed in principle.

Question 6: How will donor coordination be organized?

Examples of arrangements for multi-donor trust funds that could also be used for donor coordination for IM managed activities can be found both in the World Bank and in the UN system. The United Nations Development Programme (UNDP), for instance, through its Multi-Donor Trust Fund Office serves as the administrative interface between project implementing agencies and donors. Under its pass-through fund management modality, it signs standard administrative arrangements with donors, receives, administers and transfers donor funds to implementing agencies, and consolidates progress and final reports for submission to donors. The World Bank performs the same types of functions for a wide variety of donors and projects. If the IM's Fund were set up within the World Bank and/or the UN, donor coordination would operate through these facilities for all funds that donors would channel through the IM. If the Fund was set up within the IM, but with the World Bank acting as its Secretariat or with Bank staff working in its Secretariat, the same types of facilities could then be used within that structure.

Donors would, of course, be free to make funds for activities that would otherwise be managed or coordinated by the IM available outside that mechanism (for instance, directly to the Palestinian State or to host countries). If they did this jointly with other donors, any donor coordination directly for such projects would then need to take place outside the IM's Fund. Preferably, however, there would also be some coordination with the IM and its Fund in these situations, considering the impact that such external projects would be likely to have on the activities and operations of the IM.

Question 7: Should sub-funds be set up under the main Fund for the different purposes of the IM, i.e. compensation and other activities? Should contributions be allowed either to the main Fund or to the sub-funds?

The advantage of sub-funds and of the possibility of making earmarked contributions into them would be to offer donors choices according to their priorities and preferences and thus to enhance the level of contributions. Regarding Israel's contributions to the Fund, this might be politically sensitive if Israel decides to provide earmarked funding for property compensation only. Such a limitation might be difficult to accept for the Palestinian side who has consistently insisted on Israel's wider responsibility to pay for compensation.

Implementing the Residency Options – the Technical Committee

The implementation of the four residency options will involve different parties and activities. For the areas of return, repatriation, resettlement and integration, the IM would not be in a position to perform or even manage all the required activities by itself. In each of these areas, various degrees of support, cooperation or direct implementation by others will be required, and different levels of outside control will apply. Consequently, the role of the IM could differ for each of these areas. The two extreme options are that the IM would be made as operational as possible to take the lead in the implementation of the residency options, or its function would be limited to pure facilitation.

The Parties have tended towards an operational role for the IM, with the Joint Refugee Mechanism Paper (draft 2) at Taba culminating in the proposals for a Status-determination Committee and a Return, Repatriation and Relocation Committee, each with considerable implementation functions. In order to assess the feasibility of such an operational role, this section first summarizes the steps needed for the exercise of each of the four residency options and then examines options for different levels of IM involvement in each.[21]

Question 8: What role could the IM play in the return of refugees to Israel?

The return to Israel is probably the most sensitive and controversial issue between the Parties within the question of durable residency options for Palestinian refugees. Rex Brynen's paper on Return, Repatriation, Residency and Resettlement', Chapter 4 in this volume, summarizes how return in principle could be dealt with: all refugees could be permitted the option of return; some refugees could be permitted to return; or no refugees could be permitted to return. Since agreement on unlimited return is unlikely, the Peace Agreement may foresee return as one option for the refugees, but leave the exact number to the discretion of Israel. The Peace Agreement may also limit the number of returnees, either by a capped limit in the Agreement, or by laying down rules that would govern the rate at which refugee return could take place. In the latter two situations, the IM might play an implementation role in the application of such rules and the administration of the return (selection) process.

Along these lines, the Palestinian Position on Refugees at Taba proposed an internationally composed Repatriation Commission to guarantee and manage the implementation of the right to return, and that Commission was to determine, according to transparent criteria, who would be allowed to return in any given year, with an undetermined minimum allowed every year. The Commission would verify refugee status, determine return priorities and procedures, process applications, repatriate the refugees, and provide assistance and protection to returning refugees.[22] The Joint Refugee Mechanism Paper (draft 2) at Taba foresaw the same functions for a Technical Committee of the International Commission, the Return, Repatriation and Relocation Committee, but proposed a separate Status-determination Committee to verify refugee status.[23]

In statements since Taba, the Israeli Government has gone back to its position on refugee return as reflected in its draft Framework Agreement on Permanent Status. This draft foresaw a limited humanitarian return of some refugees for family reunification in Israel, within Israel's sovereign discretion and without any international involvement.

Considering that Israel is likely to insist on controlling the return process, the IM will either have no role in this area, or its role will be restricted. It might be tasked with ascertaining the number of allowed returns (in the case of Israel's discretion), matching that number with the refugees wishing to return and assisting refugees within the 'quota' to address the proper Israeli authorities. Whatever its involvement might be, the IM would have to face the difficult task of dealing with those refugees who might wish to return to Israel after the 'quota' has been exhausted and whom it would have to inform that they would not be allowed to return.

The implementation of the return component would require a number of challenging policy decisions and preparatory activities that include:

- Policy decisions about the key return parameters – who, how many and when?
- An extensive outreach and information campaign organized and conducted by the parties to inform, not only potential beneficiaries of the return programme but also their respective societies. While the IM and UNRWA will be in a position to support such a campaign, the two parties will need to take an active role in it as well;
- Establishment of a transparent selection process that maximizes the exercise of choice for Palestinian refugees while respecting the limitations of the return agreed upon at the political level;

- Coordination of the movement of returnees, including with the authorities of receiving communities to ensure a smooth integration of returnees into Israeli society.

Question 9: What role could the IM play in the repatriation of refugees to the Palestinian State?

The role of the IM in the repatriation of refugees to the new Palestinian State is not a controversial issue between the Parties. Apart from earlier concerns about Palestinian border crossings, Israel has not concerned itself much with this option in the negotiations. From the Palestinian perspective, the regulation of this matter will in principle be within the sovereign domain of the new Palestinian State.

In order to maximize international involvement, Palestinian negotiation documents have proposed a similar international role in the implementation of this option as for return. The Joint Refugee Mechanism Paper (draft 2) at Taba foresaw that the Return, Repatriation and Relocation Committee and the Status-determination Committee would perform the same kinds of functions in support of repatriation as they would for return.

The chapter on 'Return, Repatriation, Residency and Resettlement' refers to research that was conducted on refugee repatriation and absorption by the World Bank in 2000–2003 and that expressed concern at an overly bureaucratic approach to refugee repatriation. It warns that:

> [i]n the World Bank's view, refugees would make repatriation decisions based in large part on economic conditions and opportunities within the new Palestinian state. Given this, allowing them to migrate at a time they judged appropriate best facilitated their absorption. By linking refugee flows to bureaucratic process, it was feared, refugee repatriation flows and local economic conditions in Palestine could become uncoupled.[24]

The process foreseen in Taba would indeed require large administrative and logistical machinery and would take considerable processing time, given the number of applications that can be expected. It would also seem to assume functions that would ordinarily be performed by the authorities of the Palestinian State. The role of the IM should therefore be focused on making information available to refugees and providing assistance to those refugees who will seek it from the IM. As such, it would help refugees wishing to repatriate from a host country if the various roles of the Palestinian State, the host country and the IM in these cases were laid down, and this could, for instance, be done by way of a tripartite agreement between these parties. The IM seems best placed to initiate the conclusion of such agreements. For the IM, such agreements could foresee information tasks vis-à-vis refugees and monitoring functions concerning the implementation of the commitments under the agreement.

Given the distances in the region, it is unlikely that large numbers of refugees would need or seek assistance for the actual movement when they would repatriate. Where the IM would be approached with such a request, it could refer the refugee to an appropriate organization present in the region, such as UNRWA. Refugees seeking to repatriate from countries outside the region could also be referred to an appropriate organization with capacity in resettlement and movement. The Palestinian State might, for instance, consider seeking assistance from the IM in the screening of applicants. The IM could in turn ask IOM to perform this task which is one of its traditional activities.

If donors choose to make funds for development work for the benefit of repatriated refugees available through the IM, the IM would essentially perform trust fund functions. Development and rehabilitation projects in the Palestinian State in areas such as housing, health, education and job creation would not be implemented directly by the IM, but their implementation should be facilitated by it. In this role the IM would select reliable partners through transparent processes, request the necessary funds according to established priorities, allocate funds to the selected partners, monitor their use of the funds and ensure completion of the projects.

Irrespective of the level of the IM's involvement, the implementation of the repatriation component would require a number of challenging policy decisions and preparatory activities that include:

- Policy decisions about the key repatriation parameters – who, how many and when? Tied to these policy decisions is the general question of whether and how all Palestinian refugees will be able to obtain citizenship of the new Palestinian State;

- Development of outreach and information programmes in cooperation with current host countries;
- Depending on the repatriation parameters, the notification of selection criteria and the establishment of a transparent selection process;
- Linking the integration of repatriated refugees to development projects in the Palestinian State.

Question 10: What role could the IM play in the integration of refugees in host countries?

Host country integration of Palestinian refugees is not a topic that the Parties have dealt with in their negotiations. Although Israel and the Palestinian side are aware of both the interests of host countries in the resolution of the Palestinian refugee issue and the important roles that they will have in parts of its implementation, their negotiation documents have only suggested the membership of the host countries in certain of the IM's bodies but have not gone into the substance of these countries' roles. Since it is unlikely that host countries will be part of the negotiations, this will not change, and it will therefore be important to maintain communications prior to the Peace Agreement to take into account the respective interests and concerns and to manage expectations on all sides.

What will happen with the Palestinians living in the host countries after a Peace Agreement, both as to their legal status and concerning their political, economic and social integration, will influence their decisions on their residency choice and will thus be of concern to the new Palestinian State. At the same time, the conditions for repatriation and development in the Palestinian State will have similar influence on the residency decisions of Palestinians in host countries, and will therefore impact on those countries. The issues to be addressed in these relationships can only be discussed after a Peace Agreement, and the IM could have a role as a facilitator of such discussions.

It is difficult to predict to what extent donors will channel funds for projects for Palestinian refugees in host countries through the IM.

Where they use this facility, the role of the IM would be similar to that which it will have for development in the Palestinian State.

Another question will be how to synchronize an anticipated wind-down of UNRWA with the taking over of its functions by the respective host states. In this context, it may also be decided that certain of UNRWA's functions would (temporarily) be taken over by the IM. These matters are the subject of Chapters 3 and 5 in this volume.

The implementation of the reintegration component would require a number of challenging policy decisions and preparatory activities that would include:

- Policy decisions on status and (dual) citizenship questions for Palestinian refugees;
- Decisions on closure, re-densification or rehabilitation of refugee camps as well as on general housing, health and education policies;
- Establishment of transparent processes for the consolidation of requests for citizenship and/or the status changes within the host countries.

Question 11: What role could the IM play in the resettlement of refugees in third countries?

The Joint Refugee Mechanism Paper (draft 2) at Taba foresaw that a Return, Repatriation and Relocation Committee would also be responsible for developing resettlement procedures, processing applications and relocating refugees. It can practically be excluded that any IM will be given these functions, as the scope of third-country resettlement and its mechanisms will be determined by the receiving countries involved. The number of refugees allowed for resettlement will be set by each resettlement country, and the decision to accept an applicant will be taken by that country.

For other aspects of the process, however, the IM could be a useful partner from whose support resettlement countries could benefit. Pre-screening, movement and cultural sensitization trainings are activities that are typically outsourced by receiving countries in resettlement situations. If they did not want to enter into direct arrangements themselves, or if they wanted to coordinate their activities, countries taking in Palestinian refugees could request assistance from the IM. The IM in turn could rely for this on an organization like IOM which has been performing these activities over many years for hundreds of thousands of resettled persons and which regularly prepares information packages on countries for which it performs return and resettlement activities.

The policy decisions and preparatory activities required for the implementation of the return component would include:

- Policy decisions by receiving states of the key parameters – who, how many, when?
- Effective communication of these policies to host countries and within the refugee communities;
- Development of selection criteria and sequencing priorities for Palestinian refugees as well as establishment of transparent application and selection processes for resettlement candidates;
- Preparation of move (medical check-ups and cultural orientation trainings) and of integration in receiving communities.

Question 12: What kind of structure should be set up in the IM to support its roles in the implementation of the residency options?

Several conclusions can be drawn from the above review of the different activities required for the implementation of the four residency options and the possible roles of the IM in it. First, the IM will not have the involved and comprehensive operational role to which the Parties have tended in their negotiations, but rather draw and rely extensively on external partners to implement these activities. Second, the IM's role in all likelihood will be different with respect to each of the four residency options. Third, despite a limited operational role and an emphasis on facilitating and coordinating responsibilities, the IM will still require significant organizational capacity to perform these functions efficiently. From a technical point of view, this capacity could be provided by a strong Secretariat alone. Considering how many international partners will be involved in the implementation of the residency options, and in view of the political nature of many of the issues that are likely to arise, it is suggested that a dedicated committee with international membership be established for the purpose. This technical committee should have the possibility to defer important policy issues to the Policy Board.

The answers to Questions 8–12 have shown that the roles of the IM in the implementation of the different residency options are likely to be less operational and more of a facilitating and coordinating nature. Its role will include the prioritization and monitoring of the process within the parameters set out in the Peace Agreement and in following bilateral agreements and within the policy framework developed by the Policy Board.

In this function, the Technical Committee would rely on the experience and capacity already available in relevant governments and international organizations to take on the required activities. Where possible, it should ensure that the IM's partners will perform the necessary activities to enable the refugees' choice. One challenge for the IM will be to make the necessary financial resources available to these partners. Another will be to prioritize and plan the activities so that implementation partners can and will make the necessary capacities available on their side.

Question 13: What should be the composition of the Technical Committee, and how should its members be selected?

Given its area of activity, it would seem desirable to have representatives from the following countries and organizations on the Technical Committee: Israel, State of Palestine, Jordan, Lebanon, Syria, UNRWA, UNHCR and IOM. Who should be represented on the Technical Committee would best be decided at the 'sponsors conference' referred to above at which the Peace Agreement was to be endorsed by stakeholders. The extent of each representative's responsibilities on the Technical Committee will need to be decided with regard to each residency option.

While the members of the Technical Committee should be sufficiently high-level to have 'standing' in their coordination function vis-à-vis the IM's counterpart entities, they would ideally at the same time be experts with experience in the relevant activity areas.

The IM and Refugee Property

There is broad agreement that there will be restitution and/or compensation for the properties that Palestinians left behind when they were displaced in 1948 and that the IM will establish and regulate this process. It is less clear to what extent there should also be compensation for other losses in connection with these displacements, and if so who should be eligible. This aspect is dealt with Chapter 6 of this volume, 'Refugee Compensation: Policy Choices and Implementation Issues', which should be read in conjunction with this chapter. The following section deals with organizational and administrative *implementation questions* with respect to the restitution and compensation processes.

Question 14: Should the restitution and compensation process be dealt with directly by the IM, or should it be placed under the responsibility of an international organization such as the UN?

Various negotiation papers of the Parties have foreseen a separate body within the IM to deal with restitution and compensation. The Palestinian proposals have been more in the direction of a wider membership of states and organizations in such a body (some including the UN), while Israel has proposed a more technical type of committee, albeit for compensation only. None of the Parties has proposed to place the restitution and compensation process as such under the responsibility of an organization such as the UN.

As set out under Question 2 above, the restitution and compensation process should be dealt with directly under the IM. This would facilitate coherence and coordination, allow this part of the mechanism to benefit from the substantive experience of other parts of the IM, generate administrative synergies, and reduce the potential for duplication. In the event that the restitution and compensation process would be established directly under an organization like the UN or IOM, a number of coordination and consistency issues would have to be addressed.

Question 15: It is assumed that the Peace Agreement will regulate and provide for restitution and compensation for property losses and for fixed sum compensation for the fact of displacement. Should there be only one body to deal with both fixed sum and property loss claims, or should there be separate bodies for each of these purposes?

For the purposes of this paper, it is assumed that each Palestinian refugee will receive compensation based on the fact of his or her displacement. It is likely that this would be a fixed per capita payment, and for refugees who lost property this would be in addition to their property restitution or compensation. In these circumstances, it would be preferable to have two bodies: one dealing with property losses ('Property Loss Panel') and one with fixed sum compensation ('Fixed Sums Panel'). The reasons for this are that the procedures and methodologies for the two different types of claims will be different; the pace at which the resolution of the different claims will proceed will be different; and the expertise required from the members of the bodies will be different. Fixed sum compensation could thus be fast-tracked since this separate panel could resolve its caseload faster (and cheaper) than a single body could, who would have to deal at the same time with property losses.

Question 16: Should a multi-track system be introduced for the resolution of the property claims?

Having separate tracks for the resolution of the property claims within the Property Loss Panel would allow the introduction of a specialized process for those properties that will be restituted, a quasi-judicial process dealing with compensation for large properties that will not be restituted and that are likely to involved complex valuation issues, and a simpler and faster administrative process with per capita amounts for properties that are small and that will not be restituted. According to Fischbach, the records of the United Nations Conciliation Commission for Palestine indicate that 40 per cent of refugee families owned considerably small lands worth less than £P100 in 1948, while only a little over 1 per cent of the refugee families owned larger land exceeding £P10,000.[25] Sub-division of these holdings due to inheritance over time would have left large numbers of current heirs/owners with even smaller shares, and consequently small claims. Again, the processing methodologies for these two types of claims are likely to be different, and in particular the valuation of the 'small' claims could be done in a more standardized way.[26]

The threshold amount dividing the tracks in the above system should be decided in the Peace Agreement or by the Policy Board. If it was left for determination by the Property Loss Panel, this would complicate and slow down the latter's work since the Panel would have to perform a sampling exercise to gauge the distribution between large and small property claims so that it could organize its work accordingly.

Question 17: Will the funds available for property loss compensation be limited or open-ended?

The valuation of the property losses and the assessment of the amounts of their compensation raise a myriad of issues. This paper is not concerned with the details of the valuation standards and methodologies that should be applied or with the various ways of assessing compensation amounts, be it at the individual or the global level.[27]

One issue, however, has a particular bearing on the operation of the Property Loss Panel and on the IM as a whole. The issue is whether the funds available for the compensation of those properties that will not be restituted are assumed to be finite (i.e. a fixed total amount that will not increase over the life of the Panel), or whether it is assumed that an open-ended fund will be available that is to be resourced in function of the needs arising from the decisions of the Panel on the claims and the amounts of compensation awarded. The Palestinian side has advocated the latter. Israel has offered to make available a defined lump-sum to be agreed upfront. In the event that internationally pledged funds would contribute to this part of the IM, this would be an issue of considerable interest to donors as well. In the first scenario, the Panel might apply more standardized values to all types of claims. In addition, it may hold up the issuance of the awards until all claims are decided and the total value of the compensable property losses can be matched against the finite total funds available for the payment of the compensation, or it might make the payment of the awards in two stages. While these measures might be the fairest way to deal with this situation for the claimants as a whole, individual claimants would surely be disappointed both with the pace of the process and the instalment payments.

Question 18: Should an assessment be undertaken of the total/aggregate value of the compensable property losses? If so, by whom, when and how?

Estimates of the total/aggregate value of the refugees' property losses have varied considerably and calculations have ranged from US$3 billion to $200 billion, depending on different criteria and parameters used. Having the aggregate value of the compensable property losses and thus the total amount needed for their full compensation available when the Property Loss Panel starts its work, could help in avoiding some of the problems discussed in Question 17, even if the Panel was not formally bound by such an assessment.

Assessing the total/aggregate value of the compensable property losses independently from a review of the claims will not be an easy task. Such a global assessment could be done in a number of different ways that would, depending on the standards and methods used, lead to different results. Sources for assisting in the assessment could, among others, be the UNCCP database and the 'Custodian for Absentees' Property' records. One proposal, made at Taba, has been for a group of experts to conduct an assessment of the total value of the property losses prior to the decisions on the claims by the Property Loss Panel. If that was the case, the Property Loss Panel could devote all its resources and time to the speedy resolution of the claims and distribute this total amount over the claims it deems compensable in function of the proven losses per claim.

Should the Property Loss Panel issue higher awards than could eventually be paid out this would result in a need for pro-rata reductions. Post-award pro-rata reductions are likely to disappoint claimants' expectations as amounts paid out would be lower than what was initially awarded.

The Secretariat

None of the other bodies of the IM will be able to perform its functions without assistance from a Secretariat. The Secretariat assistance will be of varying degrees and will range from administrative support for the Policy Board, to administrative and legal support for the Claims Panels, and the performance of the majority of the work in the area of technical coordination. The Secretariat will thus play a crucial role for the overall functioning of the IM.

Both the UN and IOM have implemented international claims and compensation programmes. Both the World Bank and the UN have experience with managing multi-donor funds, and different UN agencies and other international organizations have experience with implementing the different kinds of activities related to the durable residency options. No organization has, however, dealt with the totality of the IM types of implementation and therefore none has comprehensive experience in all of the activities.

Question 19: How should the management of the Secretariat be structured and selected?

The IM will need a highly competent, efficient and neutral Secretariat, considering the number of bodies and relationships it has to support, the magnitude and complexities of its tasks, the political sensitivities, the expectations and pressures, and the numerous competing priorities it will need to balance. Given these parameters, the importance of the Secretariat for the fair and efficient functioning of the IM and the role it will play in the successful discharge of the IM's responsibilities cannot be overestimated. It will therefore also be particularly important how the management of the Secretariat will be structured and selected.

The Parties have not gone into details concerning the secretariat functions for the IM, other than with respect to the Fund. One suggestion has been that the IM should have an Executive Secretariat with a chair and high-level experts. The Geneva Accord, for instance, foresees a Secretariat with a chair to conduct the day-to-day operation of the IM. The advantage of one person at the head of the Secretariat would be clear leadership and easy decision-making.

An alternative to a chair would be management of the Secretariat by a Board of Directors, consisting for instance of three members, with rotating chair, to be appointed by the Policy Board for a fixed period of time, with the possibility of reappointment. Apart from avoiding dependence on one person only, this model would allow for more input from stakeholders into the leadership of the Secretariat. It could also introduce expertise in the three activity areas of the IM at the management level. It would, however, introduce the risk of disagreement within the Board and delay or blockage of decision-making.

Question 20: Where should the Secretariat be located? How should the regional functions of the Secretariat be organized?

Concerning the seat of the Secretariat (and thereby of the IM), the main question will be how close to or far from the region the headquarters should be. This decision will be influenced both by political considerations (proximity to stakeholders in the region and to the places of residence of many of the refugees, competing 'claims' to the seat, reach for international donors and sponsors, 'neutrality' of the place), as well as by issues of practicality (such as facilities, availability of staff and experts, language capacities and costs). Assuming that the IM will not be embedded in an existing international organization, an agreement with the 'receiving' state will be needed. In order to reduce the start-up time for the IM, options could be canvassed prior to the Peace Agreement.

To perform its functions effectively, the IM will need a presence in the countries where Palestinian refugees are residing at the inception of the IM and where they will move to during implementation. The level of this presence, which should be arranged through the Secretariat, will be different in the different locations and for the different purposes, i.e. residency options, restitution and compensation. Permanent offices are likely to be needed in the Palestinian State, Israel, Jordan, Lebanon and Syria. Depending on the volume of activities at a given time, for example, large numbers of resettlements to, or compensation claims from a particular country, offices might also have to be set up temporarily in other countries.

In this connection, there arises a question of to what extent UNRWA should and could perform such 'regional' functions for the IM and facilitate its local operations. UNRWA's knowledge of and access to the Palestinian refugees in the areas under its responsibility could provide significant support for the IM's outreach and registration activities, both for the claims and other parts. Its services could also be helpful in facilitating the integration and development activities of the IM. If the UNRWA were to be assigned such a role, this would have to be brought in line with its current and eventual future mandate.

For the outreach to and registration of refugees in countries outside the region, the Secretariat could also cooperate with organizations such as IOM, which has a world-wide net of country offices and which has for many years been involved in such outreach and registration activities, both in compensation and other contexts.

Cross-Cutting Issues

Question 21: How and by whom should the status of refugees for purposes of the residency options be established?

Several of the documents at Taba foresaw a special committee that would establish the status of a refugee for purposes of his or her residency options under the Peace Agreement. Such a centralized determination of refugee status by the IM (whether through a special committee or, what would be more practical, directly by the Secretariat) would have several advantages. It would ensure consistency, avoid duplications and provide the refugees with the possibility of having their eligibility for all options confirmed in one process.

On the other hand, given the large numbers of applicants and their geographic distribution, this process would require a large administration and would take a long time to complete, even if, as proposed, the prior registration with UNRWA would be taken as a presumption of refugee status. In addition, a central determination of refugee status by the IM is not likely to be accepted by Israel or by the receiving countries for return and resettlement activities. It therefore seems preferable to let the different components of the IM make their own determination of refugee status as they proceed, rather than holding up the provision of their respective benefits by a centralized initial 'entry examination' for all applicants.

Question 22: What measures could the IM take to maximize the choice of the refugee?

While the choice of the refugee will be the basic premise underlying the options provided for in the Peace Agreement, its practical exercise will be subject to certain constraints. It is therefore important to maximize the choice within these constraints. As such, linking the refugee's choice to the implementation activities will be a key task of the IM. This will include: (i) outreach to refugees and public information on which options are and are not available, and on their modalities; (ii) 'collection' of the refugee's choice where the IM has an active role in its implementation; and (iii) based on the choice, 'referring' the refugee and his/her descendants and family members to the entities outside the IM that will be responsible for the realization of the choice.

Further Preparatory Work

Much preparatory work has been done by the Parties and other stakeholders, as well as in policy and technical research. Based on the discussions in this paper, suggestions for additional preparatory work are listed below.

By the Palestinian side:
- Identify priority beneficiaries and priorities for the implementation of the residential options and for the restitution and compensation process;
- Identify fast-track/quick impact benefits;
- Organize evidentiary support for property claims from archives and historic records;
- Develop options for the valuation of the property claims;
- Manage the expectations of the refugees;
- Communicate with host countries and internationals.

By Israel:
- Manage the expectations of the Israeli public;
- Organize evidentiary support for property claims from archives and historic records located in Israel;
- Communicate with international partners on level of support that is required and that can be expected from them.

By international actors:
- Manage expectations of the parties, in particular those of the Palestinians, about what their contributions will and will not be;
- Coordinate and sequence the linkage between preparatory work and the negotiations;
- Close gaps in the technical knowledge;
- Research the cost of the IM;
- Consider the possible role of UNRWA in the IM and beyond;
- Encourage preparations by host countries;
- Encourage preparations by relevant international organizations;
- Facilitate discussions on ownership for IM.

Concluding Remarks

The implementation of the agreed solution to the Palestinian refugee issue will be complex. The IM will therefore require significant technical capacity. Policymakers and negotiators do not have technical implementation experience. They are likely to conclude political compromises and to leave many of the details to be decided at the implementation stage. This could be advantageous if what is regulated in the Peace Agreement is implementable and leaves the IM the necessary flexibility.

Considerable technical expertise and a body of good practices from other mechanisms are available that negotiators and creators of the IM can draw on. It will be important to consider what impact the policy decisions in the Peace Agreement will have on its implementation, as well as how the realities of the implementation should shape the policy decisions.

As soon as a Peace Agreement is concluded, there will be great expectations and enormous pressure for quick results. To avoid disappointment and backlash, all stakeholders, and in particular the Palestinian side, should identify benefits that can be fast-tracked and that will have quick impact, and they should develop strategies and plans to prioritize their implementation.

All stakeholders should consider what they might be able to prepare prior to a Peace Agreement. While the Parties' role in the negotiations must not be prejudiced, informal communication and coordination with them will help synchronize and manage expectations.

Notes

1. The views expressed in this paper are those of the authors and do not necessarily represent those of IOM.
2. For a very useful summary of past official negotiations, wider discussions among regional states and international organizations, as well as unofficial and 'second track' initiatives, see Rex Brynen, 'The Past as Prelude? Negotiating the Palestinian Refugee Issue', Chatham House Briefing Paper MEP/BR BP 08/01, (London: Chatham House, 2008), at: www.chathamhouse.org/publications/papers/view/108831
3. The relevant parts on refugees of these positions are contained as Appendices 1–6 in Rex Brynen, 'The Past as Prelude? Negotiating the Palestinian Refugee Issue', Chatham House Briefing Paper MEP/BR BP 08/01, London: Chatham House, 2008, pp. 13–23.

4. For a recent overview of the different roles that the international community has played in the establishment and implementation of claims and reparation programmes, see Heike Niebergall and Norbert Wühler, 'International Support for Reparation Processes and the Palestinian Refugee Issue', Chatham House Middle East and North Africa Programme Paper MENA PP 2012/02.

5. The Israeli draft of the Framework Agreement on Permanent Status contains the following: 'An International Commission (Commission) shall be established. Canada, the European Union, the Host Countries (Jordan, Syria, Lebanon, and Egypt), Japan, Norway, the State of Palestine, [the PLO], the Russian Federation, the United Nations, the United States and Israel shall be invited to participate therein.' Available as Appendix 1 in Rex Brynen, *supra* n. 3, p. 13.

6. The Palestinian Position on Refugees of 22 January 2001 at Taba states: 'The [Repatriation] Commission shall be composed of representatives from the United Nations, the United States, the Parties, UNRWA, the Arab host countries, the EU, and Canada…. The [Compensation] Commission shall be composed of representatives from the Parties, the United States, the EU, the United Nations, the World Bank and donor countries.' Available as Appendix 4 in Rex Brynen, *supra* n. 3, p. 15.

7. Israel's Private Response to Palestinian Refugee Paper (draft 2) of 22 January 2001 at Taba, states: 'The International Commission shall consist of the Palestinian State, Host Countries, Israel and members of the international community, including the United Nations, the World Bank, the European Union and the G8, as well as other relevant international institutions.' Available as Appendix 5 in Rex Brynen, *supra* n. 3, p. 17.

8. The Joint Refugee Mechanism Paper (draft 2), Taba, 25 January 2001 states: 'In addition to themselves, the Parties call upon the United Nations, the United States, the Parties, UNRWA, the Arab host countries, the EU, Canada, Norway, and Japan, _____ to be the members of the [International] Commission [for Palestinian Refugees].' Available as Appendix 4 in Rex Brynen, *supra* n. 3, pp. 15–17.

9. See Paragraph 54 of the Palestinian Position on Refugees of 22 January 2001 at Taba; available as Appendix 4 in Rex Brynen, *supra* n. 3, pp. 15–17.

10. The United Nations Compensation Commission (UNCC) was created in 1991 as a subsidiary organ of the United Nations Security Council. Its mandate was to process claims and pay compensation for losses and damage suffered as a direct result of Iraq's unlawful invasion and occupation of Kuwait in 1990/91. The UNCC has been the largest international claims programme to date. It resolved over 2.6 million claims submitted through 96 governments. The UNCC was set up for a limited time period and has completed the processing of claims and the payment of awards. It is now finalizing a number of residual tasks, such as archiving its records and monitoring the use of funds awarded for environmental loss and damage. For further details, see www.uncc.ch.

11. See Article 6, Paragraphs 77 and 79 of the Israeli draft of the Framework Agreement on Permanent Status, available as Appendix 1 in Rex Brynen, *supra* n. 3, p. 13.

12. See Paragraph 12 of Israel's Private Response to Palestinian Refugee Paper (draft 2), of 22 January 2001 at Taba, available as Appendix 5 in Rex Brynen, *supra* n. 3, p. 17.

13. The Joint Refugee Mechanism Paper is available as Appendix 6 in Rex Brynen, *supra* n. 3, p. 19.

14. See Paragraph 46 of the Palestinian Position on Refugees of 22 January 2001 at Taba, available as Appendix 4 in Rex Brynen, *supra* n. 3, p. 15 ff.

15. See Paragraph 10 of Israel's Private Response to Palestinian Refugee Paper (draft 2) of 22 January 2001, at Taba, available as Appendix 5 in Rex Brynen, *supra* n. 3, p. 17.

16. Ibid., see Paragraph 10b.

17. See Paragraphs 3–8 of the Joint Refugee Mechanism Paper (draft 2) of 25 January 2001 at Taba, available as Appendix 6 in Rex Brynen, *supra* n. 3, p. 17.

18. Ibid., see Paragraph 31.

19. The German Foundation 'Remembrance, Responsibility and Future' was established under German law following a wave of class action lawsuits against Germany and German companies in the United States for financial compensation for slave and forced labourers and certain other victims of National Socialist injustice. The law, the so-called German Foundation Act, also established a programme to make financial compensation available to slave and forced labourers of the National Socialist regime. For further information, see www.stiftung-evz.de.

20. This refers to several studies, carried out in two phases by the World Bank 'to gain a better understanding of the technical issues that would need to be addressed as agreed solutions to the refugee issue are implemented, and to examine the probable costs of different proposals to inform the discussion on what is feasible and over what time frame'; see Nick Krafft and Ann Elwan, 'Infrastructure scenarios for refugees and displaced persons', in Rex Brynen and Roula El-Rifai (eds), *Palestinian Refugees: Challenges of Repatriation and Development* (London: I.B. Tauris, 2007), p. 132.

21. The following paragraphs should be read in conjunction with Rex Brynen's paper on 'Return, Repatriation, Residency and Resettlement', Chapter 4 in this volume, which examines the various options and choices for permanent residency in detail.

22. See Paragraphs 7–14 of the Palestinian Position on Refugees of 22 January 2001 at Taba, Rex Brynen, *supra* n. 3, p. 15.

23. See Paragraphs 21 and 22 of the Joint Refugee Mechanism Paper (draft 2) of 25 January 2001 at Taba, Rex Brynen, *supra* n. 3, p. 19.

24. See Rex Brynen, 'Return, Repatriation, Residency and Resettlement', Chapter 4 in this volume. For a wider discussion of the key absorption and development dimensions of the Palestinian refugee issue see Rex Brynen 'Refugee Absorption and Development', Chapter 8 in this volume.

25. Michael Fischbach, *Records of Dispossession: Palestinian Refugee Property and the Arab–Israeli Conflict,* (New York: Columbia University Press, 2003), p. 129.

26. Given the large number of Palestinian refugee claims, and based on the experience of processing times from other claims programmes, more than

one commission will be needed for each of the tracks proposed here for the Property Loss Panel to be able to complete the review and decision of the claims within any politically acceptable time-frame. The same will be the case for the Fixed Sums Panel. In addition, in order to provide the necessary legal and technical support to the various commissions of these Panels, the Secretariat will require very substantial staff resources in the restitution and compensation area alone.

27. For a discussion of these matters, see Heike Niebergall and Norbert Wühler, 'Refugee Compensation: Policy Choices and Implementation Issues' Chapter 6 in this volume.

3

Whither UNRWA?

Liana Brooks-Rubin

Introduction

One set of key questions related to implementing a final status agreement on Palestinian refugees revolves around the future of the UN Relief and Works Agency for Palestine Refugees in the Near East (UNRWA). There are, according to a 2001 study conducted by Exeter University, at least two divergent schools of thought about a role for UNRWA in implementing an agreement.[1] Those in the 'UNRWA plus' school argue that UNRWA should play the lead role in coordinating and implementing so-called durable solutions for Palestinian refugees in addition to gradually handing over its functions to the Palestinian Authority (PA) and other host governments. On the other hand, the 'UNRWA minus' school argues that UNRWA's role should be limited to the provision of assistance to refugees while transferring responsibilities to host governments.

There has been no recent published analysis of UNRWA's future role, although it would be fair to say that most experts agree that a sudden termination of UNRWA would imperil the smooth transfer of services to host countries, put donor contributions at risk and spark refugee discontent, all of which would undermine the potential for success of any refugee agreement.

This chapter will address some of the key issues relating to UNRWA's wind-down, including an analysis of the Agency's capacities and weaknesses and an examination of its potential future role. Before doing so, the chapter will first focus on how past agreements have treated the issue of UNRWA, as well as the primary interests and negotiating priorities of key stakeholders.

Past Agreements

There are relatively few specifics about UNRWA in the official bilateral agreements apart from the specification (in some) about the future date by which point the Agency should cease to exist and the mention (in some) that UNRWA should be a part of an international committee or mechanism for implementing the agreement on refugees. In the Taba Accords of 2001, both Israeli and Palestinian negotiators agreed that UNRWA should be part of the International Commission for Palestinian Refugees and that UNRWA should be phased out 'in accordance with an agreed timetable of five years as a targeted period', while the Palestinian negotiators added a possible adjustment of this period subject to the implementation of other aspects of the agreement pertaining to refugees.[2] The Geneva Accords also call for a five-year phase-out period, although the Accords also stipulated that the Agency should be phased out in each 'country in which it operates based on the end of refugee status in that country' and similarly noted that UNRWA should be part of an International Commission.[3] Neither the Clinton Parameters of December 2000 nor the April 2003 Roadmap made explicit reference to UNRWA. Subsequent sections of this chapter will address the issue of a time-frame for UNRWA wind-down and the various potential role(s) UNRWA might play as part of an international body formed to implement a final status agreement on refugees.

Interests and Priorities of the Major Parties

Palestinian negotiators have traditionally been concerned about the possibility of terminating UNRWA prematurely and likely will remain committed to a gradual wind-down that is contingent on satisfactory implementation of the refugee components of an agreement. The Palestinian leadership recognizes that the vast majority of refugees (especially outside the West Bank and Gaza) consider UNRWA to represent them and would be wary of a backlash if UNRWA termination occurs too quickly.

Furthermore, Palestinian negotiators are aware of the considerable cost involved in absorbing UNRWA's services and currently lack the capacity to do so. Similarly, Palestinian negotiators are likely to advocate for UNRWA to play a significant role in implementing a final status agreement. While relations between the Palestinian Authority and UNRWA sometimes are tense, the PA believes that UNRWA is well-placed compared to other UN agencies to mediate between the desires, needs and demands of millions of Palestinian refugees on the one hand and the international community, host governments and Israel on the other.

Israeli negotiators have, in past negotiations, pressed for a quick termination of UNRWA, citing the need to end the existence of a separate refugee agency dedicated to Palestinian refugees. That said and despite frequently expressed Israeli government misgivings about UNRWA, there is reason to believe that Israel would be interested in ensuring that UNRWA's handover of services to host governments – especially the Palestinian Authority – is smooth, even if this involves a longer implementation period. By and large (and despite continuing criticisms), Israeli government officials recognize that UNRWA is a stabilizing force in a volatile region; this is especially true in Gaza, Lebanon and the West Bank.[4] Israel will want to ensure that there is no refugee backlash on the West Bank and Gaza, which could result from perceptions that termination of UNRWA is too quick. Israel will definitely be keen to ensure that there is a clear end date for the existence of UNRWA that coincides with the solution of the refugee problem. By the same token, Israeli negotiators, who previously agreed that UNRWA should have a role on an international commission to implement the agreement, may want this role to be limited to handing over its services and acting as a conduit of information between refugees and other stakeholders.

Host countries will want to ensure a gradual wind-down of UNRWA. This will be true for all three of the host countries, but particularly for Jordan, which hosts the largest number of refugees and is anxious about assuming the cost and other burdens of UNRWA's operations. If refugees in Lebanon are accorded priority for return or resettlement, the government there might not be particularly concerned with the length of wind-down. The host countries feel strongly that UNRWA should be the primary (if not the only) international organization involved in implementing a refugee agreement. In general, UNRWA has a very good working relationship with the host governments and is considered a much more trusted institution than the UN High Commissioner for Refugees (UNHCR), which works in all three countries dealing with Iraqi refugees, or the UN Development

Program (UNDP). Given Jordan's (and to a lesser extent the other host countries) strong interest in receiving compensation from the international community for hosting Palestinian refugees for over 60 years and the international communities' general opposition to this type of compensation, one issue for policymakers to consider would be how to direct development assistance to host countries (including to the Palestinian Authority) in such a way that accounts for the significant costs they will absorb once UNRWA tapers down its operations.

The international community may have divergent views on a UNRWA wind-down as well as the role the Agency should play in implementing an agreement. According to the authors of the 2001 Exeter University study, the volume and intensity of anti-UNRWA criticisms over the years has persuaded some experts in the international arena that UNRWA should have limited involvement in implementing a final status agreement.[5] Judging from more recent gatherings of policymakers and academic experts (e.g. Chatham House meetings), there seems to be growing acceptance of the fact that UNRWA should have a role in some aspects of implementation. As with the Israelis, the extent to which UNRWA continues to be viewed by key international stakeholders as a force for stability is the extent to which the Agency's call for it to play a central role in implementation will be taken seriously. Donors will want clear information about how UNRWA's budget will decrease as it transitions services to host governments. There is a legitimate concern that given the likely extended time-frame for implementation of an agreement, donors will be expected to bear the still-high UNRWA operational costs in addition to ramping up development assistance or compensation for the Palestinian Authority and host countries.

UNRWA Wind-Down: Rapid Termination, Slow Phase-Out or Open-Ended Timetable?

Regardless of the nature and extent of UNRWA's role in an international implementation mechanism, there are a significant number of operational, technical and legal issues (addressed in the next section) that stakeholders will need to understand and ultimately address in the context of designing a successful implementation mechanism. It should be noted that contrary to pronouncements by some that the transition of assets, staff and services from UNRWA to host governments is a simple paper arrangement, those immersed in studying the operational, technical and legal issues involved in an UNRWA transition estimate that this wind-down will require more than the five years envisioned in previous agreements. While recognizing the importance (symbolic and otherwise) of the dissolution of UNRWA to mark the clear end of the Palestinian refugee problem, experts seem hesitant about offering a specific time-frame, noting that in the absence of any certainty about the ultimate permanent place of residence for refugees, it is extremely difficult to plan the future of camps or health/educational facilities. Compounding this uncertainty is the oft-cited fact that candid discussions with either refugees or host governments about post-agreement scenarios, in the absence of movement on the political front, are deemed by UNRWA and policymakers alike as being at best extremely sensitive and at worst potentially explosive.

The dangers of a premature termination of UNRWA include: risking tens of millions of dollars of donor contributions, undermining the smooth transfer of services from UNRWA to host governments, and sparking massive discontent among Palestinian refugees. On the other hand, an open-ended transition period would compound UNRWA's chronic budget shortfalls as donors will probably be more interested in focusing resources on development and reintegration initiatives in the region.[6] Moreover, Israel and other stakeholders would object for political and symbolic reasons to an open-ended time-frame. Given these considerations, policymakers may want to consider that a more realistic time-frame for a complete UNRWA wind-down might be 7–10 years, although UNRWA's role will necessarily change immediately following the signing of an agreement as it begins to transition services to host governments.

In summary, the transition to a post-UNRWA period needs to be well-planned and gradual, the resource implications should be included in an overall cost analysis of implementing a successful refugee agreement, and a flexible but not totally open-ended time-frame will be key to ensuring a smooth transition, mitigating potential unrest among refugees, and taking into account the interests of key stakeholders – particularly Israel and the international community –

to have a clear end to the refugee issue, which necessarily involves the termination of UNRWA.

Key Issues and Challenges Related to UNRWA Wind-Down

As previously noted, one of the biggest challenges for planning a UNRWA wind-down are all the unknowns about what the parameters of a final agreement will look like and which choices refugees are likely to make based on those parameters. That said, there are a number of technical, legal, operational and even political issues that can be considered prior to resolution of a negotiated agreement; these issues may inform decisions about UNRWA's role in implementation, as well as the time-frame for wind-down.

Analysis of UNRWA's Capacities

Sixty years of providing humanitarian assistance and services to Palestinian refugees inarguably means UNRWA's knowledge of the refugee communities in its five fields of operation is deep and its experience negotiating complicated legal issues with host governments – particularly involving land use – is unmatched. On this basis alone, it would be difficult to argue that UNRWA should have a very constrained role in the implementation of a final status agreement on refugees.

Apart from its long-standing experience and deep knowledge of the refugee populations, one of UNRWA's more tangible assets is the fact that its staff and beneficiaries are the 'human capital' of either the future Palestinian state or neighbouring countries in a post-Israeli–Palestinian conflict Middle East. The vast majority of UNRWA's staff – teachers, doctors, social workers, sanitation workers, engineers and administrators – are Palestinian refugees themselves and their training, work experience, and presumed commitment to the health, well-being and education of Palestinian refugees represents a significant asset to the countries in the region, including the future Palestinian state. As both members of the Palestinian refugee community and representatives of an international body, area staff often play a unique and important role in bridging the numerous perception gaps between the international community and the refugee populations they serve.

UNRWA staff also bear the brunt of refugees' discontent over host government policies and practices, as well as enforcing UNRWA management decisions to cut back on or modify assistance packages due to, for example, financial constraints.

The importance of UNRWA staff members' relationship with refugees in a handover context should not be underestimated. UNRWA staff will need to continue building effective mechanisms for engaging with refugees, including communicating honestly and realistically about their options and UNRWA's changing responsibilities. Uncertainty, confusion, disappointment and frustration are emotions that are likely to be felt by many refugees in the aftermath of a political agreement governing their future and the extent to which the international community and UNRWA are prepared to bridge perception gaps and communicate openly about options is the extent to which inevitable tensions are more likely to be defused.

Although many experts envision that UNRWA area teachers, social workers, doctors, drivers and other key staff will simply make the transition from being employees of UNRWA to being employees of the public or private sector, one possible scenario is that staff members en masse will choose to leave well before wind-down is complete in order to avoid being viewed as complicit with an unsatisfactory political agreement. Considering a time-frame of up to ten years for wind-down, this scenario could significantly hamper a smooth transition. In order to mitigate the possibility of a premature mass exodus of staff, UNRWA will need to develop, in conjunction with host governments, a transitional staffing plan and an effective communications strategy. Depending upon UNRWA's role in implementation, the Agency's staffing plan might also need to plan on hiring additional staff members for jobs relating to implementation even as the Agency transfers staff members in service-provision areas to the employ of host governments.

It is also important for policymakers to consider that UNRWA is considered by a majority of Palestinian refugees to be the most trusted public institution in their lives. Most refugee experts agree that the degree to which implementing an agreement succeeds will hinge upon: the extent to which Palestinian refugees' voices are taken into consideration in the design and implementation of an agreement; the degree to which the contours of an agreement are communicated successfully to refugees; and the perception among refugees that real choices exist and that such choices are actually voluntary.

While the PLO is the official 'sole legitimate voice' of the Palestinian people, there is scant evidence to support the contention that a majority of Palestinian refugees believe that their interests are represented by the PLO or the PA. On the whole, the Palestinian leadership is perceived as being consumed with other issues that are arguably more immediately relevant to the formation of a viable Palestinian state. While perhaps obvious, it bears noting that the bilateral Israeli–Palestinian negotiating framework is constrained as it pertains to the refugee issue given both the lack of representation of refugee host governments in the negotiations and the perception among the vast majority of refugees that their leadership does not represent them. (Chapter 5 in this volume examines the positions of host governments vis-à-vis Palestinian refugees.) While the Palestinian leadership presumably could be doing more in the way of outreach and arguably should ultimately be on the hook to seek refugee buy-ins for various compensation and permanent residency options, it is unrealistic to expect that the PLO or PA will replace UNRWA as a trusted voice for refugees.

Those in the UNRWA-plus group frequently note that the Agency has demonstrated flexibility in adapting itself to changing circumstances. Indeed UNRWA, with the support of the international community, has addressed an enormous range of assistance and protection needs of Palestinian refugees resulting from conflicts, further displacement, political developments (e.g. the Hamas takeover in Gaza and subsequent international blockade). These activities go well beyond UNRWA's traditional health and education activities, which the Agency has maintained while responding to the needs arising from various emergencies.

It bears repeating that there seems to be a growing (if grudging) appreciation among policymakers and even UNRWA's long-standing critics for the Agency's contributions towards stability in a frequently volatile region. Perceptions of UNRWA as a stabilizing force are important in as much as Israelis, Palestinians and members of the international community (especially the USA) will largely determine the role UNRWA will play in implementing an agreement. The international community's perception of the Agency both as value-added and as a neutral and honest stakeholder will ultimately have some influence over decisions about the nature of UNRWA's role in implementation. When faced with persistent allegations and criticisms, UNRWA struggles to maintain adequate levels of funding from Western donors – as most recently witnessed by the Canadian government's decision in 2009 not to provide its traditional contribution to the Agency's General Fund. On the other hand, when and if key donor governments are confident that UNRWA's practices are consistent with its stated neutrality policies, there is a greater likelihood that UNRWA will be entrusted with a significant role in shaping the design and implementation of elements of a final agreement on refugees.

One area touted by UNRWA supporters as a critical element of the Agency's contribution to regional stability is its primary education programme. At present nearly half a million Palestinian refugees receive free basic education in 668 UNRWA-run elementary and preparatory schools. Historically, Palestinian refugee students in all five fields of operation consistently have achieved higher test results than students in public schools. Literacy rates among Palestinian refugees compare favourably with regional and global levels and gender equity in enrolment has been in place at UNRWA schools since the 1960s.[7] Recent educational achievement results have showed some decline among students in some fields, including Gaza, Lebanon and the West Bank, reflecting a number of factors, including disruptions caused by ongoing conflict, budget deficits, overcrowding and declining quality of educational infrastructure.

It is notable that UNRWA with Western donor support has developed a supplementary tolerance education curriculum, which since 2002 has been integrated into specific subjects at all of the Agency's schools. As a result, Palestinian refugee students enrolled in UNRWA schools are exposed to educational materials focused on principles of human rights, tolerance, conflict resolution, gender equality and diversity; these supplementary materials are unmatched in public schools throughout the region. While there has as yet not been an evaluation of the impact of the tolerance education curriculum on students' attitudes, policymakers, lawmakers, educational experts, and even some of UNRWA's critics have been impressed with both the curriculum and anecdotal evidence that many UNRWA students are absorbing the values and principles contained in the supplementary education materials.

One of UNRWA's stated aims is to inculcate staff and beneficiaries with values of neutrality and universality; these principles are woven into the Agency's employment policies and ongoing staff training modules. In a highly politicized environment where public statements are scrutinized extensively, UNRWA staff members are criticized not infrequently for failing to maintain these neutrality principles, however, it bears noting that in 2009 high-profile actions to enforce the neutrality policy in Gaza earned UNRWA and especially its Gaza field director unusual praise from long-time critic, US Congressman Steve Rothman.[8] While it is unlikely that UNRWA's record on neutrality will ever fully satisfy critics on either side of the political spectrum, its neutrality mandate and its experience navigating these issues in a complex operating environment could well be viewed as an asset.

UNRWA is on target to complete a multi-year undertaking to computerize all refugee registration records and make them accessible via an intranet service, as well as to issue individually numbered identity cards that are connected to the computerized system. The computerization of UNRWA's records will in the short-term help with more accurate determinations of who is using UNRWA's services and how often, and will ultimately be quite helpful for determining eligibility for compensation and/or residency options. It bears noting, however, that depending upon the ultimate agreed definition of a Palestinian refugee, there likely will be thousands of non-UNRWA Palestinians eligible for compensation for whom there is no centralized records system.

Analysis of UNRWA's Limitations and Key Challenges

One factor that could potentially limit UNRWA's role in implementing an agreement are the persistent criticisms that have dogged the Agency, including perceptions of its politicization as well as views that UNRWA seeks to perpetuate the refugee problem for political reasons. Other relevant criticisms often are directed at UNRWA, but are perhaps more appropriately directed at the UN General Assembly, including the fact that there is a separate UN agency for Palestinian refugees as well as a separate set of criteria for Palestinian refugees, who – among other things – are permitted to maintain refugee status even if they are citizens of a state.

Arguments aside about the appropriateness of maintaining two separate refugee agencies, it is virtually impossible to imagine that the UN General Assembly will dissolve UNRWA and replace it with UNHCR – especially in the absence of a political agreement. Furthermore, as former UNRWA General Counsel and current critic James Lindsay point out, replacing UNRWA with UNHCR would do nothing to resolve key issues of compensation and permanent place of residency that must be worked out by the parties in the context of a political agreement. Still, the persistence of these and other criticisms underscores the inherent distrust many in policy and academic circles – especially in Israel and the USA – have of UNRWA. As this author heard more than once from both Israeli and US government officials, it matters little to the hard-core critics that UNRWA continues to implement meaningful reforms, including improvements to vetting and other due diligence measures or even that UNRWA officials refrain altogether from making statements perceived as political. Most of these hard-core critics admit that they won't be satisfied until UNRWA ceases to exist.

While it is difficult to predict the impact of the criticisms on designing a post-agreement role for UNRWA, it is fair to assume that there may be one. In short, the fewer controversies UNRWA faces, the more likely it is that stakeholders will be willing to consider it as an indispensable partner in assisting the transition from refugeehood to Palestinian citizenship.

Another area that could potentially limit UNRWA's effectiveness in the future is the coordination gaps in service provision between its field offices and host authorities. Although the situation varies from field to field, it is clear that there are some significant policy and information gaps that would need to be addressed through intensive information sharing, establishment of local and national coordination mechanisms, and in some cases joint UNRWA–host government initiatives or projects. In certain fields, it is as though UNRWA is operating in a parallel universe as the relevant government ministries are largely unaware of basic information such as location of UNRWA facilities or the costs per beneficiary. By the same token, many UNRWA staff in these fields also lack basic information about Ministry of

Health and Education policies or local practices. There also exists little to no knowledge about host government capacity to eventually take over UNRWA facilities and services – something that will be of critical importance to donors who, in the absence of information about capacities, may not be willing to provide money directly to host governments as part of an overall wind-down package.

One UNRWA staff member estimates that it would take a minimum of two years to build the type of coordination necessary for a seamless handover of assets and service provision. While policy and programming coordination in advance of a political agreement would seem desirable – and indeed has started to occur in some fields – host governments by and large resist such coordination, viewing it as yet another way in which the international community is intent on imposing local integration of Palestinian refugees before an agreement exists.

Another area of potential challenge are issues related to land ownership. UNRWA does not own camp lands, but rather leases them from private landowners and, in some cases, from host governments. There is the potential for a virtual tsunami of lawsuits from private landowners unless the UNRWA wind-down process is carefully calibrated with host governments, which will expect the opportunity to buy or expropriate privately-owned camp lands and sufficient time to plan for the use of camp lands in national housing and development schemes. A measured approach for an UNRWA wind-down coupled with good coordination between UNRWA, host governments and private landowners should theoretically ensure a reasonably smooth transition process.

UNRWA does own the vast majority of its assets such as schools, clinics, community centres and offices, and there are established UN rules governing the handover of assets to host governments and other parties. UNRWA is in the process of updating the value of its assets so that information will be current to allow for a smooth handover.

Cost issues loom large; transferring camp land and other assets will be resource intensive and the longer the transition period, the more difficult it will be to sustain UNRWA's transformed operations, while ensuring adequate support for the governments absorbing these costs. UNRWA has struggled mightily with budget shortfalls for decades, donor fatigue is always a potential issue when dealing with Palestinian issues, and there remain serious disagreements about how much the Israelis will contribute. Even if all Israeli contributions are for refugee compensation, significant resources could offset the need for the international community to provide host governments with significant development assistance. Questions of overall costs as well as issues related to which parties should be responsible for bearing which costs are discussed in detail in Chapter 5 of this volume.

Finally, UNRWA's mandate, unless changed, arguably will limit the role it plays in implementing an agreement and specifically with regard to the implementation of durable solutions. UNRWA was established by UN General Assembly Resolution 302 (IV) in December 1949 to carry out 'in collaboration with local governments direct relief and works programmes', as well as to 'consult with the interested Near Eastern Governments concerning measures to be taken preparatory to the time when international assistance for relief and works projects is no longer available.'[9] Unlike Resolution 428, which established UNHCR in 1951, Resolution 302 does not provide UNRWA with a detailed mandate. UNRWA's mandate was originally envisaged as being temporary (it is renewed every three years), which may explain why Resolution 301 (IV) is sparse on details and definitions.

Since its founding, both UNRWA's mandate and its operations have evolved to match the changing situation on the ground and the needs of its beneficiaries. Early on, UNRWA interpreted 'direct relief and works', as the provision of basic nutrition, shelter, primary health care and education. The aforementioned elements have remained a very important part of UNRWA's core services, however, the Agency also has expanded its operations to include more development-oriented activities such as vocational training, large-scale jobs creation programmes, micro-finance and micro-lending programmes. Arguably, this quiet economic integration will ultimately contribute to a smoother UNRWA wind-down and the integration of refugees in the region. However, the evolution of UNRWA's activities notwithstanding, the Agency clearly does not have a mandate to seek, facilitate or implement durable solutions for refugees. While some argue that the UN General Assembly should change UNRWA's mandate in the event of a final status agreement on refugees, others believe that UNHCR – given its explicit protection role – would be better placed to serve in this role.

It is beyond the scope of this chapter to examine the mandate of UNHCR or analyse the 1951 Convention Relating to the Status of Refugees and its 1967 Protocol. However, several key issues are relevant to the topic at hand and therefore worth a mention. First, Palestinian refugees entitled to register with UNRWA are excluded from the mandate of UNHCR as well as from the protection of the 1951 Convention. The Convention directs UNHCR to

> assume the function of providing international protection, under the auspices of the United Nations, to refugees who fall under the scope of the present Statute and of seeking permanent solutions for the problem of refugees by assisting Governments and, subject to the approval of the Governments concerned, private organizations to facilitate the voluntary repatriation of such refugees, or their assimilation within new national communities.[10]

Given UNHCR's explicit mandate to implement durable solutions and its extensive experience in doing so, policymakers might want to consider a role for UNHCR in an international mechanism. This is particularly true if third-country resettlement outside the region is an option since traditional resettlement countries primarily rely on UNHCR and its partners for both refugee status determinations (although UNHCR criteria are not likely to be relevant in the Palestinian case) and referrals. These issues will be revisited later in the chapter.

Potential Roles for UNRWA in Implementing a Refugee Agreement

Based on analysis of previous agreements governing the resolution of refugee situations, experts agree that successful implementation of such agreements is characterized by the involvement of a lead agency that has a thorough knowledge of the refugee community, including its culture, traditions, concerns and aspirations, as well as a good understanding of relevant legal issues, including: access to land, occupancy rights and land title systems; legal safeguards such as amnesties; and military service obligations. UNRWA's long-standing experience serving Palestinian refugees, the trust it enjoys by and large among refugees, host governments, donor governments, and

Palestinians and Israelis (albeit the latter with serious reservations) is likely to translate into giving it a significant future role. It is clear that UNRWA is well-placed to perform the following functions:

Outreach and Communication: UNRWA is in a good position to serve as a liaison between the parties, the international mechanism and Palestinian refugees. While the PLO and host governments should arguably bear primary responsibility for managing refugee expectations, realistically UNRWA will have many more meaningful opportunities to communicate with refugees about the details of a refugee agreement, answer questions about options, support international messages and encourage refugees to take advantage of peace dividends. UNRWA could operate information centres locally, which would in turn direct refugees to other addresses, if appropriate (i.e. for compensation and resettlement). Given UNRWA's need to maintain credibility among refugees, policymakers would need to consider in advance how to empower UNRWA to be in a position to build consensus rather than fend off negative backlash.

Transition of Services/Wind-Down: As discussed, UNRWA will need to work hand-in-hand with host governments and donors on a realistic time-frame for transitioning its camps, facilities and staff to host governments. The earlier the existing gaps in coordination are bridged the smoother and less time-consuming the transition will be. Technical experts and policymakers alike should anticipate and address in advance issues such as transferring ownership of camp lands and maintaining employment opportunities for skilled area staff. UNRWA will need to continue providing assistance and services to refugees even as it transfers responsibility to host governments.

Refugee Development/Integration: During the transition period, UNRWA will need to work closely with host governments, other implementing partners and donors to develop and implement a comprehensive strategy for reintegration of refugees and post-agreement development solutions. As discussed in Chapters 5 and 8 of this volume, the PA and other host governments should include planning for refugee housing and overall integration as part of their national planning strategies. UNRWA is well-placed to act as the lead implementing partner for reintegration activities on behalf of the respective governments given its infrastructure, the scale of its current operations, its capacity and expertise. In other post-conflict scenarios, UNDP typically plays this role, while other UN agencies and NGOs implement smaller initiatives.

Other organizations that could be part of governments' comprehensive development schemes include:

- UNDP (which currently implements development programmes for non-refugees in the region);
- UNICEF (water, sanitation, nutrition);
- WHO (disease control/capacity building for Ministry of Health); and a host of NGOs;
- IOM would be well-placed to assist a lead agency in facilitated voluntary returns and could, as it does elsewhere, assist in the registration of refugees for the purposes of return or resettlement.

Role for UNRWA in Implementing Durable Solutions?

As mentioned, UNRWA's mandate would currently preclude it from implementing durable solutions, however, an argument could be made to revise UNRWA's mandate rather than to rely on organizations much less familiar with the exigencies of the population and host governments. It is interesting to note here that many of UNRWA's senior staff come from UNHCR and themselves have extensive experience facilitating voluntary repatriation in other parts of the world.

Considering UNHCR's mandate and its extensive experience in implementing large-scale repatriation operations, there is also a compelling case to be made for UNHCR involvement in the process. One idea is to second additional UNHCR staff members with relevant experience and expertise to UNRWA and another is to establish a joint UNHCR–UNRWA lead agency approach whereby each organization focuses on its primary area of expertise. The former model would necessarily involve a mandate change for UNRWA and might lead to culture clashes and or turf wars between staff in the organizations. The latter model would fit in nicely with UNHCR's approach to address the relief to development gap in previous post-repatriation scenarios, which it calls the '4Rs'. The 4Rs are: repatriation, reintegration, rehabilitation and reconstruction/development through local integration. The model aims to create successful partnerships between UN agencies, the World Bank and bilateral development partners in which international organizations and NGOs focus on their traditional implementation strengths; there is full government ownership of the process and sustained donor support is forthcoming.

In a joint UNRWA–UNHCR lead scenario, UNRWA could most reasonably be responsible for: communicating options and their implications to refugees; ascertaining refugee choice; negotiating legal status and land issues with host governments; and negotiating the particulars of transitioning services, facilities and staff to host governments. UNHCR would primarily be responsible for overseeing protection (including non-refoulement) for returnees and refugees opting to locally integrate. If third-country resettlement outside the region is an option for particular categories of refugees, UNHCR also would be responsible for overseeing this aspect of the agreement. Finally, both UNRWA and UNHCR would need to coordinate closely with a host of other implementing partners and stakeholders involved in the compensation/claims portion of an agreement, as well as with any organizations involved in transportation of refugees (e.g. IOM) and reintegration/rehabilitation/development assistance (e.g. UNDP).

In order to better illustrate how this overall concept might work in the Palestinian refugee context, it would be useful to examine in greater depth models of repatriation management.

Models of Repatriation Management

Two divergent models of repatriation management have emerged in analytical work on the Palestinian refugee issue. The first model, enshrined in the Taba non-papers and the unofficial Geneva Accords, envisages the establishment of an institutional structure to receive and determine applications for return, repatriation and resettlement. Both the Taba and Geneva Accords outline five options for refugees: return to Israel according to certain criteria and numerical limit; repatriation to areas of Israel swapped to a Palestinian state; repatriation to the Palestinian state, local integration in host countries; and resettlement to third countries outside the region. The Geneva Accords specify that there should be a Permanent Place of Residence (PPR) committee, which would receive and review applications from individual refugees and make decisions on the basis of refugees' preferences, available options and maintaining family unity. A paper issued in August 2008 by the Palestine Liberation Organization's Negotiation Support Unit (PLO-NSU) outlining the contours of an International Mechanism (IM) for implementing a 'just, agreed, and comprehensive solution to the Palestine refugee issue', argues that an international mechanism should identify refugees' chosen destinations as well as manage all operations of a repatriation, resettlement, and rehabilitation/local integration process.[11]

The second model of repatriation management emerged from comprehensive analytical work undertaken by the World Bank in the 1990s, which opposes influx controls to the Palestinian state and favours policies that would simplify refugee choice by leaving this choice largely in the hands of the refugees themselves. The World Bank researchers caution the international community against creating so-called 'perverse incentives' that would encourage movement to a Palestinian state disconnected from local economic and development conditions.[12]

Rex Brynen, who participated in the World Bank studies, wrote that

in many or most cases, (refugee) relocation decisions would be made by individuals and households based, in large part, on the relative degree of economic opportunity in the WBG, compared with conditions in their present host countries. Market mechanisms, notably price levels and unemployment rates, will act as a natural regulator of population movement.[13]

The type of model outlined in the Taba/Geneva Accords and promulgated by the PLO-NSU would, as the World Bank researchers contend, undoubtedly be overly cumbersome and ultimately population movements would be disconnected from local conditions and therefore less likely to be sustainable. However, the World Bank model contains little to no international involvement or oversight, which would leave serious protection gaps, would not adhere to international norms and may not be viewed as ending Palestinian refugeehood. An examination of past large-scale refugee repatriation operations illustrates that there is a middle ground that could be adapted successfully in the Palestinian refugee context.

As Sari Hanafi points out, large-scale refugee repatriations typically involve a 'complex legal framework and institutional arrangements as well as favourable political, economic, and social conditions.'[14] While Hanafi's characterization is true, it is also a fact that organized repatriation does not typically involve a process whereby refugees register their preferences about where they will be permanently settled with a commission as envisaged in the Taba and Geneva Accords. Instead, UNHCR with the support of the international community has developed the 'Tripartite Agreement/Commission' model in which UNHCR negotiates between the country or countries of asylum and the country of origin/return. UNHCR typically initiates negotiations as soon as there are indications that voluntary repatriation may be possible and appropriate; the negotiations should ultimately culminate in an agreement that outlines the terms and conditions of return. Voluntary Repatriation Agreements usually enshrine the principle of voluntariness, commitment of all parties to respect protection, non-refoulement and allowance of monitoring by an international organization in both the country of asylum and country of return. Voluntary repatriation agreements also stipulate that all signatories are committed to ensuring physical safety, the principle of family unity and the freedom of movement for refugees and returnees. Tripartite agreements also typically include provisions for regularizing the status of refugees opting to integrate locally in their host countries.

In the tripartite model of repatriation management, UNHCR, the country of asylum and the country of return form a commission to oversee the implementation of the agreement and address the practical or policy issues that might arise related to the terms and conditions of the agreement. Sometimes tripartite commissions involve trusted third parties as observers or participants in the commission. As in the Afghan refugee context in which separate agreements exist between UNHCR–Iran–Afghanistan and UNHCR–Pakistan–Afghanistan, separate tripartite agreements in the Palestinian refugee context would need to account for the differences in the political, legal and economic status of Palestinian refugees in their respective host countries. Tripartite agreements in the Palestinian refugee context also would need to ensure inclusion of the following: provision of some meaningful choices for refugees about their permanent place of residence; international protection and monitoring mechanisms for refugees in host countries and countries of return; and stipulation of legal rights as well as citizenship or residency status of refugees/ returnees in both host countries and countries of return. Tripartite agreements would also outline: the roles of relevant organizations in implementation; the time period of the wind-down process; and the international community's commitments in supporting integration and development programmes for refugees.

Conclusion

As this chapter underscores, one key aspect of a negotiated resolution of the Palestinian refugee issue involves the transitioning of UNRWA's responsibilities, services, assets and staff to the Palestinian Authority and other host governments that will inevitably absorb significant numbers of current Palestinian refugees. Past agreements have specified only a time-frame for UNRWA wind-down and that the Agency should be one player among many on an international commission for implementing the parameters of a negotiated agreement. A future agreement is similarly unlikely to contain many details about UNRWA's role, which could range from very narrow to quite broad.

It is important for negotiators and policymakers to understand the potential negative implications of specifying an unrealistically short timetable for an UNRWA phase-out, which could ultimately undermine the sustainability of an agreement. Ultimately, policymakers also will need to consider the appropriate role for UNRWA in implementing aspects of an agreement, as well as the potential role of other non-governmental actors. Giving the Agency too narrow a role could backfire given the likely backlash among refugees and host governments and the wasted time and resources required for another organization to scale up. On the other hand, giving UNRWA too broad a role – especially with regard to the implementation of durable solutions – not only would require a mandate change, but could also inhibit the Agency's ability to smoothly transition its services to host governments, undermine protection for refugees and significantly extend the amount of time involved in implementing a refugee agreement. In a nutshell, it will be important for stakeholders to get the UNRWA dimension right in designing an implementation mechanism.

Notes

1. Michael Dumper, 'The Return of Palestinian Refugees and Displaced Persons: The Evolution of an EU Policy on the Middle East Peace Process', pp. 15–16, online at: www.google.ca/url?sa=t&rct=j&q=dum pereupolicyonpalestinianrefugees&source=web&cd=1&ved=0CC4QF jAA&url=http%3A%2F%2Fsocialsciences.exeter.ac.uk%2Fpolitics%2F research%2Freadingroom%2FdumperEUpolicyOnPalestinianRefugees. rtf&ei=Jzr9UZKmJIX84AOwmYEI&usg=AFQjCNGxH7aQ9ki3VvKI DpYABsVj-VVuFg&sig2=jO-BBznnGC6an58NaQl4ZQ&bvm=bv.501 65853,d.dmg&cad=rja (accessed 3 August 2013).
2. Moratinos Summary of Taba, January 2001, online at: http://prrn.mcgill. ca/research/papers/moratinos.htm (accessed 11 June 2012).
3. Geneva Accord: Draft Permanent Status Agreement, October 2003, online at: http://prrn.mcgill.ca/research/documents/geneva.htm (accessed 26 December 2011).
4. For example, at the November 2009 UN General Assembly's Meeting of the 4th Committee, the Israeli delegate said the following: 'At the outset, I wish to reiterate Israel's support for UNRWA's important humanitarian mission. Over its sixty years of operation, UNRWA has displayed an enduring commitment to the extension of vital humanitarian assistance to Palestinian refugees. In so doing, UNRWA has contributed much to improving the lives of many needy people, many of whom have been tragically kept in a position of need by political forces largely beyond their control.' Statement online at: www.israel-un.org/statements-at-the-united-nations/general-assembly/184-4cunrwa031109 (accessed 11 June 2012).
5. Summary of Workshop on 'The Future of UNRWA', 19–20 February 2000, online at: http://prrn.mcgill.ca/research/papers/brynen_000219. htm (accessed 11 June 2012).
6. Ibid.
7. UN General Assembly, Report of the Commissioner-General of the United Nations Relief and Works Agency for Palestine Refugees in the Near East: Program Budget 2010–2011, Official Records of the Sixty-fourth Session, Supplement No. 13A, 2009.
8. Press Release from Congressman Rothman's Office, 'Rothman Meets with John Ging, UNRWA Director in Gaza', 22 October 2009, online at: http://rothman.house.gov/index.php?option=com_content&task=view&id=1164 (accessed 11 June 2012).
9. UN General Assembly, Assistance to Palestine Refugees, Resolution A/RES/302(IV), 8 December 1949, paragraph 7.
10. UN General Assembly, Statute of the Office of the United Nations High Commissioner for Refugees, Resolution 428(V), 14 December 1950.
11. From an unpublished PLO-NSU paper dated 12–18 July 2008. The author has a copy of this paper.

12. For a summary of the World Bank studies, see Rex Brynen, 'Refugees, Repatriation, and Development: Some Lessons from Recent Work', in R. Brynen and R. El-Rifai (eds), *Palestinian Refugees: Challenges of Repatriation and Development* (New York: I.B. Tauris, 2007), pp. 102–20.
13. Ibid., p. 103.
14. Sari Hanafi, S, 'Palestinian Return Migration: Lessons from the International Refugee Regime', in M. Dumper (ed.) *Palestinian Refugee Repatriation: Global Perspective*, (Abingdon and New York: Routledge Press, 2006), pp. 273–287.

4

Return, Repatriation, Residency and Resettlement

Rex Brynen

Introduction

The question of residence is perhaps the most sensitive and difficult aspect of the Palestinian refugee question – a question that is, in turn, one of the most sensitive and difficult of all of Israeli–Palestinian permanent status issues. The problem has its roots, of course, in the three-quarters of a million or so Palestinians who were forcibly displaced from the territory that became Israel in 1948 – a refugee population that has, over time and through generations grown to some five million or so today (see Table 4.1).[1] How can a just and durable solution be found for this population? What is the legal, political and practical context that will necessarily shape this? What degree of choice will refugees have? The question is not just one of physical residency, of who might live where in the aftermath of any future peace agreement. As well, the issue also touches upon core, even existential issues of national history and identity for Palestinians and Israelis alike. In past negotiations, the issue has also seemed to take on a strong zero-sum character: each refugee who might return has been seen as a Palestinian gain and Israeli loss, as has any acknowledgement of the legal or normative basis for refugees rights and claims.

Because of this, officials on both sides have been highly reluctant to publicly discuss the compromises they might make. During the Annapolis round of negotiations (2007–08), for example, then Prime

Minister Olmert strongly emphasized his complete unwillingness to accept even a single refugee return to Israel, declaring 'I'll never accept a solution that is based on their return to Israel, in any number.' After leaving office he later revealed that he had actually offered the return of some 1,000 refugees per year for five years, under the rubric of family reunification.[2] Similarly, Palestinian leaders have strongly emphasized the 'right of return' for all refugees in public statements – while in private have long recognized that the Palestinian side would be likely to have to make significant practical concessions on the issue in the broader context of an overall peace agreement.

Table 4.1   Estimates of Palestinian Refugee Population

	UNRWA-registered refugees (January 2013)	BADIL estimates of total Palestinian refugees and IDP population (2009)
West Bank and Gaza	1,944,544	1.8 million
Israel (IDPs)		0.3 million
Jordan	2,304,641	2.5 million
Syria	499,189	0.5 million
Lebanon	441,543	0.5 million
Other Arab countries		0.5 million
Rest of world		1.0 million
TOTAL	4,919,917	7.1 million

Source: BADIL, *Survey of Palestinian Refugees and IDPs 2008–2009* (Bethlehem: BADIL: 2009).

This paper will examine the various options for permanent residency, in the context of an overall negotiated resolution of the Israeli–Palestinian conflict. In doing so it will identify, discuss and assess the positions taken by the parties in past negotiations, as well as other possible approaches. It will also highlight the ways in which this issue might intersect with other aspects of the refugee issue, as well as other permanent status and post-agreement issues. As with other chapters in this volume, it will not attempt to make any single set of recommendations, but rather explore the possible menu of choices from which any future agreement might be built.

Residency Issues in Palestinian Refugee Negotiations

In the 1993 Israeli–Palestinian Declaration of Principles, the issue of 1948 refugees was one of the half dozen issues postponed to later negotiations on permanent status. Subsequently, the refugee issue was the subject of official discussion between the parties in the Stockholm meetings of May 2000,[3] at the Camp David summit (July–August 2000) and in the subsequent US-brokered talks that led to the Clinton Parameters of December 2000.[4] The most detailed and extensive discussions, however, took place at the Taba negotiations of January 2001.[5]

Thereafter, no permanent status negotiations were held until November 2007, when the Annapolis Round began. These lasted for approximately one year, although there was relatively little detailed discussion of the refugee issue during this time. So-called 'proximity talks' on permanent status and other issues were undertaken in 2010, but these did not address the refugee issue in any substantive way. In 2013 the parties again met in direct talks encouraged by the US.

In addition to official negotiations, a number of so-called dialogues, 'second track' and policy research projects have addressed a variety of aspects of the refugee issue, including those relating to residency.[6] Particularly important among these unofficial initiatives is the draft refugee agreement included within the Geneva Accord (2003). This reflected many of the concepts previously discussed at Taba two years earlier – unsurprisingly, given the close involvement of former Taba negotiators in the process. It also introduced a number of new elements, too.[7]

Regarding the issue of residency, the Clinton Parameters (2000) explicitly outlined 'five possible final homes for refugees'. These were:

- The state of Palestine;
- Areas in Israel being transferred to Palestine in the land swap;
- Rehabilitation in a host country;
- Resettlement in a third country;
- Admission to Israel.

Subsequent official negotiations at Taba (2001) and during the Annapolis Round (2007–08) have been based upon these options, as was the unofficial Geneva Accord (2003). Since they represent essentially all of the logical alternatives for future residency, they will be used to frame discussion in this paper too. For the purposes of clarity and consistency, however, the following terminology will be used hereafter:

- *Return* will be used to refer to the return of Palestinian refugees to the area from which the originated, namely the present-day state of Israel;
- *Repatriation* will be used to refer to refugees 'returning' to a Palestinian state, including any former Israeli areas swapped to it as part of a territorial exchange;
- *Integration* (rather than the somewhat pejorative-sounding 'rehabilitation') will be used to refer to the absorption or integration of refugees in their current host countries;
- Finally, *resettlement* will be used to refer to third country resettlement in countries other than the one in which they currently reside.

There is, of course, a substantial gap between simply identifying these options and determining their relative mix in any agreement. As will be discussed below, Israel and the Palestinians have very different positions on the question, and equally different views of the legal and normative issues involved. With several million refugees living outside of historic Palestine in Jordan, Syria, Lebanon and elsewhere, refugee host countries also have very strong interests at stake.

Interests and Priorities of the Major Parties

Palestinian Interests and Priorities

For Palestinian negotiators, a demand for recognition of their 'right of return' to 1948 areas has been a centrepiece of their negotiating position.[8] This reflects the Palestinian perception of their forced displacement in 1948 by Israel as an unambiguous moral wrong. It also reflects a view that refugee rights are clearly embedded in UN General Assembly Resolution 194 (1948) and its provision that 'refugees wishing to return to their homes and live at peace with their neighbors should be permitted to do so at the earliest practicable date', as well as Article 13.2 of the 1948 Universal Declaration of the Rights of Man ('Everyone has the right to leave any country, including their own, and to return to their country') and several other broader principles of international law. The Palestinian side also notes that refugee return has been a key element of most recent peace agreements and post-conflict peace-building, such as in Mozambique, Bosnia, Kosovo, East Timor, Afghanistan and elsewhere.

At the same time, however, past Palestinian negotiators have signalled that were recognition of the *principle* to be forthcoming, they could be flexible on the *modalities* and hence on the magnitude of any future population flows. According to an account co-written by one of the US negotiators at Camp David:

> the Palestinians are trying (to date, unsuccessfully) to reconcile these two competing imperatives – the demographic imperative and the right of return. Indeed, in one of his last pre-Camp David meetings with Clinton, Arafat asked him to 'give [him] a reasonable deal [on the refugee question] and then see how to present it as not betraying the right of return.'
>
> Some of the Palestinian negotiators proposed annual caps on the number of returnees (though at numbers far higher than their Israeli counterparts could accept); others wanted to create incentives for refugees to settle elsewhere and disincentives for them to return to the 1948 land. But all acknowledged that there could not be an unlimited, 'massive' return of Palestinian refugees to Israel. The suggestion made by some that the Camp David summit broke down over the Palestinians' demand for a right of return simply is untrue: the issue was barely discussed between the two sides and President Clinton's ideas mentioned it only in passing.[9]

Similarly, in a February 2002 op-ed in the *New York Times*, the then PLO and Palestinian Authority leader Yasir Arafat stated:

> In addition, we seek a fair and just solution to the plight of Palestinian refugees who for 54 years have not been permitted to return to their homes. *We understand Israel's demographic concerns and understand that the right of return of Palestinian refugees, a right guaranteed under international law and United Nations Resolution 194, must be implemented in a way that takes into account such concerns.* However, just as we Palestinians must be realistic with respect to Israel's

demographic desires, Israelis too must be realistic in understanding that there can be no solution to the Israeli–Palestinian conflict if the legitimate rights of these innocent civilians continue to be ignored. Left unresolved, the refugee issue has the potential to undermine any permanent peace agreement between Palestinians and Israelis. How is a Palestinian refugee to understand that his or her right of return will not be honored but those of Kosovar Albanians, Afghans and East Timorese have been? [emphasis added][10]

For Palestinian negotiators, therefore, the issue is not primarily one of resolving the condition of Palestinian exile through mass return to Israel, but rather of *securing some substantive recognition of the Palestinian experience of exile, and Israeli responsibility for this.* At the same time, this is not to say that any token and wholly symbolic number of refugee returns to Israel would necessarily satisfy Palestinian demands. There is far from any consensus among Palestinians on how much 'return' is enough, politically or morally. If the number is too small, it is likely to be seen as insulting and generate a backlash among refugees and other Palestinians. It would also thereby provide political ammunition for Palestinian opponents of the peace process.

Indeed, in considering what Palestinian interests are in negotiations for a refugee agreement, it is important to consider Palestinian public opinion and the constraints that it may impose on political leaders. Several public opinion polls show that between one-third and one-half of all Palestinians would accept a resolution of the refugee question based on the sorts of arrangements discussed in the Clinton Parameters, at Taba and in the Geneva Accord.[11] This level of support, moreover, is generally similar among refugees and non-refugees alike – highlighting the extent to which this is a national, and not merely a refugee, issue.[12] Some caution is necessary in interpreting poll results, however. On the one hand, surveys may *overestimate* the degree of support for such an outcome since they typically do not attach a specific number to the number of refugees who might return to Israel, and thus may imply much easier return than would be the case. Surveys might also *underestimate* acceptance of such a deal on the refugee issue, since they are asked in the absence of any concrete realization of Palestinian statehood. When asked if they would accept postponement of negotiations on the right of return while a Palestinian state was established, half of Palestinians in the West Bank and Gaza would agree (53 per cent of refugees, and 48 per cent of non-refugees), although only 36 per cent of refugees in Jordan and 28 per cent in Lebanon concur.[13] Overall, it is important to recognize that Palestinian public attitudes to a refugee deal will be strongly conditioned by their attitude to the broader peace agreement of which it forms a part. If the overall package is seen as positive, it seems likely that the public will be more willing to make compromises on the refugee aspect. Conversely, if the overall package is seen as weak, compromise on refugee demands would be much less likely.

As noted earlier, the political sensitivity of the Palestinian issue means that Palestinian leaders have done little to prepare their public for probable future compromise on the issue, thus limiting their flexibility in negotiations. Indeed, even casually implying that the return of refugees would be less that absolute can bring vituperative political criticism. When, for example, then Palestinian Authority Prime Minister Salam Fayyad casually suggested in an April 2010 interview that 'Of course, Palestinians would have the right to reside within the State of Palestine' – an evident truism, since it is impossible to imagine that Palestine would turn refugees away – he was attacked for having surrendered the right of return to 1948 areas.[14] Hamas even suggested that he should be placed on trial for the statement.

With regard to repatriation to Palestine, there is a strong consensus among Palestinians that the future Palestinian state ought to have *full and sovereign control over both its borders and its admission policy*. This would allow all Palestinians who wished to reside in Palestine to do so – an 'ingathering of the exiles', to use the language Israel often uses regarding Jewish immigration. Consequently, any limitations on the new state's ability to do so would not only be seen as constraints on its sovereignty, but as a fundamental violation of one of the very purposes of Palestinian self-determination. The Palestinian state would also be able to offer Palestinian passports and citizenship to those who remained in the diaspora – subject, of course, to local laws regarding residency and dual citizenship. Whether Palestinian citizens abroad would be given an expatriate vote in Palestinian elections is less clear, although this presumably is an issue to be dealt with by the new state rather than in peace negotiations.

There has been no clear Palestinian official view on how an agreement should address the issue of host country and third country resettlement. In part, this is because return and repatriation are seen as the primary mechanism for resolving Palestinian involuntary exile, and in part, because these decisions will ultimately depend on the attitude of countries who are not part of peace negotiations and over whom the Palestinian leadership has little influence. Historically, both Jordan and Syria have been quite generous to their Palestinian refugee populations and Palestinian negotiators have probably assumed that this would continue to be the case. (With the outbreak of civil war in Syria, however, the latter may no longer be a safe assumption.) The position of refugees in Lebanon has been much more precarious, however. Consequently, there has been explicit attention to the situation of Palestinians in Lebanon during past negotiations and policy planning, with a general acceptance that their needs should be prioritized in the implementation of any future peace agreement.

Israeli Interests and Priorities

On the Israeli side, *the 'right of return' is seen as anathema*, for several reasons.[15] First, substantial return of Palestinians to Israel is seen as a threat to the Jewish character of the state – the central objective of the Zionist movement, and very *raison d'être* of Israel. Second, as with other aspects of an agreement that touches upon the intangible, moral dimensions of the refugee issue, most Israelis would reject any notion of primary responsibility for the refugee problem. Instead, they argue that this was brought on by Arab rejection of the 1947 UN Partition Plan. Within Israel, the notion of a population exchange – whereby Palestinians were displaced from Israel in 1948 and Jews were displaced from Arab countries thereafter – has become broadly accepted. By this logic, the two displaced populations ought to accept current realities (an idea that, for obvious reasons, is rather less convincing to Palestinians who wish to return to Palestine). Israel typically has objections even to acceptance of a 'right of return' in principle, despite Palestinian offers of a mutually-acceptable compromise on its implementation, both because it touches upon these issues of moral responsibility, and out of legal fears that official acceptance of the 'right' could have unknown future political and legal implications. Public opinion polls in Israel show strong Jewish opposition to both the return of Palestinian refugees and to any recognition of a 'right of return'. They show somewhat greater willingness to accept partial responsibility for the refugee issue, however.[16]

While it was not advocated by previous Israeli governments in the 2000–01 and 2007–08 rounds of permanent status negotiations, one idea that has gained some currency on the Israeli far-right is that of bolstering the Jewish character of Israel by *refusing to accept the return of any refugees within Israel while simultaneously swapping areas of Israeli territory with high numbers of Israeli Arabs* to the future Palestine (and replacing their current Israeli citizenship with a Palestinian one). One vocal proponent of such a plan was former Israeli Foreign Minister Avigdor Lieberman, who has called for 'an exchange of populated territories to create two largely homogeneous states, one Jewish Israeli and the other Arab Palestinian,' coupled with 'no so-called Palestinian right of return'.[17] Such an initiative would probably face opposition from most Palestinian citizens of Israel, as well as objections from the Israeli Supreme Court. It also seems unlikely to receive a warm response from Palestinian negotiators, especially given the opposition by Palestinians in Israel to the idea.

In addition to the issue of return to Israel, some Israeli negotiators might also consider it desirable to try to exert some control over the movement of Palestinians into the new state of Palestine. The rationale given for this in the past usually focuses on immediate security interests, including both an immediate desire to keep diaspora radicals from taking up residence in Palestine, as well as a broader concern that mass repatriation would destabilize the nascent state. Through permanent status negotiations in 2000–01, *Israel gradually abandoned the notion of retaining even transitory control over Palestine's border*, however, accepting instead the idea of international monitoring. However, more hardline Israeli governments might wish to *retain permanent control over Palestinian territories in the Jordan Valley*. Prime Minister Netanyahu has suggested that Israel needs to retain long-term control over the border,[18] as has the Defense Minister Moshe Yaalon.[19] It is difficult to imagine any conditions under which this would be acceptable to Palestinian negotiators or the general Palestinian public. Indeed, doing so would be likely to delegitimize any peace agreement to a destabilizing degree, ultimately harming Israeli security interests as well as Palestinian national aspirations.

Regarding host country and third country resettlement, Israel is likely to see these as desirable ways of reducing pressure for refugee return. Given the importance of relations with the Hashemite Kingdom, it is particularly likely to take potential Jordanian concerns into account when formulating aspects of its position.

Finally, a key Israeli interest will be to ensure that any refugee agreement represents a *clear and unequivocal end of all refugee-related claims against the state of Israel*. Israeli negotiators have feared that some approaches to the refugee issue (including recognition of the right of return) might leave the issue open to be raised again at a future point. Reflecting this concern, the refugee section of Israel's proposed Framework Agreement on Permanent Status (2000) underscored the finality of claims no fewer than seven times in its 27 clauses.[20]

Host Country and Other Interests and Priorities

The host countries most affected by any future refugee agreement are those hosting the largest number of refugees: Jordan, Syria and Lebanon. The attitudes of these countries towards a refugee agreement are explored at length in Chapter 5 in this volume. However, for the purposes of this paper, several key points can be noted.

In the case of *Jordan*, some East Bankers may wish to encourage refugee return and repatriation to Israel and Palestine as a way of reducing the Palestinian share of the Jordanian population (currently comprising half or more). However, the very demographic nature of Jordan would also make it extremely difficult for the Kingdom to develop an explicit policy on this issue. Instead, Amman is more likely to encourage non-citizen Palestinians in the country to leave (comprised mainly of Gazans and West Bank Palestinians who took up residency after Jordan's 1988 disengagement from the West Bank). It is unlikely to forcibly deport these Palestinians in large numbers, however, in view of the political sensitivity of the issue. Jordan will have concerns about Palestinian citizens holding dual citizenships, and hence potential dual loyalties and obligations. Accordingly, it is unlikely to permit Jordanian citizens to hold Palestinian citizenship, and might strip citizenship from those who did return or repatriate.

In the case of *Syria*, future refugee policy has been rendered much more difficult to predict by the eruption of a bloody civil war in that country and the uncertain configuration of any future Syrian regime. However, Damascus' overall orientation to a refugee agreement, and indeed any Israeli–Palestinian peace agreement in general, may continue to be strongly conditioned by the prospects for a return of the occupied Golan Heights and an Israeli–Syrian treaty. If such an agreement comes without progress on these issues (and, indeed, threatens to further weaken Syria's position), Damascus might have considerable interest in rallying opposition to a peace deal – including its refugee component. In such a case, attacks on the Palestinian leadership for surrendering refugee rights are likely to be a major rhetorical focus. That being said, however, there is little evidence that Syria would mistreat its refugees, either by forcing them from the country or by seeking to block their ability to repatriate or return. On the contrary, the Syrian record of dealing with Palestinian refugees since 1948 has been an impressively positive one, with refugees granted almost all the privileges of Syrian citizenship. During the civil war the (overwhelmingly Sunni) refugee population has generally maintained its neutrality, or tilted towards the opposition – all of which would stand it in good stead with any future post-Assad regime. The devastation wrought by the civil war could, however, represent a 'push' factor encouraging Palestinians to repatriate to a Palestinian state.

In *Lebanon*, by contrast, sectarian-demographic sensitivities mean that there is little support for allowing Palestinians to remain or extending them citizenship. Indeed, *tawteen* (naturalization of the refugees) remains one of the great taboos of Lebanese politics. Even if a refugee agreement did not address Lebanese concerns in this area, the Lebanese government would be unlikely to deport its refugee population since, lacking a shared border with Palestine, it would largely be unable to do so. However, political pressure might build to 'encourage' the refugees to leave through limiting their (already limited) access to employment and services, and by otherwise making local conditions unwelcoming. As noted above, Palestinian negotiators have recognized this and have sought to make Palestinians in Lebanon a priority. Israel and the international community would also seem to have an interest in avoiding a crisis over the refugees in Lebanon. Refugees from Lebanon might, for example, be given priority in any third country resettlement. All parties would share an interest in reassuring the Lebanese that the issue will be addressed, thus diminishing the prospect for pre-emptive or precipitous moves.

Residential Options: Return

At the most basic level, there are three ways in which the return of Palestinian refugees to Israel could be dealt with in a future agreement: all refugees could be permitted the option of return; some refugees could be permitted to return; and no refugees could be permitted to return.

The first of these arrangements, under which all refugees who wished to take up residency could do so, would be strongly supported by Palestinians, but bitterly opposed by Israelis as 'demographic suicide' for the Jewish state. It is difficult to imagine any circumstances under which an Israeli government would agree to unrestricted return.

The third of these arrangements, by contrast, would involve the return of no refugees whatsoever. This position has been articulated by Israeli leaders from time to time and would certainly win strong support among Israeli Jews. This approach was also accepted by the Palestinian intellectual Sari Nusseibeh in his 'People's Voice Initiative' with Ami Ayalon. Specifically, that plan called for acceptance of the principle of 'Two states for two peoples' whereby 'Both sides will declare that Palestine is the only state of the Palestinian people and Israel is the only state of the Jewish people.' Consequently, 'Palestinian refugees will return only to the State of Palestine; Jews will return only to the State of Israel.'[21] On the other hand, any such agreement would face strong Palestinian public criticism for having completely surrendered the right of return – especially given that Israel itself indicated that it was prepared to accept at least some token refugee return in earlier permanent status negotiations in 2000–01 and 2007–08.

Given this, the focus of negotiations is likely to be some form of restricted return that falls between these two poles. Here, two major issues will present themselves to negotiators: how the issue of return is framed; and how the scope of any refugee to return to Israel is determined.

Framing Refugee Return

In past negotiations, Israel has expressed a preference for framing the limited return of refugees as a humanitarian gesture or a family reunification initiative, and also as a matter of Israeli sovereign discretion.[22] The Palestinians, by contrast, have preferred to frame any return in the language of rights and international legal obligations, and with explicit reference to the 'right of return'.[23] These positions reflect two very different national narratives of what happened in 1948, and hence two different positions on who bears responsibility for the refugee issue. Many of these issues of framing overlap substantially with issues of normative and intangible claims, and hence the brief discussion below should certainly be read in conjunction with Chapter 9 in this volume.

One possible approach for bridging the gap is for *Israel to declare that it accepts the Palestinian right of return in theory, while the Palestinian side agrees that it will accept constraints and limits to this right in practice*. On the Palestinian side, this option has sometimes been mooted as a way of reconciling Palestinian demands for recognition of the right of return with Israeli refusal to do so. However, it is not clear whether the declarative commitment of Israel to the right of return, coupled with explicit Palestinian acceptance of conditions, would be viewed by Palestinian public opinion as a meaningful accomplishment – or as a back-handed abandonment of refugee rights. It is also likely, as noted earlier, that Israel negotiators might have trouble accepting (or, if they did, selling to their public) that either there was such a 'right', or that it could somehow be limited once acknowledged. On the contrary, it would be seen as providing a continuing basis for refugee claims against Israel in perpetuity, and even as an existential threat.

Various ideas have been mooted for bridging this gap. An unofficial 1999 Israeli–Palestinian 'Core Group' paper, for example, suggested that 'In recognition of the Palestinian demand to exercise the right of return to historic Palestine, both parties agree that: a) this shall primarily be achieved through the voluntary repatriation of Palestinians to the Palestinian state; b) Israel shall admit a number of Palestinians who will live peacefully with their neighbours, whether as citizens of Israel, dual citizens, or as Israeli permanent residents.'[24] The Clinton Parameters suggested that the parties recognize either a right of return to 'historic Palestine', or a right of return to the Palestinian 'homeland', while making it clear that Israeli acceptance of refugees was a matter of its 'sovereign decision'.[25] According to Clinton:

> The solution will have to be consistent with the two-state approach that both sides have accepted as a way to end the Palestinian–Israeli

conflict: the state of Palestine as the homeland of the Palestinian people and the state of Israel as the homeland of the Jewish people.

Under the two-state solution, the guiding principle should be that the Palestinian state would be the focal point for Palestinians who choose to return to the area without ruling out that Israel will accept some of these refugees.

I believe that we need to adopt a formulation on the right of return that will make clear that there is no specific right of return to Israel itself but that does not negate the aspiration of the Palestinian people to return to the area.

In light of the above, I propose two alternatives:

1. Both sides recognize the right of Palestinian refugees to return to historic Palestine; or

2. Both sides recognize the right of Palestinian refugees to return to their homeland.

The agreement will define the implementation of this general right in a way that is consistent with the two-state solution.[26]

The Clinton Parameters also sought to frame this outcome by declaring that it constituted the implementation of UNGAR 194 ('the parties would agree that this implements Resolution 194'), thereby attempting to borrow the legitimacy provided by the resolution without fully embracing all of the UN resolution's substantive content.[27] A similar approach to framing was adopted in the Geneva Accord, which recognized UN General Assembly Resolution (UNGAR) 194, along with UN Security Council Resolution 242 and the Arab Peace Initiative, as representing 'the basis for resolving the refugee issue' while also stating that 'these rights are fulfilled according to [the refugee Article] of this Agreement.' As for the 2002 Arab Peace Initiative itself, it balances the same elements by calling for 'a just solution to the Palestinian refugee issue to be agreed upon in accordance with UN General Assembly Resolution 194,' effectively conditioning any outcome on what Israel could consider acceptable (through inclusion of the requirement that it be 'agreed').

During 2000–01 there was also some thought given to framing the potential *repatriation of refugees to swapped territories* – that is, current Israeli territory that would be exchanged to the Palestinian state in exchange for Israeli annexation of the major Jewish settlement blocs near the Green Line – as *fulfilling the goal of a right of return to 1948 areas*. It seems highly unlikely, however, that refugees would view it as such, especially those refugees coming from other areas of Israel. This would especially be the case if the areas swapped to Palestine were those, such as those adjacent to Gaza, that were not considered especially valuable or having much history of substantial Palestinian inhabitation.

Modalities: Setting the Numbers

Unless one assumes agreement on the unlimited return of refugees to Israel – an unlikely outcome, given what would be fundamental Israeli objections – a refugee agreement would contain provisions somehow determining, limiting, or shaping the nature and magnitude of refugee flows. Several models have emerged in past negotiations for limiting the future flow of returnees.

The first of these is to set an *upper limit or numerical cap* on refugee return, as was proposed in Israel's draft Framework Agreement on Permanent Status (2000) and in the Israeli 'Private Response' paper presented at the Taba negotiations (January 2001). While the formal version of the latter contained no final number, verbally the Israeli team suggested that 25,000 refugees might be accepted over three years, or 40,000 over five years. For Israel, such an approach has the advantage that it makes it clear in advance what the magnitude of refugee return would be, and avoids any sort of long-term commitment. For the Palestinians, however, a number might seem to run counter to the principle of realizing refugee rights, and could become a lightning rod for criticism if it were deemed too low by the Palestinian public.

It was also suggested at Taba that Israel's offer could also be seen in the context of a 15-year time-frame for implementing a refugee deal – an ambiguous formulation that might suggest that the eventual return could be as high as 120–125,000.[28] While ambiguity can help gloss over differences during negotiations, it can prove problematic once the agreement is subject to public debate. This is especially true in the Israeli–Palestinian context where statements by leaders to their constituents on one side are almost immediately reported on by the media on the other side. As already noted, by the time of the Annapolis negotiations (2008), Israel's willingness to accept returnees had been reduced to a mere 5,000 in total, under the rubric of limited family reunification.

Another possibility would be to set an annual rate of refugee return for an indefinite period, rather than a total cap – for example, 5,000 per year. The PLO proposals on refugees at Taba (2001) initially suggested such an approach, but did not explicitly state what the number would be. An open-ended commitment like this would likely be very unpopular in Israel, however, unless the annual numbers were very low.

The Geneva Accord (2003) took a somewhat different approach to the issue. While a numerical cap was also suggested, this was not to be determined in the peace agreement itself. Rather, Israel would unilaterally declare the number of refugee returns that it would permit, but in so doing *would link this to third country resettlement by others*:

> [admission to Israel] shall be at the sovereign discretion of Israel and will be in accordance with a number that Israel will submit to the International Commission. This number shall represent the total number of Palestinian refugees that Israel shall accept. As a basis, Israel will consider the average of the total numbers submitted by the different third countries to the International Commission.[29]

Such an approach has strong advantages to Israel, in that it would be allowed to set almost any number it wished, no matter how low. As worded in the agreement, it was only required to 'consider' the numbers accepted by third countries. For the Palestinians this could prove highly problematic. However, there might well be some interesting possibilities, differently worded, for linking return, third country resettlement, and even donor contributions for refugee development and compensation so as to create positive pressures on Israel and donor countries to be more generous than might otherwise be the case.

It has also been suggested at times that the number of refugees accepted by Israel could be tied to the number of Israeli settlers who were permitted to remain in the territory of the new Palestinian state. Some Palestinian negotiators have expressed discomfort with linking the two, concerned that it would seem to imply some sort of moral equivalence between the actions of illegal Jewish settlement in the occupied Palestinian territory and the refugees' legal and normative right of return. Nonetheless, even if not made explicit in an agreement, the two issues could become paired in negotiations. Similarly, the number of Palestinian residents of East Jerusalem who would come under Palestinian sovereignty as citizens of a Palestinian state could also be raised in negotiation by the Palestinian side in an effort to encourage Israel to accept a higher rate of refugee return. If Israel were to accept 100,000 refugees and withdraw from occupied East Jerusalem (with over 200,000 Palestinian residents), for example, the net effect would be 100,000 fewer Palestinians resident in Israel after the establishment of a Palestinian state.

This sort of ethnic bargaining is typically distasteful to the Palestinian side, who are understandably unsettled by the idea of trying to maximize the Jewish character of the state of Israel – in their view, it is the very same ideological impulse that lay behind the forced displacement of refugees in 1948. On the other hand, one cannot ignore that this consideration is an important one for most Israeli Jews. Indeed, as noted earlier, some Israeli politicians have gone further and argued that an agreement should seek to dramatically reduce the number of non-Jews resident within Israel through an exchange of populations. It is not clear how feasible this would be. It would be difficult to draw practical boundaries that wouldn't include some Jewish population areas. More importantly, many (and probably most) Palestinian citizens of Israel would probably be strenuously opposed to being stripped of their citizenship in a high-income country to become part of the new, underdeveloped Palestinian state. The political and legal obstacles to such a move, including those posed by the Israeli Supreme Court, would be formidable.

Modalities: Setting the Rules

An alternative approach to assigning explicit numbers to refugee return in an agreement is to instead focus on the rules that will govern – and, in effect, limit – the rate at which this could take place. Many Palestinian negotiators have expressed a preference for this approach, suggesting (for example) that the actual magnitude of refugee return to Israel would be limited in practice by the existing integration of many refugees in their current places of residence, as well as by the requirement that refugees returning to Israel would have to acquire

Israeli citizenship. Because of such factors, the number who *would* return would be much lower than the number who, in theory, *could* return. By embedding modality-based restrictions in an agreement, rather than focusing on caps and ceilings, it becomes easier for the Palestinian leadership to sell an agreement to their constituents – although it would be at the cost of making it harder for an Israeli government to win public support on their side.

This sort of approach was embodied in the initial PLO position at the Taba negotiations (2001), which stated that 'all refugees who wish to return to their homes in Israel and live at peace with their neighbors have the right to do so. The right of every refugee to return shall be exercised in accordance with the modalities set out in the agreement.' (Article XXX.5.a)[30]

It is possible to imagine a number of different modalities that could be agreed upon by the parties to determine which refugees would (and, by implication, which would not) be able to return. These criteria could be agreed upon in advance between Palestine and Israel, made subject to future negotiation or determined unilaterally by Israel within the confines of agreed principles. Possible criteria might include:

- On a *first come, first-served* basis.
- On the basis of *age*. Thus, first-generation refugees (those born before 1948) would receive priority over subsequent-generation refugees, and older refugees would generally receive priority over younger refugees. This was proposed verbally by the Israeli side in the 2001 Taba negotiations, since it would also allow the agreement to be framed as having fulfilled the 'right of return' for those actually displaced in 1948. Unspoken, perhaps, was also the fact that first generation refugees would be past reproductive age, and hence pose no 'demographic threat' to the Jewish character of Israel. The Palestinians have rejected the idea as unworkable, given the difficulty of elderly Palestinians moving to Israel without the support of their extended family. Today, the pool of surviving first generation refugees (estimated by the World Bank at 220,000 in 1997)[31] is dwindling rapidly to a fraction of this as the survivors die.
- On the basis of *current area of residency*. Palestinians residing in Lebanon and other inhospitable locales could, for example,

receive priority over others. The need to prioritize Palestinians in Lebanon was put forward by the Palestinian side during final status talks in 2000–01, with the PLO proposing at Taba (2001) that 'all refugees who currently reside in Lebanon and choose to exercise the right of return in accordance with this Article shall be enabled to return to Israel within two years of the signing of this Agreement.' (Article XX.15). In its written response, the Israeli negotiating team instead suggested that 'priority [be] accorded to those Palestinian refugees currently resident in Lebanon,' as well as stating that 'Israel notes its moral commitment to the swift resolution of the plight of the refugee population of Sabra and Shatila camps,' (Para 8.a). The unofficial Geneva Accord (2003) proposed that 'Priority [with regard to all residential options] shall be accorded to the Palestinian refugee population in Lebanon.' (Article 7.4.v.d).

- On the basis of *sponsorship*. Refugees with strong family connections to relatives currently residing within Israel, or those with other local sponsors, would receive priority. In its draft Framework Agreement on Permanent Status (2000), Israel suggested that any refugees admitted to Israel 'shall be reunited with their families in their present place of residence in Israel, accept Israeli citizenship, and waive their legal status as refugees,' (Article 6.75).
- According to procedures developed by an *international commission*. This approach was put forward in the initial PLO position at Taba (2001), which proposed that 'The Commission shall determine, according to transparent criteria, who will be allowed to return in any given year, in Accordance with Paragraph 16 of the Article.' (Article 18). Paragraph 16, in turn, established a minimum number of returns per year (but 'without prejudice to the right of every refugee to return to Israel'.) Refugees would have five years to declare their intent to return, but would not be limited as to when they could exercise this (Article 17);
- On the basis of *ease of integration* (determined by language, age, skills, employability, possibly measured by some kind of system of allotted points for particular characteristics). This would have the advantage, for Israel, of securing the most economically productive segment of the Palestinian refugee population – and

94

would be disadvantageous to Palestine and host countries in equal measure;

- Using a *lottery system*, whereby the annual quota is determined randomly from all applications received.
- Some combination of these.

Sequencing and Implementation

In addition to the complex issue of what numbers and modalities would be agreed upon by the parties, there is also the question of sequencing and implementation. Should everything with regard to refugee return be decided at the time of, and in the text of, a permanent status agreement? Or could and should some things be left for later?

First, the parties *could agree at the time of a final status agreement* on either a total number of returnees, an annual rate of return, and/or the criteria for admission, as well as the modalities and procedures to be used. An advantage of initial agreement is that the refugee issue can be linked to other aspects of permanent status negotiations, and there may thus be greater pressure on the parties to be flexible in the interests of an overall agreement. A disadvantage of initial agreement is that the sensitivity and complexity of the refugee issue could delay or derail the achievement of a permanent status agreement.

Alternatively, the parties could agree *on the principle of limited return, but postpone to subsequent negotiations any detailed agreement* on the actual totals, rates, criteria, and the modalities and procedures to be used. The advantage of a delayed agreement is that it does not require Palestine or Israel to announce the actual total number of returnees at the time that a permanent status agreement is signed. By postponing agreement on numbers and criteria, Palestine might reduce any political backlash caused by the numbers being too low, and Israel might reduce any political backlash caused by the numbers being too high. Also, the consolidation of Israeli–Palestinian peace might increase the political willingness of Israeli public opinion to accept the return of some 1948 refugees.

The disadvantage of delayed agreement is that it creates an opportunity for Israel to stall, and indefinitely postpone, practical agreement. Such stalling was a characteristic of the quadripartite negotiations on the return of 1967 displaced persons to the West

Bank and Gaza. Although Israel agreed to such repatriation in 1993 (and, indeed, in 1979), it never agreed on definitions, numbers or procedures. As a consequence, not a single displaced person has ever returned under this provision.

Finally, *Israel could be permitted to unilaterally determine totals, rates, criteria, and modalities and procedures*. Israel is likely, in any event, to insist that setting immigration criteria and procedures is a sovereign prerogative and not a subject for diplomatic negotiation. However, if Israel were to be permitted to set all criteria and procedures, the Palestinian side would fear that it might subvert any agreement on limited return by creating bureaucratic impediments and delays in implementation. Consequently, Palestinian negotiators would be likely to push for some Israeli commitment to transparency and timeliness, and/or to some international monitoring mechanism to assure that Israeli commitments are being met.

With regard to implementation, both the PLO position at Taba and the subsequent joint mechanisms paper there envisage that *an international commission would play a major role in administering all residential options, including that of return*. Under the initial PLO model, the 'Repatriation Commission' would 'guarantee and manage implementation of the right of return,' (Article XX.7), variously determining priorities and procedures, processing applications, and actually repatriating/returning refugees. The 'Return, Repatriation, and Relocation Commission' proposed in the subsequent joint refugee mechanism paper at Taba is broadly similar. By contrast, Israel's draft Framework Agreement on Permanent Status (2000), which was more reflective of mainstream government thinking on the issue, foresaw *no international role at all in the implementation of a limited, humanitarian return of some refugees to Israel*, emphasizing instead that who and how many might be accepted was solely a matter of Israeli sovereign discretion. The unofficial Geneva Accord (2003) attempted to bridge the two positions, calling for the establishment of a Permanent Place of Residence Committee by the international commission, but making all return to Israel subject to Israel's sovereign discretion.

In general, the Palestinian side would like to maximize the role of the international community in implementing return to Israel, while the Israeli side would like to minimize it. The hybrid model proposed in the Geneva Accord, while attempting to bridge the gap, might instead bring about the worst of both possible worlds, whereby the Commission has a mandate to implement return but has no way of overcoming Israel's sovereign veto. In such a case, prolonged political negotiations and delays might be the result, with members of the Commission being partly blamed by refugees and host countries for the stalemate.

Residential Options: Repatriation

A second major element of the residency component of any future refugee agreement will concern repatriation to the new Palestinian state. Here, several issues will present themselves. How will refugees (and others in the diaspora) avail themselves of this option? What implications might this have for the stability of the new state and to what extent should the absorptive limits of Palestine be reflected in the text of an agreement? What ancillary issues might arise from the establishment of a Palestinian nationality?

As with refugee return to Israel, several models of refugee repatriation to the Palestinian state – such as the Taba mechanisms paper (2001) and the Geneva Accord (2003) – envisage that the permanent residential preferences of refugees will be collected, processed and somehow determined by a committee of an international commission. Israel generally has not concerned itself greatly with this issue, at least not in its negotiating position on the refugee component of a peace deal. It has, however, sometimes sought to exercise *control over Palestinian border crossings* for a period of time, something that would give it some effective control over the ability of Palestinians to repatriate. According to the summary prepared by EU Special Representative, Miguel Angel Moratinos, at the conclusion of the Taba negotiations,

> The Palestinian side was confident that Palestinian sovereignty over borders and international crossing points would be recognized in the agreement. The two sides had, however, not yet resolved this issue including the question of monitoring and verification at Palestine's international borders (Israeli or international presence).[32]

As noted earlier, in subsequent years a number of Israelis – including Prime Minister Netanyahu – have insisted that Israel retain longer, and possibly permanent, control over the Jordan Valley. This might well give Israel effective control over all Palestinian immigration. As also noted earlier, any such proposal would face fundamental Palestinian opposition.

Research conducted on refugee repatriation and absorption by the World Bank in 2000–03 expressed concern at an excessively bureaucratic approach to refugee repatriation, such as the sort proposed at Taba and in the Geneva Accord. In the World Bank's view, refugees would be likely to make repatriation decisions based for a large part on economic conditions and opportunities within the new Palestinian state. Given this, allowing them to migrate at a time which they judged as appropriate would be best for facilitating their absorption. By linking refugee flows to bureaucratic process, it was feared that refugee repatriation flows and local economic conditions in Palestine could become uncoupled. While this makes considerable development sense (and is discussed in much more detail in Chapter 8 on 'Refugee Absorption and Development' in this volume), it is possible that Jordan – fearing adverse complications arising from migration and dual citizenship, or wishing to minimize the transit of non-citizen Palestinians through its territories – could put in place various kinds of border controls and restrictions. Ironically, these might actually work against Jordan's longer-term economic and even political interests, even if they appeared useful at the time to Amman.

Residential Options: Third Country Resettlement

In the past, the international community has undertaken large-scale, comprehensive and coordinated projects of third country refugee resettlement, such as those involving Ugandan Asians and the Indo-Chinese boat people in the 1970s. The present context is likely to be rather different, however. The political sensitivities of immigration policy, economic uncertainties and post-9/11 security concerns make it very unlikely that third countries will offer to accept large numbers of Palestinian refugees. Moreover, what refugees they do accept are likely to be processed on a gradual, relatively laborious, case-by-case basis.[33] Given this, third country resettlement is not likely to be a major demographic element in resolving the refugee issue, although it might still have utility as an indicator of international support for a peace agreement, as a way of encouraging Israel to accept refugee return (as, for example, the linkage put forward in the Geneva Accord), and as a way of addressing some of the most pressing or problematic humanitarian cases (such as refugees in Lebanon).

Moreover, whatever the scope of third country resettlement, its mechanisms will probably lie outside the parameters negotiated by Israelis and Palestinians in a peace agreement. Instead, it will remain (as the Clinton Parameters noted) subject to the sovereign discretion of the countries involved. Certainly, an International Commission might have a role in this. The joint Refugee Mechanism Paper drawn up by the two sides at Taba in 2001 envisaged that the 'Return, Repatriation, and Relocation Committee' of the 'International Commission for Palestinian Refugees' be responsible for determining procedures, processing applications and relocating refugees. However, it is doubtful that it would or could have done all of this, given the unwillingness of third countries to surrender their prerogatives in this way. Indeed, the complex mechanisms proposed at Taba risked adding an additional unwieldy layer of bureaucracy to the process.

A more effective role for an international mechanism might be to standardize some application procedures and inform refugees of their options for applying for third country resettlement. Assistance could also be provided to refugees. Existing international organizations (UNRWA, UNHCR, IOM) seem best placed to do this, in conjunction with donors and national refugee and immigration authorities.

Residential Options: Host Country Integration

As noted earlier, the attitudes, interests and positions of the three largest Palestinian refugee host countries differ sharply. Whatever the domestic debate within Jordan, it seems likely that the position of the 95 per cent or more of Palestinian refugees in Jordan, who currently hold Jordanian citizenship will be secure. The situation of others is less certain. In Syria there has been little reason to believe that the Syrian government would adversely treat Palestinian refugees, even if Damascus opposed an Israeli–Palestinian peace agreement. However, full legal integration – and the possibility of naturalization and citizenship – might have to await both an end to the civil war and Israeli–Syrian peace. In Lebanon there will be strong pressures to reduce the Palestinian population as quickly as possible, and little support for naturalization. However, if it is apparent that the bulk of Palestinian refugees in Lebanon are able to return, repatriate and resettle outside of Lebanon, political conditions might become more auspicious for extending Lebanese citizenship to those refugee children with a Lebanese mother.[34] In all three countries, the eventual wind-down of UNRWA and the transfer of many of its services to the host government would be a further complicating factor.

As with the question of third country resettlement, there are stark limits on the degree to which these issues can be addressed in a bilateral Israeli–Palestinian agreement. Many of them will inevitably need to be discussed and resolved in cooperation with host countries after any agreement is reached. It certainly seems unlikely that either Israel or the Palestinians would bring other regional parties into what is certain to be a highly sensitive and secretive negotiating process. Nonetheless, both Israel and the Palestinians do have an interest in understanding the concerns and interests of neighbouring host countries, and in trying to anticipate these. Open lines of dialogue and communication, both through formal channels and less formal ones (such as Chatham House's long-standing 'Minster Lovell Process' of refugee and host country meetings)[35] can help to minimize surprises and enhance the prospects for smooth implementation of a deal once one is reached.

Conclusion

This chapter has sought to identify the main issues with regard to permanent residency that will arise in any current or future Israeli–Palestinian negotiations on the refugee issue, highlighting both the interests of the various parties and the practical and other issues that might bear on the various possible approaches. In doing so, it must be remembered that *no aspect of the refugee issue, nor the refugee issue in general, can be adequately treated in isolation from other elements of the peace process.*

This will be particularly evident with regard to the degree of compromise the parties are willing to make on recognizing some degree of Palestinian right of return, as noted earlier. If an overall peace agreement is shown as delivering a viable Palestinian state, based on the 1967 borders and including East Jerusalem, Palestinian willingness to be flexible on this issue will be greater. Conversely, if a peace agreement delivers much less than this, flexibility on the refugee issue is likely to be much more limited too.

These sorts of linkages also exist within the various components of a refugee deal. Greater Israeli willingness to address Palestinian normative and intangible needs could well generate greater Palestinian flexibility (both in negotiations, and at the level of public opinion) on material issues such as return and compensation. Similarly, *the scope and nature of a compensation package could well have a substantial effect on refugee repatriation, resettlement and integration*. Any compensation paid to host countries, for example, could be formally or informally conditioned on their cooperation in implementing an agreement. Even if no state compensation is included in a deal, the desirability of integrating refugees into a host country could be influenced by the generosity of individual refugee compensation. Were US$20 billion in compensation to be paid to the 4.9 million UNRWA-registered refugees, for example, this would represent a potential capital infusion of up to US$12 billion into the economies of Jordan, Syria and Lebanon – if the refugees remained there. Conversely, under that same scenario, the new Palestinian state would have a heightened interest in attracting Palestinians to repatriate, given the potential investment capital that Palestinian refugee families would possess. In all cases, the social and economic ease of return, repatriation, resettlement and integration would all be facilitated by the possession by refugees of compensation funds. Indeed, compensation payments to former refugees residing in, or repatriating to, Palestine could potentially equal or exceed the entire GNP of the Palestinian territories.

One final aspect of permanent refugee residency that must be considered is how best to involve and inform the refugees themselves, and in so doing maximize the degree of informed choice that they are able to exercise in selecting a durable solution. Such choices will inevitably be constrained by the nature of an agreement, and by political and economic context. Nonetheless, to the extent that engagement and informed choice is maximized, outcomes are likely to be more positive and enduring for all concerned. Palestine, host countries and the international community will, post-agreement, play a key role in this. Given its high degree of credibility among refugees,

UNRWA (or some kind of 'Ibn UNRWA' successor implementation agency) is likely to pay an especially important role in this regard.

Finally, throughout the implementation process it will be important to avoid the natural tendency of governments to overpromise. There will be inevitable obstacles, roadblocks and delays in making a refugee agreement work, generating frustration and blame. Being frank about these will not prevent them. It may well reduce the adverse political effects consequence of inflated and unmet expectations, however – thereby enhancing the prospects for a successful transition to peace, and with it a just, lasting and mutually-acceptable resolution of the Palestinian refugee issue.

Notes

1. Some critics of UNRWA charge that the Agency's count of registered refugees is high because of an underreporting of refugee deaths. UNRWA rejects this criticism, however, and notes that its data for the age distribution of refugees closely matches that reported by census data for Palestinians in the occupied Palestinian territories and Jordan. Moreover, UNRWA registration is only open for refugees in UNRWA's area of operation, meaning that refugees and descendants living further afield are not counted. The BADIL numbers presented in Table 4.1, by contrast, attempt to estimate the total number of refugees worldwide, but may include some significant double-counting. In Lebanon, for example, the actual number of refugees currently residing in the country is unofficially estimated (even by UNRWA sources) as around 250,000, with the remainder having migrated to other countries (for example, as migrant labour in the Gulf). BADIL's numbers also include both refugees who fled in 1948, as well as other IDPs (including, for example, Palestinian citizens of Israel who were forcibly displaced in 1947–49 but who remained within Israeli borders, as well as 1967 displaced persons and other Palestinians who found themselves unable to return after 1948).
2. 'Diplomacy: "It has not been the easiest year"', *Jerusalem Post*, 29 March 2007, online at: www.jpost.com/Home/Article.aspx?id=56529; and 'Ehud Olmert Still Dreams of Peace', *The Australian*, 28 November 2009, online at: www.theaustralian.com.au/news/opinion/ehud-olmert-still-dreams-of-peace/story-e6frg76f-1225804745744. The Israeli offer is also recorded in an internal report by the PLO's Negotiation Support unit (31 August 2008), online at: www.ajtransparency.com/files/4736.PDF
3. For some details, see Gilead Sher, *The Israeli–Palestinian Peace Negotiations, 1999–2001: Within Reach,* (London: Routledge, 2006).
4. The refugee sections of both Israel's draft Framework Agreement on Permanent Status as well as the Clinton Parameters can be found in Rex Brynen, 'The Past as Prelude? Negotiating the Palestinian Refugee Issue', Chatham House Briefing Paper MEP/BR BP 08/01, London: Chatham

House, 2008, online at: www.chathamhouse.org/publications/papers/view/108831.

5. For the text of the PLO proposal on refugees, the Israeli 'Private Response', and the two sides' joint refugee mechanism paper, see Brynen, 'The Past as Prelude?'.

6. For an overview, see Brynen, 'The Past as Prelude?'; See also Chatham House, 'The Regional Dimension of the Palestinian Refugee Issue: Simulation Exercise Report', (June 2008), online at: www.chathamhouse. org/sites/default/files/public/Research/Middle%20East/12092_prsimulation0608.pdf

7. For the full text of the Geneva Accord and its various annexes, see the official website at: www.geneva-accord.org/. For additional discussion, see Rex Brynen, 'The Geneva Accord and the Palestinian Refugee Issue', unpublished paper, February 2004, online at: www.idrc.ca/uploads/user-S/12075984591geneva_refugees__Brynen_2.pdf

8. For additional discussion, see Abbas Shiblak, 'The Palestinian Refugee Issue: A Palestinian Perspective', Chatham House Briefing Paper MENAP/PR BP 2009/01, London: Chatham House, 2009, online at: www.chathamhouse. org/publications/papers/view/108973

9. Robert Malley and Hussein Agha, 'Camp David and After (2: A Reply to Ehud Barak)', *New York Review of Books*, 13 June 2002, online at: www. nybooks.com/articles/archives/2002/jun/13/camp-david-and-after-an-exchange-2-a-reply-to-ehud/

10. Yasir Arafat, 'The Palestinian Vision of Peace', *New York Times*, 3 February 2002, online at: www.nytimes.com/2002/02/03/opinion/the-palestinian-vision-of-peace.html

11. Palestinian Center for Policy and Survey Research, 'Joint Israeli–Palestinian Public Opinion Poll', June 2010, Press Release, 29 June 2010, online at: www.pcpsr.org/survey/polls/2010/p36ejoint.html. Since 2003, Palestinian support for the refugee component of a deal has ranged from 39 per cent (August 2009) to 48 per cent (June 2010), and is typically a few points lower than support for the overall package of final status arrangements.

12. Palestinian Center for Policy and Survey Research, 'Result of PSR Refugees Poll in the West Bank/Gaza Strip, Jordan and Lebanon on Refugees' Preferences and Behavior in a Palestinian–Israeli Permanent Refugee Agreement, January–June 2003', Press Release, 18 July 2003, online at: www.pcpsr.org/survey/polls/2003/refugeesjune03.html

13. Palestinian Center for Policy and Survey Research, 'Result of PSR Refugees Poll in the West Bank/Gaza Strip'.

14. 'Palestinian PM to Haaretz: We Will Have a State Next Year', *Haaretz*, 2 April 2010, online at: www.haaretz.com/print-edition/news/palestinian-pm-to-haaretz-we-will-have-a-state-next-year-1.283802; 'Report: Hamas Wants to Try Fayyad over Haaretz Interview', *Haaretz*, 3 April 2010, online at: www.haaretz.com/news/report-hamas-wants-to-try-fayyad-over-haaretz-interview-1.283868

15. For additional discussion of Israeli interests and perspectives, see Orit Gal, 'Israeli Perspectives on the Palestinian Refugee Issue', Chatham House Briefing Paper MENAP/PR BP 2009/01, London: Chatham House, 2008, online at: www.chathamhouse.org/publications/papers/view/108833

16. According to one August 2003 poll of Israelis, 'the overwhelming majority – 68% – are not prepared to allow a single refugee to return and 16% are prepared to allow only a few thousand. Only small percentages are prepared to allow larger numbers of refugees to return (7% do not know). [...] The Jewish public's opposition to a return of the refugees is so strong that a clear majority of 66% are not prepared to recognize the right of return in principle, even if this recognition does not mean that refugees would actually be able to return to Israel and even if such recognition was the last obstacle to reaching an agreement with the Palestinians. Under such conditions, 27% would be ready for Israel to recognize the right of return in principle (7% had no opinion on the matter). The majority of the Jewish respondents – 44% – believed that the major reason for the Jewish opposition to the Palestinian right of return is the demographic danger. 31% pointed to the security risk as the main reason, 10% attributed this to the prevalent view that the Palestinian have no such right and 7% saw all these reasons as of equal importance.' Palestinian citizens of Israel, by contrast, overwhelmingly supported the refugees' right of return. The survey also found that 'A more specific question about the circumstances of the refugees' flight in 1948 revealed that a majority of the Jewish public – 56% – pin the blame on the Arab side. Thus, 29% put it on the Arab leadership for telling the Palestinians to leave, 23% on the refugees for leaving on their own initiative, or on the two factors together (4%). Seventeen percent attribute the flight to expulsion by Israeli forces. Eighteen percent did not know, and small percentages ascribed the problem to other causes or other combinations of these factors.' See: 'Peace Index: August 2003', Tami Steinmetz Center for Peace Research, Tel Aviv University, online at: www.tau.ac.il/peace/

17. Avigdor Lieberman, 'My Blueprint for Resolution', *Jerusalem Post*, 23 June 2010, online at: www.jpost.com/Opinion/Op-EdContributors/Article. aspx?id=179333

18. See 'Netanyahu: Israel will Never Cede Jordan Valley', *Ha'aretz*, 2 March 2010, online at: www.haaretz.com/news/netanyahu-israel-will-never-cede-jordan-valley-1.266329

19. For typical arguments in favour of permanent Israeli control over the Jordan Valley, see the various contributions to Dan Diker, (ed.), *Israel's Critical Security Needs for a Viable Peace*, (Jerusalem: Jerusalem Center for Public Affairs, 2010), online at: www.jcpa.org/text/security/fullstudy.pdf

20. Sher, *The Israeli–Palestinian Peace Negotiations*, pp. 247–50.

21. For the full text of the plan, see www.jewishvirtuallibrary.org/jsource/Peace/peoplesvoiceplan.html

22. The Israeli draft Framework Agreement on Permanent Status (2000) noted that 'The parties are cognizant of the suffering caused to individuals and communities on both sides during and following the 1948 War. Israel further recognizes the urgent need for a humane, just, and realistic settlement to the plight of the Palestinian refugees [...]' through 'possible return to the State of Palestine, integration within host countries, and immigration to other third countries.' It added that 'In light of the new era of peace, the Palestinian Party recognizes that the Right of Return shall

apply solely to the state of Palestine,' but also stated that Israel would allow the phased entry of a limited number of refugees 'on humanitarian grounds.'

23. The initial Palestinian refugee proposal at Taba (2001), for example, stated that 'Israel recognizes its moral and legal responsibility for the forced displacement and dispossession of the Palestinian civilian population during the 1948 war [...]' and that 'Israel shall bear responsibility for the resolution of the refugee problem.' It went on stress that 'A just settlement of the refugee problem [...] must lead to the implementation of United Nations General Assembly Resolution 194.'

24. See 'Resolving the Refugee Issue: A Discussion Paper', unpublished paper, 13 July 1999. For more information on the activities of the Core Group, see Rex Brynen (with Eileen Alma, Joel Peters, Roula el-Rifai and Jill Tansley), 'The Ottawa Process: An Examination of Canada's Track Two Involvement in the Palestinian Refugee Issue', paper presented at the Stocktaking II Conference on Palestinian Refugee Research in Ottawa, Canada, 17–20 June 2003, online at: http://web.idrc.ca/en/ev-123242-201-1-DO_TOPIC.html

25. Text in Brynen, 'The Past as Prelude? Negotiating the Palestinian Refugee Issue'.

26. Ibid.

27. A limited right of return would not, of course, really represent a full implementation of UNGAR 194. On the other hand, any future Israeli–Palestinian peace agreement would likely win UN Security Council endorsement, including its refugee component.

28. Akiva Eldar, 'Moratinos Document – The Peace that Nearly Was at Taba', Ha'aretz, 14 February 2002, available online at: http://prrn.mcgill.ca/research/papers/moratinos.htm

29. Text in Brynen, 'The Past as Prelude? Negotiating the Palestinian Refugee Issue'.

30. Ibid.

31. See World Bank, 'Palestinian Refugees: An Overview', unpublished paper, (Washington DC: The World Bank, 2001), p. 8.

32. Eldar, 'Moratinos Document'.

33. As an illustration of this, it took the international community over six years to find places for most of the three thousand Palestinian refugees from Iraq that were trapped on the borders with Syria and Jordan (2003–10).

34. At present, Lebanese nationality law only allows the father to pass on Lebanese citizenship to his offspring. While there has been pressure to reform this in the interests of gender equality, the refugee issue has been an obstacle, with some Lebanese politicians arguing that allowing all Lebanese-Palestinian couples to naturalize their children as Lebanese citizens represents a step in the direction of *tawteen*.

35. For details of the Minster Lovell meetings, see 'Chatham House Project on the Palestinian Refugee Issue', online at: www.chathamhouse.org.uk/research/middle_east/current_projects/palestinian_refugees/minster_lovell/

5

An Offer They Can Refuse: Host Countries and the Palestinian Refugee Issue

Roula El-Rifai and Nadim Shehadi

Introduction

The majority of Palestinians who fled their homes in 1948 after the establishment of the State of Israel – numbering more than 700,000 – found themselves in adjacent Jordan, Lebanon, Syria, the then Jordanian-controlled West Bank and the Egyptian-administered Gaza Strip. These locations have been the official hosts of what are now almost 5 million registered Palestinian refugees (See Table 5.1). According to the United Nations Relief and Works Agency (UNRWA), which provides assistance to these refugees, almost one third of them – some 1.4 million – live in 61 recognized refugee camps.

Jordan, Lebanon and Syria have thus hosted large numbers of Palestinian refugees for most of their existence as independent states. For Jordan and Lebanon in particular, the relationship among the refugees, the Palestinian leadership and the host countries has had fundamental effects on the political and economic development of both countries.

Several factors have shaped this relationship. The first and most obvious has been the size of the refugee population relative to that of the host country. In Jordan, for example, approximately one-third of the population consists of registered refugees, and a majority of the entire population is believed to be of Palestinian origin. The strength of the authoritarian state, the dominant ideology of governance and the underlying structure of society and politics have also been important factors. In Syria for example, refugees were – until the onset of civil war in 2011 – dealt with in the context of a strong state that articulated an Arab nationalist ideology which facilitated granting them extensive civil and economic (if not political) rights in the country. The collapse of Syria into civil conflict, by contrast, has generated new vulnerabilities. In Lebanon, a weak state and the sectarian politicization of demography has long rendered the Palestinian presence a sensitive issue. In Jordan, the monarchy has long viewed Palestinian nationalism as a threat and while proclaiming the unity of all Jordanians has at the same time very much depended on 'East Bankers' for its core political support.

Table 5.1   Estimates of Palestinian Refugee Populations in Host Countries

Field of operations	Official camps	Registered refugees	Total registered persons	% of registered persons in camps	Registered persons as a % of host country population
Jordan	10	2,034,641	2,110,114	18	33
Lebanon	15	441,543	474,053	50	11
Syria	9	499,189	528,711	30	2
West Bank	19	741,409	895,703	24	33
Gaza Strip	8	1,203,135	1,263,312	43	71
Agency Total	*61*	*4,919,917*	*5,271,893*	*29%*	

Source: UNRWA (1 January 2013), CIA World Factbook.

The political dynamic between host governments and the Palestinian movement (especially the Palestinian Liberation Organization, but increasingly Hamas too) has also shaped the situation of refugees. All three states have had turbulent relationships with the PLO, at times marred by violent conflict, including the civil war in Jordan in 1970–71 and in Lebanon from 1975 until the 1982 Israeli invasion. The PLO has had an open conflict with the Syrian regime that has been ongoing since the 1970s. More recently, Hamas has become alienated from Damascus in the context of the civil war.

Host countries have a major interest in the shape of any agreement on the Palestinian refugee issue because each country will be deeply affected by the content and form of that agreement. Politically, the absence of any peace agreement between Palestinians and Israelis or an agreement on a resolution of the refugee problem is complicating the relationship among host governments, the Palestinian leadership and refugee populations. In Jordan, the consequences of any agreement would be existential and would have profound political, economic and demographic implications for the Hashemite Kingdom. In Lebanon, following the 1989 Taif Agreement, which ended the civil war, there is strong consensus against the permanent settlement (*tawteen*) of Palestinian refugees, most of whom are Sunni Muslims. In Syria, any eventual resolution of the Palestinian refugee issue would likely be linked to the prospects of a Syrian–Israeli peace and the future of the Israeli-occupied Golan Heights.

This chapter will discuss Palestinian refugee issues from the perspectives of each of the three major host countries: Jordan, Syria and Lebanon. In doing so, it will first explore in greater detail some of the general policy issues that arise for host countries from the refugee issue, as well as the ways in which hosts have generally been absent from past negotiating processes. Next, the discussion will move onto the specificities of each of the three cases. The chapter will conclude by addressing the implications of current trends, most notably the continuing regional ramifications of the Arab Spring, the bloody civil war in Syria and the absence of a meaningful peace process.

Host Country Interests and Refugee Negotiations

While there are many complex potential linkages between the outcome of any future refugee negotiations and the interests of host countries, these essentially boil down to five sets of core issues: residency (including repatriation, return and resettlement), financial implications, the future of UNRWA, implementation mechanisms, and implications for political stability.

With regard to *residency*, any refugee agreement that might be reached will have implications for how many Palestinians might continue to reside in Jordan, Syria or Lebanon, and how many might either return to Israel, be repatriated to a Palestinian state, or even be resettled in other third countries.[1] Historically, both Jordanian leaders and Lebanese politicians have – quite apart from any normative commitment to the refugees' 'right of return' – preferred that substantial numbers of refugees leave their countries in any future agreement. Syrian officials have also strongly upheld the right of return, but have tended not to see the refugees as a burden or political problem per se, and demographic concerns have not been a major determinant of policy.

In the case of *financial implications*, some host countries have argued that the past costs of hosting refugees ought to entitle them to compensation or donor assistance in the event of a refugee agreement. The Jordanians have been especially outspoken in this regard. Host countries would also be affected by any reparations or compensation that were paid directly to the refugees, which could amount to many billions of dollars. This could represent a significant boost to local economies but could also create friction in some areas. Host countries would also have concerns about the eventual wind-down of UNRWA as part of any agreement. The burden of provision of services and protection of refugees would shift to them.

Because of the importance of both population movements and the financial dimensions of any agreement, host countries would have considerable interest in the design of the *implementation mechanism* for any refugee agreement. On the one hand, they might wish to be directly involved in whatever steering body helped oversee this. On the other hand, too close a relationship might prove politically risky if the agreement itself was unpopular among refugees, or if problems arose in implementing its terms.

Financial concerns would be a major factor in host countries' attitudes towards the *future of UNRWA*. Currently the Agency spends approximately more than US$250 million per year and employs some 13,000 refugees to deliver health, education and social services to refugees in these three countries. These costs would probably devolve to local governments in the event of a peace agreement and those authorities would also need to consider what to do about the Agency's infrastructure and employees. Local governments would also become the object of new demands from their Palestinian populations. The issue is not simply a material one, however. Host countries would generally favour a very slow phase out of UNRWA so as to maintain some palpable sign of international commitment to fully resolve the refugee issue.

For its part, UNRWA has generally sought to align both its programmes, for example, school curriculum and pay scales, with the local public sector, in part to facilitate any future transition.

Finally, cross-cutting all of these dimensions is the overriding concern of *political stability*. Host regimes would want to ensure that an agreement enhanced rather than undermined political stability. In Jordan and Lebanon, demographic concerns would be part of this. In all three countries there would be considerable unwillingness to be openly associated with a refugee agreement that was deeply unpopular among the refugees themselves. Any deal perceived as involving a compromise on the right of return, for example, would carry a heavy political cost – especially if it were not offset by other elements of the peace agreement.

Host Countries and the Negotiation Process

Despite these many substantial and varied interests, host countries have generally been marginal to Palestinian–Israeli peace negotiations, from the Declaration of Principles reached between Israel and the PLO in Oslo in 1993, through the permanent status negotiations of 2000–01, to the failed Annapolis round of negotiations in 2007–08.[2] In essence, host countries and their populations have been part of the problem but they have not been and will not be participants in developing the solution. Instead, they will have to develop policies to deal with, and possibly pre-empt, the outcome of the refugee component of the Middle East Peace Process. The options for the host countries are limited; on the one hand, they are under no obligation to accept any deal that they did not participate in negotiating. On the other hand, they also bear the repercussions of the absence of a deal with the increased tension and frustration of their refugee population and the political tensions which that uncertainty creates. At best, host countries will be confronted with a package agreement that they will have to react to, despite having had no formal input to it. At worst, they will have to cope with the fallout of there being no refugee package at all. Their only real option or prerogative is to refuse to endorse the outcome of negotiations and not to cooperate with the implementation of any agreement.[3]

Some – including senior host country officials – argue that not being formally part of the negotiations process has its advantages. For example, if a refugee agreement were negatively received by the host country populations, including by the Palestinian refugees, host countries could avoid blame for an agreement, which they did not negotiate and would not have to bear the cost of the political compromise on the refugee issue. The negotiators, Israel and the PLO, as well as the United States – the most likely key sponsor of the negotiations – might also prefer not to have the host countries formally involved in the process because that would give them a de facto veto power, which would further complicate the process of reaching agreement. The USA and negotiators could argue that the priority is to first reach an agreement and then to worry about selling it to the host countries. From their perspective, formally including the host countries in the process would empower the spoilers.

One avenue for dealing with the dilemma of host country exclusion could be an active Track II mechanism that informally feeds host country positions into the negotiating process. During the early rounds of negotiations leading up to the Taba talks and the Quartet roadmap, senior Palestinian negotiators noted the need to bridge the gap between the PLO and host country positions on the refugee issue and called for a third party to launch a Track II process to establish regular lines of communications between the PLO and Jordanian officials on the Palestinian refugee issue. The objective was to inform the PLO position to avoid them entering into an agreement out of synch with Jordanian interests.

The marginalization of the host countries is a direct result of the bilateral structure of negotiations after Oslo. The problem is best seen as a contrast between the mechanism of negotiations in the Middle East Peace Process initiated in Madrid in 1991 and that of the Oslo process between the PLO and Israel in 1993. Madrid was inclusive of all the neighbouring Arab states and aimed at a comprehensive agreement that would be signed collectively between the Arab countries and Israel. The ensuing multilateral track of negotiations, which aimed to complement the bilateral negotiations, also aimed at addressing issues common to the region and at involving Palestinians,

Israelis and the regional parties as well as any other interested country in the international community.[4] Host countries were formally part of that track through the Canadian-led Refugee Working Group (RWG). Under Madrid, the PLO was not the principal negotiator and was part of the Jordanian delegation. The Madrid process was an Arab–Israeli one as opposed to the Oslo process, which was Palestinian–Israeli, initiated by secret bilateral negotiations between the PLO and Israel and excluding any of the Arab states.

One outcome from Oslo was the further fragmentation of the Arab position and the creation of competing bilateral tracks. But host countries were never able to fully use the multilateral RWG forum to present their views, mainly due to the broad nature of participation but also because of an agenda that was perceived by them to exclude the political dimension. Moreover, Lebanon and Syria never participated in this track and in 1997, the Arab League called for a boycott of the RWG to protest Israeli policies. This led the RWG to officially suspend its formal activities in 2000.[5]

Under Oslo, the refugee issue was part of a final status package to include Jerusalem, borders, refugees, water rights, settlements and other issues of common interest between the PLO and Israel. However, both Jerusalem and refugees cannot be considered as purely bilateral issues between Israel and the PLO because they are of interest to other parties and it is generally argued that these two issues represent key stumbling blocks to resolving the Arab–Israeli conflict. The intangible moral and religious aspects of any negotiations over Jerusalem are of global interest for Christians, Jews and Muslims, however, the practical aspects of access and borders as well as local governance can be more easily resolved bilaterally between Israel and the PLO. The Palestinian refugee issue is unique in that it is the only permanent status issue that is not fully resolvable through bilateral negotiations between Israel and the PLO. Whatever the two parties agree on will have an impact on the host countries and on the refugees outside the PNA; these are major stakeholders who formally have had no input in the negotiations process, and to-date, there is no formal mechanism for them to influence its outcome.

Stage three of the Road Map for Peace announced by President George W. Bush on 24 June 2002, includes an international conference where regional stakeholders will participate and launch final status talks. This would have been an occasion for the host countries to put their positions forward before the negotiations and set their own parameters for a solution to the Palestinian refugee issue. This was possibly the only mechanism for addressing host country concerns in the negotiations after Oslo, but is now considered dated.

Over the years, there have been some informal Track II processes that have tried to address the exclusion of host countries from the negotiations process. Chatham House in the UK led a project which argued that the exclusion of the perspective of host countries and their refugee populations from a bilateral agreement could be costly and could make for an unsustainable agreement. The project, which began in 2000, tried to complement that structural gap in the negotiations process through research and a series of informal Track II meetings, which came to be known as the 'Minster Lovell Process'.[6]

Host countries have different priorities when it comes to the implementation of an agreement. Their main concern would be the impact or fallout from the agreement on their internal politics and on their relations with the refugees.[7] There are three key policy issues that must be addressed in the near and long terms by regional and international stakeholders. The first relates to the structure of the negotiations, which as discussed above, resulted in a failure to represent the interests of the host countries, specifically on the Palestinian refugee issue. The question is how should future negotiations be designed so as to include the interests of host countries? The second relates to the importance of finding a way to ensure the cooperation of the host countries in the implementation of any future agreement, even if they are not part of the negotiations or do not approve of their outcome. The third issue relates to the need to manage the situation in host countries in the meantime; in the context of little or no progress in the Middle East Peace Process and in the absence of negotiations, it has left host countries and refugees to bear the brunt of the repercussions of this limbo situation. The events in Syria and the displacement of a large number of Palestinian refugees there, many of whom went to Lebanon, complicate matters further.

The Arab Peace Initiative

One important regional element in the Palestinian–Israeli conflict is the Arab Peace Initiative (API), which was proposed and endorsed at the 2002 Arab Summit in Beirut and later reaffirmed at other Arab summits. The API is the most important regional initiative since Madrid and offers Israel recognition and normalization after it reaches an agreement with the Palestinians which would: (a) include complete withdrawal from the occupied Arab territories, including the Syrian Golan Heights, to the 4 June 1967 line and the territories still occupied in southern Lebanon; (b) attain a just solution to the problem of Palestinian refugees to be agreed upon in accordance with the UN General Assembly Resolution No. 194; and (c) accept the establishment of an independent and sovereign Palestinian state in the Palestinian territories occupied since 4 June 1967 in the West Bank and Gaza Strip with East Jerusalem as its capital. In return the Arab states will do the following: (a) consider the Arab–Israeli conflict over, sign a peace agreement with Israel, and achieve peace for all states in the region; and (b) establish normal relations with Israel within the framework of this comprehensive peace.[8]

Both the wording and the content of the API are important. They represent a compromise reached after heated debates and several drafts. Concepts such as the right of return and the prohibition of permanent settlement (*tawteen*) were included so as to leave the negotiators more room to manoeuver. The discussions of the amendments to the API during the Arab League Summit were mainly related to the wording on the right of return. The compromise formula, which mentions Resolution 194 as the basis of a 'just solution' that would be 'agreed upon' by both Israel and the PLO, leaves its implementation in the hands of the PLO leadership while adding language that any deal should be acceptable to both parties. Furthermore, the API 'assures the rejection of all forms of Palestinian patriation which conflict with the special circumstances of the Arab host countries.'[9]

In essence, the API conveys the message that a comprehensive regional peace is possible if some conditions are fulfilled. It reflects the position that any compromise involving both Jerusalem and the refugees, reached in the negotiations between the PLO and Israel, would be endorsed as long as it is acceptable to the parties. This implies that members of the Arab League would not get involved in the political cost of reaching an agreement on these two issues. Rather, responsibility will be borne by the PLO leadership as the negotiators on behalf of the Palestinians.

The API was in a large part initiated by one of the host countries, Jordan, and then adopted by Saudi Arabia which presented it at the Arab League Summit in Beirut where the two other host countries, Syria and Lebanon, played a role in amending the paragraph on the refugees to include a mention of United Nations General Assembly Resolution (UNGA) 194. It thus represents indirectly a compromise endorsed by the three host countries and by the Arab League and later by the Organization of the Islamic Conference.

At the time, the announcement of the API was overshadowed by the reoccupation of the West Bank by Israel in April 2002, as well as by the lack of Israeli interest in reaching a deal. Since then, however, there have been several attempts to revive it. It is widely reported that the Obama administration will be basing its new approach to the negotiations on the API, bringing the API back to the fore.

Host Countries: Specific Circumstances

While it is possible to identify general areas of interest shared by all or most of the three major host countries, the specific priorities and concerns of each vary with their national circumstances. Consequently, it is important to examine each in turn.

Jordan: An Existential Concern

The Hashemite Kingdom of Jordan is the only one of the three host states that has a peace treaty with Israel, which was signed shortly after Oslo. The 1994 treaty is a bilateral one and includes a clause on refugees which places Israel under an obligation to discuss the humanitarian issues relating to refugees with Jordan itself: 'Recognizing that the above human problems caused by the conflict in the Middle East cannot be fully resolved on the bilateral level, the Parties will seek to resolve them in appropriate forums, in accordance with international law ....'[10]

Of the three host countries, Jordan hosts the most Palestinian refugees with a total population of over 2 million and their proportion to resident population is the highest. Some 18 per cent of UNRWA-registered refugees live in the ten official and three unofficial refugee camps in Jordan and the rest live in urban areas, particularly around Amman, which is home to around half of all residents of Jordan.

Jordan conferred formal citizenship en masse to the 1948 Palestinian refugees residing in its territory. The population of Jordan before 1948 was roughly 400,000 people, to which were added about 70,000 Palestinian refugees who crossed the river in that year. Following the 1948 Israeli–Arab war, Jordan formally annexed the West Bank and the total population of the Kingdom including the West Bank was around 900,000 people. Following the 1967 Arab–Israeli war and the Israeli occupation of the West Bank and East Jerusalem, Jordan hosted a further estimated 240,000 who were displaced for the first time and fled to Jordan. In July 1988, Jordan formally severed all administrative and legal ties with the occupied West Bank resulting in additional flows of refugees – some were displaced to the Kingdom. A further number of Palestinians, expelled from Kuwait in 1991 following the Gulf War, moved to Jordan; some of them already had Jordanian citizenship.

Even though there are no official statistics on Palestinians in Jordan and numbers differ depending on sources, some observers estimate that the number of Jordanians of Palestinian origin to be around 43 per cent of the total population of the Kingdom. Other observers believe the proportion to be higher, reaching about 60 per cent.[11] For this reason alone, the question of Palestinian refugees is one of the most sensitive in the Kingdom.

Palestinian refugees living in Jordan have four different legal statuses:

1. '1948 refugees', regardless of whether or not they are registered with UNRWA as 'Palestine refugees';
2. '1967 West Bank displaced': those whose main place of residence has been the East Bank of the River Jordan since 1967;
3. The 1967 'Gazan displaced': either 1948 Palestine refugees or those displaced from Gaza in 1967: UNRWA estimates their population to be around 120,000;
4. West Bankers: those who have sought residence in the East Bank since July 1988.

The first two categories – and their descendants – are officially regarded as Jordanian citizens, while the others are regarded as 'foreigners', but with various complex legal statuses and entitlements. Because most Palestinians in Jordan are Jordanian citizens, the government (far more so than in Syria or Lebanon) asserts its right to represent their interests in political and diplomatic negotiations. Paradoxically, the domestic sensitivity of the issue means that Jordan has no particular desire to be involved in formal talks on the subject, where it might share blame with the Palestinians for any compromises made.

Institutionally Jordan has a well-established department of refugee affairs, which is part of the Ministry of Interior. It includes over 240 employees in addition to representative offices in every refugee camp.

Palestinians in Jordan are generally fully integrated into the economy. Indeed, it is widely believed that they have a disproportionate presence in the private sector. However, political integration has lagged. Jordanians of East Bank origin have a larger share of government jobs and have disproportionate representation in the Jordanian parliament.[12] While the state has emphasized the unity of all Jordanians, it has also depended on East Bankers for its core support, and manipulated Palestinian–East Banker tensions at times (for example, in attempting to blunt post-Arab Spring calls for political reform).

The defining event of the relationship between the Jordanian state and the Palestinians was the civil war of 1970 when the PLO and various other Palestinian factions attempted to overthrow the monarchy in what is known as Black September. The violence lasted from September 1970 until July 1971 with thousands of casualties and the expulsion of the PLO leadership to Lebanon. Tight security control by the secret services (*mukhabarat*) and the prohibition of any overtly Palestinian political activity are part of the legacy of what came to be called 'Black September'. Since then, Islamist opposition parties provide the common platform where Palestinians and Jordanians can belong equally. Also, there have been over the years declarations by various Israeli right-wing politicians suggesting that 'Jordan is Palestine' and should be the future home of all Palestinians – thus solving the problem of their 'right of return' and the demographic problem of too many Palestinians in the West Bank and Gaza. These all add up to components that are at the root of Jordanian–Palestinian tensions. For Jordan the issue of the future of Palestinian refugees is existential.

The Jordanian position on the issue of refugees in the Middle East Peace Process is the best defined among the host countries and rests on several principles. One is that the Palestinians in Jordan are Jordanian citizens and should be represented by the Jordanian state in any negotiations relating to compensation. Jordan, as all host countries, will greatly benefit from compensation payments to Palestinians from Jordan, through taxing income, as well as through the economic benefit from consumption. The second is the categorical rejection of any formula that involves dual citizenship, i.e. both Palestinian and Jordanian, for fear of divided loyalties and as a way to limit Palestinian numbers in Jordan. Palestinians in Jordan will be given the right to choose which side of the river they want to belong to but Jordan will probably strip Palestinians of their citizenship if they decide to repatriate to a Palestinian state. The 'foreigners' in Jordan are likely to be asked to repatriate to a Palestinian state in the event of a peace agreement. But given Palestinian demographics in Jordan, it will be politically risky and sensitive to develop and implement such policies.

Third, Jordan also has the most advanced position on state compensation for hosting the refugees. It has proposed figures that some describe as unrealistic claims that don't take into account the substantive economic benefit which Palestinians have brought to Jordan over the years. This demand by Jordan and other host countries is likely to be dealt with by the donor community, which will invest in the host countries following an agreement – what some have called the 'peace dividend' for these countries.

The idea of an eventual Jordanian–Palestinian federation has always been part of the debate but is officially rejected on both sides, especially prior to the establishment of a Palestinian state in the West Bank and Gaza with Jerusalem as the capital.[13] It is possible that once that state is established, the federation option can be examined in its own right by two sovereign states without the burden and the legacy of Jordanian–Palestinian relations and tensions.

To date, Arab Spring type protests against the government in Jordan have not been related to the Palestinian presence in that country and have not been identified with the Jordanian–Palestinian divide. Rather they have been focused on demands for political and economic reform. Uncertainty over the future in Jordan is high and the risk of growing Islamist influence would affect the balance of power inside

from Jordan following Black September in 1971. This brought the PLO to clash with the Lebanese army in 1973 and with Lebanese factions, a clash which was considered to be the trigger of the civil war in 1975. Israeli invasions in 1978 and 1982 ultimately resulted in the expulsion of the PLO leadership to Tunis and clashes between Palestinians and the Syrian regime finished the job. Ultimately, the PLO's total withdrawal from the country came in 1993 after the Oslo Accords, when the PLO stopped paying salaries and pensions and shut down most of its institutions. This has been a major contributor to the deterioration of living conditions among the Palestinians in Lebanon. The PLO was said to have employed a majority of the Palestinian workforce and provided most social services through its institutions.

The vacuum created by the departure of the PLO was large and was never filled. It left Palestinian civilians behind without any protection and at a time when the Lebanese state itself was recovering from near total collapse after the civil war ended in 1990. Moreover, Palestinian camps suffered from much destruction and became the scene of factional fighting between pro-PLO and pro-Syrian armed groups with no reconstruction plans for the camps.

The 1989 Taif accord, which ended the civil war in Lebanon and became the country's informal amended constitution, included a clause prohibiting the permanent settlement of the Palestinians in Lebanon. In 1991 the Lebanese Government set up a ministerial committee to conduct discussions with Palestinians and regulate the presence of Palestinians in Lebanon; these discussions were interrupted by the Middle East Peace Process negotiations in Madrid and only resumed in 2005. The Lebanese perspective was that the basis of the Madrid talks of 'land for peace' according to UN Resolutions 242 and 338 calling for Israel's withdrawal from territories it occupied in 1967, did not deal with the Israeli occupation in Southern Lebanon or with the refugee issue. Given this, there was a debate about whether Lebanon should participate in the Madrid process. Ultimately, Lebanon justified its participation by arguing that its presence would help highlight the need to address the refugee issue and to lobby for the implementation of UNSC Resolution 425 of 1978 calling for Israeli withdrawal from the south of the country. The absence of discussions on refugees in both the Madrid and Oslo processes exacerbated the Lebanese fears of permanent settlement.

The Lebanese government addressed the issue of Palestinian refugees for the first time in 2005 following the withdrawal of Syrian troops from the country. The government set up an inter-ministerial working group that later became known as the Lebanese–Palestinian Dialogue Committee (LPDC) to deal with outstanding Palestinian refugee issues in the country. The mandate of the group was to improve the living conditions of Palestinians in Lebanon, to initiate a dialogue about Palestinian arms inside camps and put an end to Palestinian arms outside camps, and finally to work to establish formal diplomatic relations between Lebanon and Palestine. The group was supported by an externally-funded technical team. Given its lack of executive authority, the LPDC was never able to move on the key thorny issues of the right to employment and to property ownership for Palestinians. The slow progress on the regulation of Palestinian status in Lebanese laws, especially in relation to these rights, has proven to be the main source of tension. The battle of Nahr el Bared between the Lebanese army and a terrorist group that took over the Palestinian refugee camp in north Lebanon in 2007 awakened all the fears and anxieties of both the Lebanese and Palestinians.[21]

Lebanon remains institutionally weak when it comes to the administrative infrastructure for dealing with the refugee issues. The Directorate of Palestinian Refugee Affairs at the Ministry of Interior contains some two dozen employees compared to its counterparts in Syria and Jordan with at least ten times that number. The LPDC is dependent on donor funding, has less than a dozen staff and has limited political influence.

Lebanon's position vis-à-vis the MEPP is also maximalist, rejecting any form of settlement of refugees in the country, and progress on the legal front is often paralyzed by the political debates about fears of de facto permanent settlement fuelled by the lack of progress in the peace process. Lebanon is thus so far institutionally ill-prepared to participate in the implementation of an agreement.

Palestinian refugees in Lebanon deserve special attention for the political significance of the community there. Lebanon is the only place in the region where refugees have had the opportunity to develop their own political and civil society institutions and where one can find the broadest spectrum of Palestinian political opinions and organizations. In fact, Palestinian politics exists in Lebanon much more than it does in Ramallah, Gaza, Damascus, Amman or in the West, where there is also an active Palestinian diaspora. The PLO and Fatah have regained some of their presence after Syrian withdrawal in 2005 and coexist with Hamas and other rejectionist factions. Despite restrictions on freedom of association for Palestinians, there is a vibrant Palestinian civil society operating in Lebanon and several research centres, publishing houses and media outlets. This makes Beirut the political capital of Palestinian diaspora politics and an essential component of a future solution.

The Palestinian refugee issue will remain a hot topic in Lebanon and is bound to trigger controversy whenever it is raised. Although there has been some improvement in Palestinian–Lebanese relations since 2005, the impact of that is yet to be felt by the residents of the refugee camps. Their condition is governed by the default options in most instances and where detrimental laws cannot be changed, they are simply not applied. The policy options for Lebanon are also not clear, should an agreement be reached. The Lebanese state is bound to cooperate with the implementation mechanism of an agreement while rejecting certain components dealing with permanent settlement, which is prohibited by the constitution of their country and by the Taif Agreement.

Lebanon needs to develop its institutional capacity to deal with the Palestinian refugee issue and manage Palestinian–Lebanese relations until a solution is reached. The government of Lebanon needs to develop a policy towards such a solution as well as the capacity to participate in the implementation and to safeguard its interests in that process. Open discussion of the refugee issue is possible in the country but it easily gets caught up in political and sectarian rivalries. Of all the host countries, Palestinians in Lebanon are the most dependent on international support and on UNRWA services.

The special situation of Palestinians in Lebanon has been recognized by the PLO and the international community and past agreements (including the Taba and the Geneva Accords) have made Palestinians in Lebanon a priority, especially in relation to the option of third country resettlement – something some Jordanian officials reject given the small number of refugees in that country compared to those in Jordan. Given that Lebanon would not have a border with a future Palestinian state, it is unlikely that in the event of an agreement, Lebanon would move to deport Palestinians; but it is likely to continue with its measures against Palestinians such as restricting their right to employment, in order to encourage them to leave the country. Lebanon, however, needs to develop a policy towards those Palestinians who will wish to remain in that country, including those who are married to Lebanese.

Conclusion

In some ways, the current diplomatic stagnation of the 'peace process' provides an opportunity for host countries to more fully develop their policy options, so as to be better prepared for any future talks and for their part in the implementation of an agreement. They will almost certainly not do so, however. Syria, after all, is enmeshed in a bloody and prolonged civil war. Lebanon also has more pressing policy issues confronting it. In Jordan, there seems little incentive to address the sensitive issue of the future status of Palestinian refugees in the country, especially at a time when the Arab Spring and the Syrian civil war have the Hashemite monarchy on edge.

The Arab Spring itself will have important implications for the refugee issue. These will be most acutely felt in Syria, with the refugees – likely Syrians themselves – facing sustained violence and humanitarian crisis. While Palestinian groups contend they are not taking sides, it seems inevitable that given their degree of assimilation they will be as involved as other residents of Syria. Lebanon has, as noted earlier, seen tens of thousands of Palestinian refugees from Syria (and Syrian refugees) flee to that country. While the Lebanese state has not tried to close its borders and prevent the inflow of refugees, it has at the same time not been able to provide them with services. Their flight has only accentuated the burden on UNRWA and on the poor, overcrowded Lebanese-Palestinian refugee communities that have provided them with aid and shelter. The political and sectarian polarization generated by the war in Syria could spread to refugee communities too, something already evident on a small scale within the Palestinian community.

For its part, Jordan has generally tried to block entry to Syrian-Palestinian refugees for fear that it might host them indefinitely, thus further eroding the East Bank share of the population. This concern may have driven, in part, the Kingdom's decision to facilitate the supply of weapons and training to friendly Syrian opposition militias in southern Syria, in order to establish a buffer zone north of its border.

A major concern of the host countries is the decline in UNRWA services and the crisis that the institution is constantly going through. UNRWA itself has been under attack by various lobby groups, both for its internal managerial problems and for its very existence, which is interpreted as perpetuating the Palestinian refugee problem rather than helping resolve it. While UNRWA recognizes that it is in need of a major strategic overhaul and reform, it is also difficult to undergo any medium- or long-term planning while the institution is in crisis, living from hand to mouth.

While ongoing negotiations raise the concerns of the host countries about the type of solution that might be imposed on them, the absence of negotiations or a stagnation in the process also raises concerns but of a different nature. The absence of negotiations increases tensions and divisions within the Palestinian community and, when it is accompanied by a decline in UNRWA services, also raises anxieties within the host state. This situation, often described as limbo, creates an atmosphere where even humanitarian or developmental initiatives acquire a political dimension by raising suspicions that they are part of an overall plan for permanent settlement. Such fears were expressed in the reconstruction of Jenin camp in the West Bank, in the improvements done to infrastructure in camps in Jordan as well as in Syria as in the case of improvements in the refugee camp of Nairab near Aleppo and in Lebanon during the reconstruction of Nahr el Bared camp.

While former occurrences of the limbo phenomenon happened when the Palestinian–Israeli conflict was hot and on the agenda, we are now experiencing an unprecedented period during which the Palestinian–Israeli conflict as a whole is marginalized and is no longer a priority given the different developments in the region and in the Arab Spring.

Notes

1. On aspects of repatriation to a Palestinian state, see Rex Brynen and Roula El-Rifai (eds), *Palestinian Refugees: The Challenges of Repatriation and Development* (New York: I.B. Tauris, 2007).

2. For an overview of negotiations on the Palestinian refugee issue, see Rex Brynen, 'The Past as a Prelude: Negotiating the Palestinian Refugee Issue', Chatham House, June 2008, at: www.chathamhouse.org/publications/papers/view/108831

3. See two meeting reports from the Chatham House project: 'Refugees and Host Countries in International Law', report of a consultation workshop held on 7–8 September 2002, at: www.chathamhouse.org/sites/default/files/public/Research/Middle%20East/070902summary.pdf; and 'Host Country Workshop', report from a meeting held in November 2007, at: www.chathamhouse.org/sites/default/files/public/Research/Middle%20East/1107report.pdf. See also Nadim Shehadi, 'Palestinian Refugees: The Regional Perspective', Chatham House, April 2009, at: www.chathamhouse.org/publications/papers/view/109047

4. For background on the multilaterals, see Joel Peters, *Pathways to Peace: The Multilateral Arab–Israeli Peace Talks* (London: Royal Institute of International Affairs, 1996); and Dalia Dassa Kaye, *Beyond the Handshake: Multilateral Cooperation in the Arab–Israeli Peace Process, 1991–1996* (New York: Columbia University Press, 2001).

5. The Gavel of the RWG, held by Canada, continued informal Track II activities. IDRC, which supported Canada's role as the Gavel organized two Stocktaking meetings in 1997 and 2003 and supported a broad range of policy-relevant research and dialogue activities which came to be known as the 'Ottawa Process'.

6. For details of the Minster Lovell Process, see the Chatham House website at: www.chathamhouse.org/research/middle-east/current-projects/minster-lovell-process

7. See Nadim Shehadi, 'Palestinian Refugees: The Regional Perspective', Chatham House, April 2009.

8. For the text of the API, see www.guardian.co.uk/world/2002/mar/28/israel7

9. Ibid.

10. Clause 1, Article 8 on Refugees and Displaced Persons, at: www.kinghussein.gov.jo/peacetreaty.html

11. Listening to Palestinian Refugees/Displaced Persons in Jordan: Perceptions of their Political and Socio-Economic Status, January 2009, unpublished report by Al-Quds Centre for Political Studies.

12. Ibid.

13. See Mustafa Hamarneh, Rosemary Hollis and Khalil Shikaki, *Jordanian Palestinian Relations: Where to?: Four scenarios for the future*, (London: Royal Institute of International Affairs, 1997).

14. See Adnan Abu-Odeh, *Jordanians, Palestinians and the Hashemite Kingdom in the Middle East Peace Process*, (Washington DC: United States Institute of Peace, 1999).

15. See Yehuda Greenfield-Gilat, 'A Renewable Energy Peace Park in the Golan as a Framework to an Israeli–Syrian Agreement', United States Institute of Peace Briefing Report, Washington, DC, 10 July 2009.

16. See Ghada Hashem Talhami, *Syria and the Palestinians: The Clash of Nationalisms*, (Miami: University Press of Florida, 2001).

17. On the red lines see Efraim Inbar, *Israel's National Security: Issues and Challenges since the Yom Kippur War,* (London: Routledge, 2008), p. 19.
18. See Jaber Suleiman, 'The Current Political, Organizational, and Security Situation in the Palestinian Refugee Camps of Lebanon', *Journal of Palestine Studies*, Vol. 29, no. 1, p. 66.
19. UNRWA, 'Syria Crisis Situation Update', No. 56 (29 July 2012), at: www.unrwa.org/etemplate.php?id=1836
20. The term is used by Yezid Sayigh in *Armed Struggle and the Search for State: The Palestinian National Movement 1949–1993,* (Oxford: Oxford University Press, 1999).
21. See Nadim Shehadi, 'A Staircase in Nahr el Bared: The future of Palestinian Refugees in Lebanon', Washington DC, Aspen Institute, October 2010, at: www.aspeninstitute.org/publications/staircase-nahr-el-bared-future-palestinian-refugees-lebanon

6

Refugee Compensation: Policy Choices and Implementation Issues

Heike Niebergall and Norbert Wühler[1]

Introduction

ompensation for Palestinian refugees has been seen as an integral part of a comprehensive solution to the Palestinian refugee issue since the first attempts to end this refugee crisis.[2] The need to compensate Palestinian refugees for the losses that they have suffered has been acknowledged in one form or another during all negotiations over the past decades and a Palestinian–Israeli Peace or other Agreement ending the refugee crisis is expected to set out the key parameters of such a compensation scheme and of the mechanism to implement it. The parties acknowledge or insist that compensation represents only one remedy that is to be provided along with other reparation and rehabilitation measures. At the same time, the question of what these other measures should entail and to what extent they should include restitution of property rights and the right to return to Israel as one of the durable residency options, represents one of the most bitterly disputed issues between the parties.

While acknowledging the close and complex linkage that exists at all levels between restitution, compensation and the exercise of durable residency options, this chapter focuses on compensation alone and looks at the possible parameters of a compensation scheme for Palestinian refugees as they have transpired during the negotiations, and on the policy and implementation issues that would be faced in such a scheme.[3] The authors wish to stress, however, that most policy issues and implementation challenges that will be discussed relating to compensation could equally apply to restitution. As such the considerations below regarding eligibility, evidentiary standards, inheritance issues and to a large extent also organizational structures are equally relevant when considering a property restitution scheme for Palestinian refugees.

Drawing on experiences from past and current compensation claims programmes,[4] the chapter aims to set out the issues and questions that the designers and implementers of a compensation scheme for Palestinian refugees are likely to face:[5] What losses will be compensated? Who will receive compensation? What types of compensation will be provided? How will compensable losses be valued? What are suitable models for the compensation component of an implementation mechanism? What are the options for the underlying funding schemes?

Given the negotiation positions so far, the provisions on compensation in the Agreement are likely to reflect a difficult political compromise that could be the result of important policy issues being left to be decided at the implementation stage. This political compromise might also result in compensation provisions that are less than optimal from a technical standpoint and could delay the distribution of compensation benefits. Once an Agreement has been concluded, however, quick results will be needed in order to avoid a backlash among the Palestinian refugees, that in turn could threaten the sustainability of the Peace Agreement.

The implementation should therefore foresee the fast-tracking of certain benefits in order to achieve quick impact and to at least meet some of the expectations on the side of the beneficiaries without delay. As such, the chapter also discusses what could be prepared by the various stakeholders prior to such an agreement in order to assist the efficient and speedy implementation of the compensation part and with it ensure a quick positive impact for Palestinian refugees following an agreement.

Negotiating Positions

The complex linkage between the different remedies discussed in the context of a resolution of the Palestinian refugee issue is reflected in the negotiating positions of the parties.

The Palestinian side has insisted that a solution for Palestinian refugees has to be built on the universal principles and best practices of international law and that return, restitution and compensation must be recognized as cumulative and at the same time separate entitlements dealing with distinct aspects of the Palestinian refugee issue.[6] Without such recognition, Palestinians believe that even the discussion of compensation would be perceived as the acceptance of compensation as a trade-off for the rights of return and restitution. In addition to this, they have stressed the importance of Israel itself, rather than the international community, taking on the responsibility of providing the funds for Palestinian refugee compensation.

The Israeli side, while accepting that compensation is owed to Palestinian landowners for property that will remain with Israel, is wary of participation in any further compensation for Palestinian refugees, as this could be seen as an acceptance of a moral and legal responsibility for the forced displacement of the Palestinian refugees. Israel rejects the act of restitution of property inside Israel. It demands that the Peace Agreement will settle all claims in a final and definitive way, ending all claims and closing the refugee file. This not only requires that all refugee-related demands are comprehensively addressed in the Peace Agreement and that nothing is left to a later post-agreement phase, it also raises complex questions regarding the extent a bilateral Israeli–Palestinian Agreement can be binding on third parties, e.g. Palestinian diaspora and host countries.

Despite these conflicting positions on compensation-related issues, the principle that some compensation would be part of a resolution of the Palestinian refugee issue has been accepted since the Beilin-Abu Mazen understandings of 1995. Later negotiations and position papers at the Camp David Summit in 2000, the Clinton Parameters of the same year and during the Taba negotiations in 2001 all saw compensation for refugees as part of a comprehensive solution.[7]

The early discussions, proposals and negotiations focused on compensation for the value of property that Palestinian refugees lost when they were displaced in 1948. At Taba, a second compensation element was added, and the Parties generally agreed on two types of compensation, i.e. compensation for the value of lost property that would not be restituted on the one hand and compensation for suffering and losses as a result of displacement on the other. As mentioned above, the Parties were, and still are however, far apart concerning the extent to which compensation rather than restitution of the property rights would apply, the assessment of the value of the Palestinian property losses, and the question as to how the compensation should be funded, who should contribute and how much; and when and how these questions should be answered.

Much preparatory and technical work has been done to facilitate the Parties' negotiations of these issues, by the Parties themselves, but also through so called 'Track II' and independent research activities. The preparatory work relates to issues such as the availability and status of property records to support and verify future property claims; the methods of how to calculate individual losses; the assessment of the total value of the properties; the registration of refugees that would be eligible for compensation; payment modalities; and the impact of significant compensation payments on the refugees and their host or home societies and economies.[8]

Main Compensation Parameters

This section discusses the substantive features of the compensation scheme that will be relevant for the eligibility of Palestinian refugees to receive compensation, by looking at the following questions: For what types of losses will compensation be paid? Who is entitled to receive compensation? And, what type of compensation will be provided?

Types of Losses Compensated

As mentioned above, past negotiations have identified two very distinct types of compensation for Palestinian refugees.

The first type of compensation to be looked at here is compensation for the suffering and losses resulting from the displacement. In the Palestinian refugee context, this compensation is usually referred to as 'compensation for refugeehood'. Compensation for refugeehood would constitute the primary reparative measure for economically assessable damage which Palestinian refugees have suffered as a result of the displacement. As such, it could encompass physical and mental harm; lost opportunities, including employment, education and social benefits; material damages and loss of earnings, including loss of earning potential; and moral damage.[9]

The Parties' negotiations have not addressed the question of which damages exactly would be redressed by compensation for refugeehood. In the Joint Refugee Mechanism Paper (draft 2) at Taba, it was stated that a fixed per capita compensation for suffering and losses incurred as a result of the physical displacement would be provided.[10] This indicates that a standardized approach would be foreseen to jointly redress the different damage types under the refugeehood umbrella. Experiences of other compensation schemes, such as the 9/11 Compensation Fund, show that the valuation of individual losses would require different sets of evidentiary standards for different loss types as well as very complex methods for their valuation, in particular regarding the compensation for lost opportunity.[11] While addressing the different damage types jointly under the refugeehood umbrella would seem reasonable in light of the large number of cases, there should still be clarification of exactly which types of losses would fall under the refugeehood umbrella. Lack of clarity in this respect would create the risk of a disparity between Palestinian refugee expectations and the remedies the compensation programme will ultimately provide and as such could pose a serious threat to legal closure.

The second type of compensation would address the real property rights that Palestinians lost when they were displaced. Here compensation would constitute the 'substitute reparative measure' for those cases in which the 'primary reparative measure', i.e. the restitution of the right to the property is not granted.[12] Under this category, compensation would be provided to the original owners of land, houses and apartments.

Given the distribution of land within Palestinian society before 1948, concerns have been raised that a compensation scheme based solely on property losses, more precisely the loss of *ownership* rights to real property, would reaffirm and even aggravate the inequalities in Palestinian society where landownership was traditionally in the hands of a few rich families.[13] Those hit hardest by the displacement, the refugees residing in refugee camps, would not benefit from the scheme. Additionally, given the prevailing patterns of ownership, women would be largely excluded from this type of benefit.

These concerns are not unique to the Palestinian context. One way to at least partially address them would be to include compensation for the loss of real property rights other than those of ownership, such as the right to use land. Examples for such an approach can be found in other property claims programmes which faced the issue that landownership was limited to few and that other types of real property rights, such as possession or the right to use land, were equally relevant in the specific local laws. For example, the claims programme established in Iraq in 2003 to resolve property disputes arising out of the arbitrary and forced dislocation of civilian populations during the Baathist regime, at least initially not only dealt with ownership rights, but also with other rights to real property recognized in Iraqi civil law, such as rights of use and right of *usu fructus* or servitudes.[14] Also, the Housing and Property Directorate and the Housing and Property Claims Commission in Kosovo established through United Nations Security Council Resolution 1244 (1999) of 10 June 1999 was concerned with different types of rights to residential real property, i.e. possession and occupancy rights.[15]

While there have been programmes that have also included compensation for the loss of personal property and business property, these types of losses have not been included in any of the negotiations and are therefore not addressed in this chapter.

Who Will Be Eligible to Receive Compensation?

The question of who will be eligible to receive compensation needs to be addressed separately for the different types of compensation.

The compensation for property of which refugees were deprived as a result of their displacement would primarily go to the original right holders. However, given the length of time that has passed since the displacement and the decreasing likelihood that the original title-holders will still be alive at the time when the compensation scheme is implemented, it would be necessary to extend the eligibility to the heirs or legal successors.

The provision of property compensation to heirs and legal successors would, however, add considerable complexity to the compensation process, as it will require the consideration of inheritance rights as part of the eligibility determination. The issue of inheritance rights is an area that is usually not considered or that is highly underestimated at the pre-implementation stage. Yet, it has proven to be one of the most time- and resource-consuming aspects of claims processing.

The fact that in the Palestinian refugee context the majority of claimants for property compensation will consist of children and grandchildren of the original owners, and that in many cases that members of the same family might be dispersed all over the world, with different legal systems applying to questions of inheritance and personal estates adds considerable complexity to the determination of eligible heirs for property compensation.

In order to avoid time-consuming and costly legal determinations for the Palestinian refugee compensation process, negotiators should consider and ideally foresee already in the Peace Agreement the development of standardized inheritance rules. These rules would not only define which of the family members would be the legal successors of the original right holders and who would thus be entitled to receive the property loss compensation, but would also regulate potentially controversial questions such as the validity of a will, and the marital status or the legal status of adopted children and of children born out of wedlock. These standardized rules would apply to all claims irrespective of the claimants' and the refugee family's past and current place of residence. They would avoid the need for complex legal research and thus enable the compensation mechanism to deal with all claims in a more efficient manner. Standardized inheritance rules could also ensure that attention is paid to gender issues and address concerns that many women would be excluded from property compensation if traditional inheritance laws or local customs and practices that might discriminate against female family members were to be applied.[16] While the development of standardized inheritance rules would be challenging, it is one of the areas that could be prepared and researched ahead of the establishment of a compensation scheme.

For refugeehood compensation, the question of eligibility seems more straightforward, as it is tied to the present situation, i.e. the fact that the refugee is displaced. Nevertheless, important policy decisions will need to be made which will have a fundamental impact on the character and extent of this benefit and which therefore should not be left to the implementers.

Above all, a decision will be required as to whether the requirement of 'refugeehood' is equal to being a Palestinian refugee or whether an additional element of vulnerability or neediness will be required. Given the very large number of beneficiaries, individual proof of refugee status in each claim would be extremely time-consuming and resource intensive. What will therefore have to be agreed upon is how the refugee status of the claimants can be verified in a more 'global' manner, in particular through a comparison with information on Palestinian refugees in other records and archives.[17] The most likely source for such a repository of 'verification data' would be the database which UNRWA maintains of Palestinians who have registered with the agency. If UNRWA's registration were taken as a starting point, what would have to be determined is how to deal with the refugees who have not registered with the agency. Again, the potential use of this and other repositories of verification data is an area that can be researched and prepared ahead of the establishment of a compensation programme.

Type of Compensation

The last parameter relates to the type of compensation that will be provided by the compensation scheme and whether it will consist of financial payments[18] only or also involve in-kind benefits such as training, educational support or the provision of material goods, e.g. building material.

There are pros and cons to both options. Providing compensation in the form of in-kind benefits would most obviously link the refugee compensation scheme with general rehabilitation and development measures. This might attract more support from international donors who are interested in ensuring long-term sustainability of their assistance and who in the past have expressed reluctance to support refugee compensation or even refugee-specific development efforts. The implementation of in-kind benefits is, however, challenging, requires considerable and varied technical expertise, needs to cooperate and coordinate with large numbers of outside partners, and is relatively expensive. In addition, it may no longer be perceived by its recipients as reparations but rather be equated with 'extra' development assistance, and this could in turn lead to envy and animosity in the rest of Palestinian society.

Cash payments, on the other hand, are easier to implement and generally provide much greater flexibility to refugee families. They are less sensitive to timing and could be administered and executed independently from other aspects of the solution for the refugee, in particular for the question of where the family will take up permanent residence. Even so, challenges exist in the implementation of cash payments as well. It will have to be determined whether the most efficient and cost-effective manner would be the actual handing out of cash, the issuance of cheques or the transfer into bank accounts. Different methods may be used depending on the country and claims population concerned, and in the region an organization like UNRWA could again play an important role in this respect.[19]

The compensation type that is provided will have a significant impact on the funding structures and the organizational features required for the implementation mechanism. It will also impact the sequencing of the implementation of other aspects of the overall solution for Palestinian refugees, in particular the residency options. It is therefore necessary that this parameter is decided by the negotiating Parties and addressed in the Peace Agreement.

Mechanism and Procedures

Considering the different models that have been used in the practice of national and international claims programmes, a multitude of options and variations is conceivable for the organizational set-up of the implementation mechanism for the compensation component.[20] While lessons can be learned from the experiences of past programmes, the uniqueness of the situation of the Palestinian refugees would require specific solutions. First and foremost, is the requirement that the implementation structure should allow for and facilitate the coordination of the compensation measures with other aspects of the refugee solution, in particular the exercise and implementation of residency choices. For a more comprehensive discussion of the organizational and administrative aspects of the implementation mechanism and the issues raised during the parties' negotiations, the reader is referred to Chapter 2 in this volume, 'Implementation

Mechanism: Policy Choices and Implementation Issues' by the same authors.

Implementation Structures for the Compensation Component

With regard to the compensation component, various negotiation papers of the Parties have foreseen a separate body within the IM to deal with refugee compensation. The Palestinian proposals have been more in the direction of a wide membership of states and organizations in such a body (some including the UN), while Israel has proposed a more technical type of committee. None of the Parties has proposed to place the refugee compensation as such under the responsibility of an organization such as the UN.

Experience in other compensation programmes shows that two separate bodies should deal with the two types of compensation that are being assumed for the purposes of this paper, one dealing with property losses ('Property Loss Panel') and one with fixed sum compensation ('Fixed Sums Panel').

The procedures and methodologies to be used to ensure fair and transparent and at the same time efficient claims resolution processes will be different for the two types of compensation. The types of documentation required in support of a claim will be different, and so will be the standards of evidence. Property loss compensation might involve complex valuation exercises while refugeehood compensation is likely to be awarded as a standard fixed-sum amount. As a result, the pace at which the resolution of the different claims will proceed will be different; and the expertise required from the members of the bodies and their support staff will also be different. Most importantly, if dealt with by two different bodies, the fixed sum compensation for refugeehood could be fast-tracked, ensuring that at least a part of the remedies foreseen reaches the refugees as promptly as possible.[21]

Assuming that the question of property restitution is decided either prior to the implementation of the compensation scheme or by a separate body within the property loss panels, the system should be further differentiated within the property compensation. Small property claims, i.e. those relating to small pieces of land of relatively little economic value, could be resolved in a simpler and faster administrative process while a more involved quasi-judicial process could be established for 'large' claims; the processing methodologies for these two types of claims might be different, and in particular the valuation of the 'small' claims may be done in a more standardized way.[22]

The threshold amount dividing the two tracks in the above system should be decided in the Peace Agreement or by the Policy Board of the Implementation Mechanisms based on existing data on Palestinian ownership distribution in 1948.[23] If it were left to be determined by the Property Loss Panel, this would complicate and slow down the latter's work since the Panel would have to perform a sampling exercise to gauge the distribution between large and small claims, so that it could organize its work accordingly.

An important component of the implementation structure will be the Secretariat supporting the compensation part of the mechanism. Considering the number of panels and commissions it will service, and the processing and valuation methods it will need to apply, the skills of its staff will have to comprise expertise in law, valuation, accounting, IT and process management, in addition to language and general support services.

Verification and Processing Techniques

Despite their different backgrounds and institutional settings, compensation programmes generally share the common goal of providing effective remedies for a large number of individuals who suffered losses, damage or injuries. Recent programmes have been expected to accomplish this task in a shorter period of time and with more efficiency than would be possible through case-by-case decisions in domestic courts. As a result, it has been crucial that the design of the claims process strike an appropriate balance between efficiency and fairness and individual justice. As part of this, claims programmes have extensively relied on innovative mass claims processing methods and techniques, while providing for the necessary independence of decision-makers and for other safeguards for due process.[24]

Central to this is the process established to verify claims. While the verification process lies at the heart of implementation, there are a number of questions that should be considered before the programme is established, so that the legal framework and the procedural rules can be tailored to the circumstances on the ground, and to the specific needs and situations of Palestinian refugees.

How efficiently and successfully the verification process can be implemented will depend on a number of factors, in particular on the evidentiary standards that are being applied, and the extent to which external verification data sources are available, can be used and integrated into the claims review process in an efficient manner. For refugeehood compensation, it can be expected that the verification of claims will mainly consist of the verification of the refugee status and possibly of the additional criteria of neediness. More complex verification issues will arise for the compensation of property rights.

As in all reparation claims programmes, there will be an inherent tension in the verification process between making the programme's remedies accessible to as many Palestinian refugees as possible and protecting the process against fraudulent claims. In the Palestinian refugee context, the verification process will have to acknowledge the diverse living conditions of Palestinian refugees today, the different fate families have suffered over the past decades, and the effects that these have had on their ability to support their claims for property compensation with documentation. In light of this, what will need to be considered is to what extent the evidentiary requirements should be relaxed, in order to facilitate the refugee's task of proving a claim and to ensure that the process is open and accessible to all Palestinian refugees, in particular to the neediest who are living in disadvantaged conditions. In an effort to assist claimants, other programmes have developed and applied presumptions to fill the gaps in the evidence provided by claimants by piecing together information received from individual claims and/or from historical research conducted by or on behalf of the compensation mechanism.[25]

Another factor is the extent to which the claims mechanism will successfully establish cooperation with holders of relevant information repositories, such as the UNCCP and UNRWA records, in order to verify or supplement information provided by refugees in support of their compensation claims. In this regard, the negotiating Parties should ideally agree on which external data repositories would be acceptable verification tools. Furthermore, they should provide in the Peace Agreement that those data repositories will be accessible for the compensation mechanisms without additional administrative or financial burdens.

To allow for an efficient verification process involving external sources, it is necessary that the verification can be conducted by way of computerized data matching. A manual case-by-case verification would not be feasible given the large number of claims expected. This in turn requires that external verification data has been 'cleaned', researched and consolidated, and is residing on suitable technical platforms so that the custom-built database system of the compensation claims mechanism can 'communicate' with them.

Finally, the large number of claims expected for property compensation might make it necessary to develop standard valuation methodologies, in order to speed up the review of claims and to ensure consistency and reliability throughout the process. The individual valuation of losses is time-consuming and costly. It also requires a certain amount of information to substantiate the losses; this is information which many of the Palestinian refugees today might not have. Standard valuation methodologies could be developed by accountants, loss adjusters and other technical experts for the purpose of the standardized verification of claims and quantification of compensation award. Such methodologies would be particularly helpful if a two-track system were to be introduced for the property compensation with a simpler and faster administrative process, with standard amounts for the resolution of (sub-categories of) 'small' property claims.

The most extreme example of standardized compensation is the compensation of per capita amounts. Here, claimants do not need to substantiate their loss at all and there is no need for the programme to gather, review and evaluate information about individual losses, as every claimant who is eligible for compensation will receive the same amount of money. This method would certainly make the most sense for the refugeehood claims. While such fixed compensation awards might be perceived as particularly unfair by refugees in connection with property losses, they might still be the most transparent and workable approach for small property claims, in a situation where the mechanism is faced with large numbers of claims and limited evidence available on the one hand, and strong political pressure to deliver results quickly on the other hand.

Funding Arrangements

A solid funding arrangement is crucial to the success of any compensation programme. At the same time, however, it has been the experience of past programmes that securing adequate funding is often difficult. Funding arrangements for a compensation programme on the one hand concern the availability of sufficient financial resources to satisfy all compensation claims and on the other hand refer to the technical modalities of the funding structures underlying the compensation scheme.

Available Compensation Resources

Regarding the first, work on Palestinian refugee compensation has tended to assume that once the Parties can agree on a deal, 'someone', being either Israel or the international community, will pay for it.[26] However, for the success and sustainability of the compensation scheme, it will be important to have clear answers to the questions of who is going to pay for the compensation and how much. This requires that the Parties engage with potential supporters during the negotiations and that the funding aspects of the compensation scheme are vetted by the international donor community. Experiences in other programmes has shown that while governments are usually willing to pledge money during the early stages of a programme, the focus of the international donor community tends to move on quickly to other 'emergencies', making it more and more difficult to motivate donors and to maintain the required level of funding.

As mentioned before, it is necessary to distinguish between the two types of compensation: refugeehood and property losses.

Estimates of the total/aggregate value of the refugees' property losses have ranged from US$3 billion to US$200 billion, depending on different criteria and parameters used. Knowing the aggregate value of the compensable property losses, and thus the total amount needed for their full compensation early on, would have a number of advantages; above all, it would avoid the risk that the available compensation resources might fall drastically short of the needs halfway through the programme. On the other hand, assessing the total/aggregate value of the compensable property losses will not be an easy task and could be done in a number of different ways that is likely to lead to different results. Sources for assisting in such a global assessment could, among others, be the UNCCP database and the 'Custodian for Absentees' Property' records, both of which contain information on Palestinian properties in 1948, including on the location, type, size and their ownership.

At Taba, it was proposed that an assessment of the total value of the property losses should be conducted prior to the decisions on the claims by the Property Loss Panel, presumably with the latter then distributing this total amount over the claims it will determine to be compensable in function of the proven losses per claim. Again, while such an early assessment would have its advantages, the composition of the group of experts, the criteria and methods it would apply, and the time and resources it would need, would all pose their own challenges.

In addition, various estimates have been made during the negotiations as to the sum that would be made available for Palestinian refugee compensation.[27] In a multitude of donor meetings, representatives of donor countries have expressed doubts that their governments would be willing to contribute to compensation for property that will not be restituted, as it is seen to be the responsibility of Israel as the possessor of these properties to pay for this compensation.

International donor support for the refugeehood component will depend on the overall structure of the Palestinian–Israeli Agreement. The latter will influence the extent to which international support will be channelled to refugee compensation payments as opposed to other support, e.g. development projects in the new Palestinian State and integration projects in host countries.

As such, the overall funding level available will depend as much on political as on economic considerations.

Funding Structures

The funding structure underlying the compensation scheme relates to the question of whether the funding will consist of a finite sum or an open arrangement. In the case of a finite sum, the total compensation amount is known and available at the outset of the compensation scheme, while in an open arrangement the financial needs are assessed and met as the programme is being implemented. The Palestinian side has advocated the latter; Israel has offered to make available a defined lump sum to be agreed upfront. As internationally pledged funds would contribute to the compensation payments, this would be an issue of considerable interest to donors as well.

While an open funding arrangement allows for more flexibility in responding to unforeseen needs as they evolve throughout the implementation, it is unlikely that Israel or international sponsors will commit to an automatic replenishment regarding either of the two compensation types. Without this commitment, there would be a need to continuously justify financial needs and to fund-raise for the compensation, which would be a daunting task that would place a heavy burden on the implementers and force them to devote considerable time and energy to this. In such case, a decision would have to be made by the negotiators as to who should and could most efficiently shoulder the burden of mobilizing additional funding. Would it be the highest body of the implementation mechanism, the 'Policy Board' whose responsibilities are likely to encompass the representation of the IM at the highest political level and whose members might be best connected to relevant donor governments? Or, would it fall on the International Fund whose central role so far has been seen in the management of the funds and donor coordination for development, reintegration and rehabilitation projects relating to Palestinian refugees?

The biggest challenge regarding a finite sum is that it is being agreed upon when the number of compensable claims or eligible claimants is not yet known. In such a case, the compensation levels stipulated in a constituting framework will have to be based on estimates and bear the risk of changing considerably as the process develops. This would be particularly necessary, if the administrative costs of the implementation mechanism for the refugee component have to paid from the same pot of money. Experience has shown that programme budget estimates developed at the political level tend to be based on the number of expected eligible claimants and tend to ignore the considerable costs associated with the processing of claims that have no merits and that will not result in a compensation payment.

In addition, finite sums bear the risk that the funds are exhausted before all eligible claimants have been compensated and with that, the risk of a serious backlash within the intended beneficiary community. Facing similar issues, past programmes have tried to mitigate the risk by holding up the issuance of the awards until all claims are decided and the total value of the compensable property losses can be matched against the finite total funds available for the payment of the compensation. Another measure has been to pay out compensation awards in instalments and with it to reserve the option of a pro rata reduction of the final compensation sum to be paid. However, while these measures might be the fairest way to deal with this situation for the claimants as a whole, such schemes create a considerable extra administrative burden and the delays involved in receiving the benefit can be extremely frustrating for claimants.

The considerations above support the call for the Parties to regulate certain priorities in the Peace Agreement, i.e. to include decisions on the prioritization of loss types or beneficiary groups during the implementation process to ensure that particularly needy refugees will receive benefits without delay and benefit from quick impact measures.

Closure

The desire for closure is usually one of the main motives and goals for the creation of claims restitution or compensation programmes following a conflict or crisis. As mentioned above, it has been one of the central demands from the Israeli side that the Peace Agreement would comprehensively and with finality address all refugee-related issues and would bring a formal end to all refugee claims.

From a legal point of view, this would require that the compensation scheme established by the Peace Agreement would provide the exclusive and final forum for all compensation claims from Palestinian refugees and would thus preclude any possible lawsuits or other legal remedies in domestic or international fora. Legal closure will need to be addressed comprehensively in the Peace Agreement, in particular with regard to its effect on third parties. At the same time, the technical aspects of its implementation would need to be dealt with through special measures and procedures at the implementation stage.

In past programmes, such measures have included the signing of waivers by successful claimants as a precondition for receiving compensation or the termination of parallel litigation in other fora. Both measures applied for the property programme of the German Forced Labour Compensation Programme executed by the German

Foundation 'Remembrance, Responsibility and Future'. All claimants who were eligible to receive compensation under the programme had to sign waiver and indemnification undertakings before the compensation amount was paid out to them, which became operative once the claimants received the compensation payments.

Threats to the legal peace from third parties, on the other hand, were dealt with at the highest political level. Prior to the establishment of the programme, the US Government and the Federal German Government had agreed that the Foundation was 'to be the exclusive remedy and forum for the resolution of all claims that have or may be asserted against German companies arising from the National Socialist era and World War II.'[28] As a result of this political Agreement, the US Government filed a Statement of Interest in all pertinent proceedings against German companies before the US courts, notifying the court that it would be in the foreign policy interest of the United States for the German Foundation to be the exclusive forum and that it would recommend dismissal on any valid legal ground.

In addition to this, other parties involved, in particular the lawyers who originally submitted the class action law suits, signed a 'Joint Statement' accepting the common objective that German companies would receive all embracing and enduring legal peace. In signing the statement, they also undertook the obligation to file motions to dismiss with prejudice all the related lawsuits they had filed, which were currently pending in US courts.

There is another aspect of closure that refers to the end-point of a reconciliation process. A compensation process might contribute to or even play a major role in such a process, although, depending on the history of the conflict and the extent of violations suffered, it can rarely be the sole measure in the support of reconciliation. Chapter 9 on 'Intangible Needs, Moral Acknowledgement and the Palestinian Refugee Issue' in this volume further examines the key aspects and requirements of the reconciliation process of the Israeli and Palestinian people.

Suggested Preparatory Work Relating to Compensation

The following list summarizes the suggestions for certain additional preparatory work touched upon throughout the chapter:

By the Palestinian side:

- identify priorities for the compensation payments to avoid disappointment and a backlash (benefit types, prioritize certain beneficiaries);
- prepare existing data repositories for their role as a verification tool in a compensation claims programme;
- develop options for the standardized valuation of (small?) property claims;
- work towards mitigating the gap between the expectations of the refugees and what the solution will offer;
- engage with international donors regarding their support for refugee compensation;
- prepare for the development of standardized inheritance rules.

By Israel:

- engage with the Israeli public about financial responsibilities connected to a Peace Agreement;
- prepare existing data repositories for their role as a verification tool in a compensation claims programme;
- engage with internationals donors regarding their support to refugee compensation.

By international actors:

- engage with the Parties and their respective populations about the likely contributions to refugee compensation;
- coordinate and sequence the linkage between preparatory work and the negotiations;
- close gaps in technical knowledge.

Notes

1. The views expressed in this chapter are those of the authors and do not necessarily represent those of IOM.
2. Compensation was mentioned already in United Nations General Assembly Resolution 194 of 11 December 1948, A/RES(194 (III), which instructed the United Nations Conciliation Commission for Palestine (UNCCP) that:

> [...] the refugees wishing to return to their homes and live at peace with their neighbors should be permitted to do so at the earliest practicable date, and that compensation should be paid for the property of those choosing not to return and for loss of or damage to property which,

under principles of international law or equity, should be made good by the Governments or authorities responsible.

3. This chapter only deals with compensation for Palestinian refugees. For a discussion of potential compensation of host countries or compensation of Jews who were displaced from Arab countries, see Chapter 5 in this volume: Roula El-Rifai and Nadim Shehadi, 'An Offer They Can Refuse: Host Countries and the Palestinian Refugee Issue', as well as Chapter 7: Michael Fischbach, 'Addressing Jewish Claims in the Context of a Palestinian–Israeli Agreement'.

4. For a more detailed comparative overview of different features of restitution and compensation programmes, see Norbert Wühler and Heike Niebergall, *Property Restitution and Compensation: Practices and Experiences of Claims Programmes*, (Geneva: International Organization for Migration, 2008).

5. Certain other aspects of Palestinian refugee compensation are also addressed in other chapters in this volume. See in particular Chapter 4 by Rex Brynen, 'Return, Repatriation, Residency and Resettlement'; Chapter 8 by Rex Brynen, 'Refugee Absorption and Development'; Chapter 9 by Michael Molloy and John Bell, 'Intangible Needs, Moral Acknowledgement and the Palestinian Refugee Issue'; and Chapter 2 by Heike Niebergall and Norbert Wühler, 'Implementation Mechanism: Policy Choices and Implementation Issues'.

6. In this regard, it has been argued that the right to restitution of property lost does not equal the right of return, the former referring to the restoration of property titles, the latter referring to the right to go back to one's original home.

7. For a comprehensive description of the negotiations of the Palestinian refugee issue, as well as excerpts of relevant negotiation positions, see Rex Brynen, 'The Past as Prelude? Negotiating the Palestinian Refugee Issue', Chatham House Briefing Paper, MEP/PR BP 08/01, June 2008.

8. Annex 7 to the Geneva Accord presents the most involved and detailed proposal for the organization, structure and procedure for refugee compensation, but unlike the Geneva Accord, it was not signed by any of the Palestinian members.

9. In this regard, see UN Basic Principles and Guidelines on the Right to a Remedy and Reparation for Victims of Gross Violations of International Human Rights Law and Serious Violations of International Humanitarian Law, adopted and proclaimed by UN General Assembly Resolution 60/147, UN Document A/RES/60/147, 16 December 2005.

10. Paragraph 25a of the Joint Refugee Mechanism Paper (draft 2), at Taba, 25 January 2001, available at Rex Brynen, *The Past as Prelude?*, p. 19.

11. For further details on the valuation methodologies applied in past compensation claims programmes, see Norbert Wühler and Heike Niebergall, *Property Restitution and Compensation: Practices and Experiences of Claims Programmes* (Geneva: International Organization for Migration, 2008), Chapter G, at: www.iom.int/jahia/webdav/site/myjahiasite/shared/shared/mainsite/published_docs/books/Property_Restitution_and_Compensation.pdf

12. The so-called Pinheiro Principles on Housing and Property Restitution for Refugees and Displaced Persons, adopted by the UN ECOSOC Commission on Human Rights, Sub-Commission on the Promotion and Protection of Human Rights in 2005, UN Document E/CN.4/Sub.2/2005/17, 28 June 2005, state in Principle 2.2 that 'States shall demonstrably prioritize the right to restitution as the preferred remedy for displacement and as a key element of restorative justice.' As such, under international law, compensation would apply to those cases only, where restitution is not possible or not wanted by the displaced.

13. Rex Brynen, 'Palestinian Refugee Compensation: Connection and Complexities', in Rex Brynen and Roula El-Rifai (eds), *Compensation to Palestinian Refugees and the Search for Palestinian–Israeli Peace* (London: Pluto Press, 2013).

14. The programme in Iraq was set up after the fall of the Saddam Hussein regime, following the 2002/2003 Iraq War, to deal with the consequences of the forced displacement and expropriation policies of the Baathist regime. Initially, a commission was established by the Coalition Provisional Authority. The programme was restructured twice, based on a national law, and in 2010 the commission was renamed the Real Property Claims Commission (RPCC). The RPCC has jurisdiction over claims regarding properties that were confiscated and seized since the late 1960s for political, ethnic, religious or sectarian reasons, or that were expropriated without proper consideration. The principal remedy is restitution of the property; in certain cases, compensation can be awarded. Since the start of its operations in 2004, the RPCC has decided 60,000 out of 160,000 claims, but more than 20,000 appeals are pending. For further information, see www.crrpd.org. Given the volume of cases before this Iraqi Commission, it has de facto only dealt with ownership rights.

15. The property restitution programme in Kosovo was established following United Nations Security Council Resolution 1244 (1999) of 10 June 1999 which gave the Special Representative of the Secretary General in Kosovo (SRSG) the authority to establish institutions responsible for the restitution of residential property that had been lost during or as a result of the armed conflict that occurred between 27 February 1998 and 20 June 1999. The SRSG acted upon this authority with UNMIK Regulation 1999/23 establishing the Housing and Property Directorate (HPD) and the Housing and Property Claims Commission (HPCC). The HPD/HPCC was operational from November 1999 until March 2006. During this period, it collected and resolved approximately 29,000 claims for the repossession of residential property.

Following UNMIK Regulation 2006/10, on 6 March 2006 the staff and assets of the HPD were subsumed by the newly-established Kosovo Property Agency (KPA) which assumed responsibility for the implementation of all claims that were still pending before the HPD at that time. The Regulation also established the Kosovo Property Claims Commission (KPCC). The KPCC's mandate is to resolve claims resulting from the 1998–1999 conflict in respect of ownership over private immovable property, including agricultural, residential and commercial property. The KPA has received approximately 42,000 claims. Almost three-quarters of these have been decided by the KPCC to date. See www.hpdkosovo.org and www.kpaonline.org

16. These issues will be even more relevant in restitution awards and their enforcement.

17. Electronic data-matching of this type has been done on a similarly large scale by the United Nations Compensation Commission and in the German Forced Labour Compensation Programme.

18. While financial compensation is usually understood as cash payments to beneficiaries, it could also consist of preferential loans or government bonds.

19. For payments in over 90 countries, the German Forced Labour Compensation Programme, for instance, used an international bank with a worldwide net of branches and cooperating partner banks in places where it was not represented.

20. For an overview see Pablo de Greiff (ed.), *The Handbook of Reparations* (Oxford: Oxford University Press, 2006) and Howard M. Holtzmann and Edda Kristjánsdóttir (eds), *International Mass Claims Processes: Legal and Practical Perspectives* (New York: Oxford University Press, 2007).

21. Given the number of expected claims, the experience of processing times from other claims programmes show that, even with the application of streamlined mass claims processing methodologies, more than one commission will be needed both within the Property Loss Panel and the Fixed Sums Refugeehood Compensation Panel, to complete the work within any politically feasible time-frame. A calculation using average processing times from comparable programmes shows that for the Fixed Sums Refugeehood Compensation Panel, for instance, one Commission would need approximately nine years to deal with the caseload. Increasing the number of Commissions to three would allow for the completion of the caseload within approximately three years.

22. The Property Claims Commission under the German Forced Labour Compensation Programme, for instance, used a valuation methodology that standardized the compensation amounts using parameters such as the location, size, age and the use of the property.

23. The records of the United Nations Conciliation Commission for Palestine indicate that 40 per cent of refugee families owned considerably small lands worth less than P£100 in 1948, while only a little over 1 per cent of the refugee families owned larger land exceeding P£10,000. See Michael Fischbach, *Records of Dispossession: Palestinian Refugee Property and the Arab–Israeli Conflict,* (New York: Columbia University Press, 2003), p. 129.

24. Regarding the tension between mass claims processing goals and modern human rights standards, see Matti Pellonpää, *Due Process in Mass Claims Proceedings and Article 6 of the ECHR,* in Jürgen Bröhmer (ed.), 'The Protection of Human Rights at the Beginning of the 21st Century', Colloquium in Honour of Professor Dr. Dr. Dr. h.c. mult. Georg Ress on the Occasion of his 75th Birthday, (Baden-Baden: Nomos Verlag, 2012).

25. For an overview of evidentiary standards used in past reparation programmes, see Heike Niebergall, 'Overcoming Evidentiary Weaknesses in Reparation Claims Programmes', in Carla Ferstman, Mariana Goetz and Alan Stephens (eds), *Reparations for Victims of Genocide, War Crimes and Crimes against Humanity*, (The Hague: Martinus Nijhoff, 2009), pp. 145 ff.
26. See Brynen, 'Palestinian Refugee Compensation: Connection and Complexities'.
27. Ibid.
28. Article 1 of the Agreement between the Government of the United States of America and the Government of the Federal Republic of Germany concerning the Foundation 'Remembrance, Responsibility and the Future', Berlin, 17 July 2000, *Federal Law Gazette* 1372, Year 2000 Part II No. 34.

7

Addressing Jewish Claims in the Context of a Palestinian–Israeli Agreement

Michael R. Fischbach

Introduction

Among the issues that Israel has brought up in connection with a resolution of the Palestinian refugee question generally, and the issue of compensation specifically, is the matter of claims against Arab states for property abandoned by Jews during their exodus from those states. Most of the approximately 800,000 Jews who left Arab states during 1948 and the 25 years thereafter immigrated to Israel. Some of these persons sustained property losses during the process of their emigration from the Arab world. Starting in 1951, at a time when tens of thousands of Iraqi Jews who moved to Israel had their property sequestered by the Iraqi government, Israel – which in 1949 had declared that it would compensate the 1948 Palestinians for the property they left behind and that was confiscated by the Israeli government – announced that henceforth it would factor in the value of lost Jewish assets in Iraq and elsewhere when the time came for it to compensate the Palestinians. Despite the fact that the Palestinian refugees were not themselves responsible for these Jewish losses, Israel linked the resolution of the two respective sets of property losses.

The subject of how to deal with Jewish property claims has arisen at various points during the Israeli–Palestinian peace talks that began in 1993. In 2000, the two sides discussed the joint resolution of both sets of claims through an international fund that would entertain claims and pay compensation to both Jewish and Palestinian claimants. By 2001, however, both sides seem to have agreed that the subject of Jewish claims is not a subject for further bilateral Israeli–Palestinian talks.

The Nature and Value of Jewish Claims

Approximately 800,000 Jews left Arab countries during and after the first Arab–Israeli war of 1948. Most of these Jews moved to Israel, although others left for Europe, the Americas and elsewhere. The reasons for this huge emigration varied by country and, within each country, by factors such as social class, commitment to Zionism and so forth. Over the years, a degree of controversy has emerged among Jews from Arab countries and other Jews over the question of whether or not to refer to these Jews as 'refugees' who fled the Arab world. Some have insisted that they are refugees who fled Arab oppression or actually were expelled by the Arab states, while others have insisted that those who left the countries of their birth moved to Israel out of their Zionist convictions. Still others have noted that the circumstances of these persons' decisions to leave were more complex and nuanced than such an either–or proposition.[1]

Some of the Jews who left the Arab world sustained property losses upon their departure. In some cases, most notably Iraq in 1951 and Libya in 1970, Jews waiting for emigration or those who already had emigrated had their property frozen or sequestered, rendering them unable to expatriate their assets. In Egypt in 1956, the government sequestered the property of certain Jews and then expelled them. In other cases, Jews leaving Arab countries simply abandoned their property before leaving or sold it at deflated prices. Countries such as Tunisia and Egypt nationalized the property of Jews (and non-Jews) as part of their socialist economic policies. In yet other cases, Arab governments limited the amount of currency that Jews (and non-Jewish citizens) could take out of the country. In the case of Lebanon, Syria, Jordan and areas of the West Bank and Gaza which are under Palestinian control, some pre-1948 Zionist Jewish property (as opposed to indigenous Jewish property) was cut off from its owners in Israel by the first Arab–Israeli war. Finally, throughout the Arab world, considerable communal property (such as cemeteries, schools, synagogues and religious artefacts) was abandoned or left behind in the care of the remaining Jewish communities, most of which since have left as well.

It is worth pointing out that even in the cases where Arab governments formally sequestered Jewish emigrant property, this property has remained legally sequestered in the absence of subsequent legislation formally confiscating it. It thus remains 'sequestered' but not actually 'confiscated' (the case of Libya is an exception, where a 1970 law formally confiscated the assets of certain Jews, and offered compensation). There are no good, complete statistics available for the scope and value of Jewish property in Arab countries that can help quantify any claims to this property. In 1949, the Israeli government tried to register property claims against Arab countries, and renewed this effort on several occasions in the 1950s, both on its own and through 'public' (but technically non-governmental) bodies. However, only a small percentage of Jews from Arab countries living in Israel responded to these requests for registration, and the data collected was woefully incomplete. Needless to say, Jews outside Israel were not solicited for such information. Even the statistics that were gathered represented self-reported losses, usually without any way to verify the claims through official documents.[2] In 1969, the government created a special unit within the Ministry of Justice to collect and maintain data on these losses. This office was closed in 1999, but reopened in 2002.[3] In 2010, the Ministry of Pensioners' Affairs created an office for this purpose, although it is not clear if it has taken over the records previously collected by the Justice Ministry.[4]

For their part, various Jewish non-governmental organizations outside Israel have tried to collect statistics on Jewish property losses beginning in 1957 with an attempt to catalogue Egyptian Jewish financial losses. Periodic efforts to register losses in Arab countries have continued into the 2000s.[5] These groups, too, have not succeeded in producing complete and reliable statistics, and the numbers that they have floated represent guesswork at best.

No Arab government has permitted the opening of its archives for the purposes of determining what, if any, information it possesses relevant to Jewish property.

Positions of the Parties

Palestinian refugees and Palestinian negotiators have steadfastly refused to accept any linkage between their property losses and claims, and those of Jews who left the Arab world. Their argument is that, as displaced and dispossessed refugees themselves, they cannot be saddled with the additional political and financial liability for what Arab governments did to their own Jewish citizens. Aggrieved Jews should seek redress for any claims from those governments concerned, this argument goes, or through other means. Palestinian compensation should not be compromised by Jewish claims. Nor should any claims that Jews who left Arab countries are 'refugees' impact any other Palestinian refugee rights, including the right of return. Some Palestinians argue that most Jews left the Arab world voluntarily, and not as refugees who were expelled or who fled from war in their homeland.

Diplomatically, the PLO always has insisted that the question of Jewish claims therefore cannot be linked to Palestinian refugee compensation or any other aspect of bilateral Israeli–Palestinian peace talks. PLO negotiators stated this as early as the second plenary of the Refugee Working Group (RWG) that was held in Ottawa in November 1992, the RWG having been established as part of the multilateral talks that commenced after the October 1991 Madrid Conference. The Palestinian position always has been that Palestinians were not responsible for the loss, seizure, sequestration, etc. of Jewish property at the hands of Arab states. Therefore, the question of Jewish claims is not a suitable topic for bilateral Israeli–Palestinian talks and must be pursued by Israel in talks with the specific Arab countries where those losses occurred. PLO negotiators continued to articulate this stance at Camp David in 2000 and in Taba in 2001.

For their part, some Israelis and various Jewish non-governmental organizations outside Israel have contended that on a regional level, a Jewish–Arab population and property exchange has occurred in the Middle East because of the events of 1948 and the ongoing

Arab–Israeli conflict. They say that because of the 1948 war and the ongoing conflict, Israel was emptied of most of its Arabs, who took up residence in the West Bank, Gaza and the surrounding Arab countries. Soon thereafter, the Arab world was emptied of most of its Jews, who largely took up residence in Israel. Both the Palestinian refugees and Jews fleeing the Arab world sustained property losses so that in the end, according to this argument, the situation ended up as a draw: an even exchange of people and property. If Israel is therefore required to compensate Palestinians in the Arab world, the Arab world must compensate their former citizens in Israel.

Israel first linked Jewish property claims with compensation claims of Palestinian refugees publicly in March 1951 during the mass Jewish exodus from Iraq. Although no serious Arab–Israeli negotiations occurred after the Paris Conference of 1951, the policy of linkage remained, at least on paper, a basic Israeli diplomatic principle for decades thereafter. However, Israel's policy of linking Jewish claims with Palestinian claims has changed after the 2001 Taba talks, as is detailed in the section below.

The Issue in Past Negotiations

After decades of war and diplomatic inertia, Israel eventually signed peace treaties with two Arab states: Egypt, in March 1979, and Jordan, in October 1994. Formal peace meant that Israel finally could, if it desired, press for redress for Jewish property losses sustained by Israeli citizens in those two countries. Yet despite the fact that Article 8 of the Israeli–Egyptian peace treaty created a mutual claims commission by which both countries could pursue financial claims against one another, Israel never did use the commission to raise the issue of property compensation for those Egyptian Jews who moved to Israel and became Israeli citizens (despite pressure from within in Israel to do so). Years later in July 2000, the Israeli negotiator Elyakim Rubenstein told one of his Palestinian counterparts that Israel had not broached the question of Jewish losses with the Egyptians because 'We decided to keep this subject for the talks on the Palestinian refugees.'[6]

Similarly, although Article 25 of the Israeli–Jordanian peace treaty also called for a mutual claims commission, Israel never has exercised its right to seek redress for Jewish losses sustained in Jordan either.

Conversely, the Israelis went to great lengths to prevent Jordanian citizens (especially Palestinian refugees who possessed Jordanian citizenship) from using the peace treaty to seek redress for their own property losses in Israel. To this end, the Israeli Knesset passed a law on 1 February 1995 stating that Jordanian citizens who had been declared 'absentees' (and thus subject to having their property in Israel confiscated) prior to the peace treaty would remain classified as such.[7] Israel clearly wished to keep the question of Jewish claims for any eventual peace settlement with the Palestinians.

The September 1993 Oslo Accords began the process by which Israeli and Palestinian negotiations started discussing several so-called final status questions in preparation for an eventual Israeli–Palestinian peace treaty. It was in the context of the talks on the 1948 Palestinian refugees that Israel finally could employ its policy of linkage and bring up the matter of Jewish claims when the Palestinians raised their claims for refugee compensation. Linking Jewish claims with those of the Palestinians was designed to limit Israel's financial obligations to the Palestinians, as was revealed in a statement made by the Israeli negotiator Zalman Shoval, who in 1993 declared, 'Israel would agree to cancel the Jewish claims if the Palestinians would give up their compensation demands.'[8]

The first time that the two sides seriously examined the Jewish claims question was during the Camp David II summit in July 2000. At this meeting, Israel changed its long-standing policy of linkage in an important way. Instead of talking about deducting the value of Jewish claims from what it would pay the Palestinians, Israel advocated establishing an international fund that would pay out claims to all those persons who sustained losses as a result of the conflict. The idea was floated that international donors would contribute to the fund, which would pay out claims to individuals (not governments) that filed them. Article 6, Item 82 of a draft, internal Israeli negotiating document entitled 'Framework Agreement on Permanent Status' spelled this idea out by noting that

> The parties agree that a just settlement of the Israeli–Arab conflict should settle the claims by Jewish individuals and communities that left Arab countries or parts of Mandatory Palestine due to the 1948 war and its aftermath. An international mechanism affiliated

with the above Commission and Fund [discussed earlier in the document] will be established to deal with such claims.[9]

The document also contained an 'end of claims' clause that stated that all Jewish claims against the Arab world would have to be settled by this fund, and that no additional claims could be presented after the proposed commission and fund had finished their work.

Israeli press reports asserted that the international fund idea originated with the Americans, and was part of a plan that read, 'an international organization will be established for the compensation and rehabilitation of refugees in their current location; Israel will participate in its financing.'[10] President Bill Clinton reportedly told the Israeli negotiator Elyakim Rubenstein that such a fund might total US$10 billion or more.[11] The Palestinian negotiator Mahmud Abbas (Abu Mazin) claimed that the Israeli side insisted that the money in the fund be divided equally between Palestinian and Jewish claimants.[12]

What motivated the Israeli side to change the policy of linkage from one in which Israel would deduct the value of Jewish property from what it would pay Palestinian refugees, to one in which claimants from all sides would petition for compensation from a third party (an international fund)? Two reasons suggest themselves. The first was the sheer scale of the imbalance in the compensation figures which each side would present. Israel did not possess much hard data on Jewish claims, and what statistics it did have indicated a much smaller amount than that claimed by the Palestinians. A 'deeply involved source' in the negotiators told an Israeli journalist in December 1999 that a confidential Israeli foreign ministry study had shown that, based on the incomplete records the Israeli government possessed on Jewish losses in the Arab world, Palestinian claims were likely to dwarf them by a ratio of 22:1.[13] Given this disparity, the Israeli side no doubt felt that insisting on the original concept of linkage would still leave Israel owing a considerable amount of money. Instead, the international fund would relieve them of this burden because even though they would 'participate in its financing', the Israelis would not be responsible for coming up with all the money themselves.

A second reason for the change in linkage strategy no doubt was that it would relieve Israel of the burden of creating an implementation mechanism for deciding what Palestinian claims were valid, determining who should receive how much, and other such technical issues. Israel also would be absolved of having to pay compensation to its own citizens for property lost in Arab countries, as some Israelis had been demanding for years.

In response to the presentation of the fund idea, Palestinian negotiators at Camp David angrily rejected the entire idea of linking their refugees' property claims in any way with those of Jews from Arab countries. This reflected a longstanding position that Israel must take up Jewish claims against Arab countries with the respective nations involved; it was not a matter for bilateral Israeli–Palestinian talks inasmuch as the Palestinians were neither responsible nor liable for any such losses.

The question of linking Jewish and Palestinian claims in some shape or form took another historic turn during the subsequent Taba talks in January 2001. At Taba, the PLO negotiators continued to insist that the subject of Jewish claims was not appropriate for bilateral Israeli-Palestinian talks, and the Israelis seemed to agree. While both sides ended up agreeing to creation of an international fund to pay compensation for Palestinian refugees, the Israeli side took a further step away from the historic policy of linkage by conceding that the Jewish claims would not be addressed within the context of bilateral Israeli–Palestinian talks. The Israeli proposal presented at Taba stated this clearly:

> Although the issue of compensation to former Jewish refugees from Arab countries is not part of the bilateral Israeli–Palestinian agreement, in recognition of their suffering and losses, the parties pledge to cooperate in pursuing an equitable and just resolution to the issue.[14]

The two parties appear to have adhered to this 'de-linking' of Jewish and Palestinian claims in subsequent talks. For example, the unofficial December 2003 Geneva Accord does not mention Jewish claims at all. On the other hand, the Israeli Knesset, responding to lobbying by Jewish groups claiming to speak on behalf of Jews from Arab countries, enacted a resolution several years later in February 2010 calling for the Israeli government to insist upon some form of linkage between

Palestinians and Jews from Arab countries in future negotiations. The resolution reads, in part:

> The state of Israel will not sign, directly or by proxy, any agreement or treaty with a country or authority dealing with a political settlement in the Middle East without ensuring the rights of Jewish refugees from Arab countries according to the U.N.'s refugee treaty.
>
> In any discussion where the Palestinian refugee issue is brought up in the framework of peace negotiations in the Middle East, the Israeli government will bring up the issue of compensation for loss of property and giving equal status to Arab refugees who left their property after the state was established and to Jewish refugees from Arab countries.[15]

In April 2012, two years after the Knesset resolution, the Israeli Ministry of Foreign Affairs issued a document stating that it henceforth would begin campaigning on behalf of linking the post-1948 Palestinian and Jewish experiences, and that 'the issue of Jewish refugees should be raised in every peace negotiation framework whether it is opposite the Palestinians or Arab governments.'[16]

It remains to be seen what impact, legal or otherwise, these Israeli governmental actions will have on Israeli negotiation strategies in the future. It also is not clear what the resolution means by 'ensuring the rights of Jewish refugees', or what 'bring[ing] up the issue of compensation' for Jews during negotiations actually means.

The Issue as it Has Been Addressed Outside of Arab–Israeli Negotiations

It is worth noting that not all Jews formerly from Arab countries, both in Israel and elsewhere, have agreed with the notion that it should be the Israeli government that represents their claims. The question of how best to seek compensation or restitution of property lost in the Arab world has been addressed in other ways over the decades, including bilaterally, unilaterally and through the courts of third parties. Foreign governments, Jewish non-governmental organizations and individual Jews have sought redress for losses on their own, outside of Israel, outside of the diplomacy of the Arab–Israeli conflict, and outside of the context of linkage with Palestinian refugee claims. Some of these cases saw governments work out arrangements for compensation on their own where they saw themselves as liable for damages. The first such case involved the British government compensating the Jews of Aden for property losses sustained during anti-Jewish disturbances in November 1947. British colonial authorities in Aden entertained Jewish claims and paid out at least part of the value of these claims.[17] More recently, the Iraqi government enacted legislation in 2006 allowing Iraqis to seek compensation or restitution for property that had been seized by the Baathist government between 1968–2003 (but not property seized prior to that, a category that included most of the Jewish property that had been seized).[18] Lastly, calls and even law suits have arisen within Israel demanding that the Israeli government itself compensate its own citizens from Arab countries for their losses, much as it provides financial assistance to European Jewish Holocaust survivors.[19]

Governments outside the Middle East have been involved in Jewish property claims as well. After Egypt expelled stateless persons and those holding certain European passports in 1956, the governments of Italy, France and the United Kingdom reached financial arrangements with the Egyptian government in 1957, 1958 and 1959, respectively. These agreements provided some financial relief for their aggrieved nationals who lost property in Egypt. Jewish nationals of those three nations thereafter were eligible for compensation or were allowed to transfer out funds from Egypt.[20] Finally, the French government enacted laws to pay compensation for the property that French citizens, including Jews, left behind during their hasty flight from Algeria, just prior to Algeria's declaration of independence in 1962.[21]

Lastly, individual Jews and Jewish organizations have sought compensation/restitution of lost property. In early 1957, four Jewish organizations – the American Jewish Joint Distribution Committee, the World Jewish Congress, the American Jewish Committee and the Jewish Agency – formed a joint committee to register 1956–57 Jewish property losses in Egypt in order to seek compensation. However, no concrete actions resulted outside of gathering data on the losses. More recently, individual Jews and organizations, both in Israel and elsewhere, have sued for property damages in Egyptian, American and even Israeli courts (in the latter case, attempts were made to force the

Israeli government to press for compensation of their claims bilaterally with the Arab states involved).[22]

Policy Options and Cost-Benefit Analysis

Conceivably, an international fund that would be created for compensating Palestinian refugees could also allow Jews to submit claims as well. However, it really is not feasible – politically or practically – to connect Jewish property claims against Arab countries to Palestinian refugee property claims, nor to connect, formally, other claims about the 'refugeehood' of Jews formerly living in Arab countries in negotiations about Palestinian refugees. Politically, the circumstances surrounding the Jewish exodus from the Arab world during and after 1948 vary from the circumstances that befell the Palestinians (and vary from Arab country to Arab country). In any case, the Palestinian refugees were not responsible, and therefore not liable, for the Jewish exodus from the Arab world, nor for the property losses that some of these Jewish emigrants sustained as a result.

It can also be argued (and has been argued) that the State of Israel has no right to negotiate on behalf of all Jews from Arab countries, no matter where they live and no matter what happened to their property. A final political problem with this idea is that the Israeli and Palestinian sides have already agreed that the two sets of claims will not constitute part of any future bilateral Israeli–Palestinian negotiations and thus of any future peace agreement.

Beyond politics, including Jewish claims within the rubric of an international fund would face potentially insurmountable practical problems as well. The most important of these is the lack of reliable statistics about the scale and value of Jewish losses throughout the Arab world. Moreover, it would be a daunting task for the fund's managers to determine who is a Jewish 'refugee' (as opposed to someone who left for other reasons, including economic) when this is a debatable issue even among Jews from Arab countries themselves.

Given these problems, the best solution for Jewish claims might be to seek compensation and/or restitution through negotiations outside the Palestinian–Israeli arena. In the case of Israel, this would involve bilateral talks with the individual Arab states involved. As noted above, treaty rights already give Israel the right to do this in the cases of Jordan and Egypt. At least while it was governed by Mu'ammar al-Qaddafi, Libya indicated its willingness to compensate Jews, and Israel maintains friendly – if not formal diplomatic – ties with other Arab states such as Morocco. Another option would be for individual Jews or Jewish groups to press for compensation from individual Arab states, which would be a move that would satisfy the needs of Jews living outside of Israel, and one that would avoid the problem of the lack of diplomatic relations between Israel and most Arab states.

As for the Israeli–Palestinian context, a symbolic policy option might, for the narrative portion of an agreement on refugees, include a reference to the suffering of Jewish emigrants from Arab countries. This is in line with what was discussed at Taba. Foreign Minister Tzipora (Tzipi) Livni offered possible language on this point in her remarks at the November 2007 Annapolis summit:

> The right thing to do is to build a shared future in two separate states: one – the State of Israel, which was established as a Jewish state, a national home for the Jewish people; and the other – Palestine, which will be established to give a full and complete solution to Palestinians wherever they may be... waiting for a sense of belonging to a national state, the same feeling of wholeness that the establishment of the State of Israel gave to Jewish refugees who were forced to leave Arab countries.[23]

Notes

1. For a discussion of this question, as well as a thorough study of the entire question of Jewish property losses in the Arab world, see Michael R. Fischbach, *Jewish Property Claims Against Arab Countries*, (New York: Columbia University Press, 2008).
2. Fischbach, *Jewish Property Claims*, pp. 101–3 and 130–9.
3. Fischbach, *Jewish Property Claims*, pp. 139, 181, 228–32 and 252–8.
4. Benjamin Joffe-Walt, 'New Office Begins Investigating Lost Property of ME Jews', *Jerusalem Post*, 28 July 2010, online at: www.jpost.com/Israel/Article.aspx?id=182837 (accessed 3 August 2013).
5. For further information on these various campaigns, see Fischbach *Jewish Property Claims*.
6. Amnon Kapeliouk, 'Camp David dialogues', *Le Monde Diplomatique*, September 2000, online at: http://mondediplo.com/2000/09/08 campdavid (accessed 3 August 2013).
7. Law of Implementation of the Peace Treaty, Article 6.b.

8. Peter Hirschberg, 'Private Property; Keep Out!', *Jerusalem Report* 27, (September 1999).

9. The document was published by Israeli negotiator Gilead Sher in his English-language book *The Israeli–Palestinian Peace Negotiations, 1999–2001: Within Reach*, (London: Routledge, 2006), pp. 247–8.

10. *Report on Israeli Settlement in the Occupied Territories*, Foundation for Middle East Peace, vol. 10, no. 5, (September–October 2000), p. 2, online at: www.fmep.org/reports/archive/vol.-10/no.-5/PDF (accessed 3 August 2013).

11. Charles Enderlin, *Shattered Dreams: The Failure of the Peace Process in the Middle East 1995–2002*, (New York: Other Press, 2003), p. 198.

12. *Al-Hayat*, 23 and 24 November 2000, cited in Middle East Media Resource Institute, *Special Dispatch*, no. 157, 28 November 2000.

13. Itamar Levin, *Locked Doors: The Seizure of Jewish Property in Arab Countries*, (Westport, CT: Praeger, 2001), p. 223.

14. For the text of the Israeli proposal, see Appendix 5 of Rex Brynen, 'Past as Prelude? Negotiating the Palestinian Refugee Issue' (London: Chatham House, 2008), online at: www.chathamhouse.org/publications/papers/view/108831 (accessed 3 August 2013).

15. Rachelle Kliger, 'Israel vies to Bring Mideast Jewish Refugees into Talks', *Jerusalem Post* Internet edition, 18 February 2010, online at: www.jpost.com/JewishWorld/JewishNews/Article.aspx?id=169043 (accessed 3 August 2013).

16. Israeli Ministry of Foreign Affairs, 'Jewish refugees from Arab and Muslim countries', 3 April 2012, online at: www.mfa.gov.il/MFA/Peace+Process/Guide+to+the+Peace+Process/Jewish_refugees_from_Arab_and_Muslim_countries-Apr_2012.htm (accessed 3 August 2013).

17. Fischbach *Jewish Property Claims*, pp. 139–41.

18. Ibid., p. 216.

19. Ibid., pp. 175, 187 and 247–50.

20. Ibid., pp. 152–4.

21. Ibid., pp. 154–8.

22. Ibid., pp. 175–9 and 219–22.

23. Paul Lungen, 'Jewish Refugees Briefly Mentioned at Annapolis', *Canadian Jewish News*, 6 December 2007.

8

Refugee Absorption and Development

Rex Brynen

Development Issues in Refugee Negotiations

The central aim of any future Israeli–Palestinian agreement on the refugee issue will be to find a durable solution to the situation of the more than 4.9 million refugees. In achieving this, development issues will loom large. Refugees who might return or be repatriated will have to be absorbed and integrated into their new places of residence. Similarly, it will be important that refugees who remain in their current host countries also see an improvement in their current situation as a consequence of peace. Done properly, the refugee absorption efforts will be a key part of both consolidating peace and of promoting socio-economic development. Done poorly, however, they have the potential to fuel refugee discontent, adversely impact local economies, antagonize host countries, and ultimately destabilize the peace agreement itself.

The development aspects of the refugee issue have generally been seen as predominately arising in the implementation phase of the peace process, after the parties have reached formal agreement. They have not, for example, figured explicitly in past negotiating texts, nor are they likely to do so in future. On the other hand, it is important to recognize that the decisions which the parties make on such key issues as a permanent place of residency, compensation, international mechanisms and the future wind-down of UNRWA, will all have important developmental implications. Pursuing a narrow legal or political approach to these issues without attention to their longer-term social and economic viability could result in reaching an agreement that proves deeply problematic in the long run.

This chapter will address some of the key absorption and development dimensions of the Palestinian refugee issue, highlighting the costs and benefits that might be associated with different approaches. Before doing so, however, it will first focus on the major interests and negotiating priorities that the parties are likely to bring to bear on the matter.

Interests and Priorities of the Major Parties

For *Palestinian negotiators*, a key interest in negotiations is to maximize both the degree of residential choice and the scope of property restitution and compensation contained in any agreement. They are unlikely to agree to any sort of restrictions on repatriation to a future Palestinian state, with the inevitable consequence that absorption issues will therefore be a major policy challenge for Palestinian leaders and officials in the aftermath of independence. Palestinian negotiators will wish to see a slow and gradual wind-down on UNRWA, contingent on full resolution and implementation of the refugee issue – both because of the Agency's status as a symbol of refugees' needs and rights, but also because of the substantial cost of assuming responsibility for UNRWA services in the West Bank and Gaza. Overall, the Palestinian side is driven largely by the political and refugee-rights component of an agreement, but it would certainly like to see the issue dealt with in a way that generates tangible improvements in the conditions of refugee communities and development gains for the new Palestinian state.

Typically, the Palestinian negotiating team has operated with little input from experienced development planners, increasing the risk that components of the agreement are suboptimal from this perspective. On the other hand, considerable work was done in the past on possible absorption models by the PA Ministry of Planning, some of it in conjunction with the World Bank.[1] A more effective integration of this expertise into future Palestinian negotiating teams would undoubtedly be an asset.

For *Israeli negotiators*, priorities have typically been to reduce Israeli legal and financial liabilities, minimize any refugee return to Israeli territory, and ensure that an agreement results in a permanent end of claims on the issue. Israel, however, would also have a geostrategic interest in assuring that the mechanics of a deal do not destabilize either the Palestinian state or neighbouring countries, especially Jordan.

In the Taba round of negotiations (and later in the non-official Geneva Initiative), both sides developed fairly complex provisions regarding implementation mechanisms, as well as possible models for compensation. By contrast, the Israeli draft *Framework Agreement on Permanent Status* (2000–01) had rather less to say on the modalities of either.

For *host countries*, and especially for *Jordan*, compensation paid to host states as well as to the refugees directly has been a key interest. Jordan would also have considerable interest in shaping issues of repatriation, especially as they related to refugees who were Jordanian citizens. *Syria*, by contrast, has not articulated any substantial position on refugee permanent status issues. Although some of its interests would undoubtedly overlap with Jordan, its cooperation is likely to be more fundamentally conditioned upon the prospects for an Israeli–Syrian peace agreement. Neither country would want to see a rapid wind-down of UNRWA that would require it to assume the burden for service provision. The primary concern of *Lebanon* has been to avoid pressures to naturalize its refugee community. As a result, and also because of limited policy planning capacity and the inherent sensitivity of the issue, it has really not addressed other interests that it might have, especially as they relate to compensation, the future of the refugee camps, and especially the possibility that some refugees might wish to remain in Lebanon post-agreement.

In the case of the *international community*, the most immediate interest would be that the parties reach a mutually acceptable resolution of the issue. However, other interests are likely to come to bear, especially in the implementation stage. Donors may have significantly different perspectives on the mechanics of aid implementation, the degree and types of coordination, the use of pooled funds versus bilateral aid projects (or, for that matter, transitional budget support), and the fate of UNRWA. There may also be some degree of national rivalry involved, especially insofar as membership in an international mechanism or leadership of aid coordination is involved.

Key Absorption and Development Issues

The negotiation and especially implementation of any future refugee agreement will have to address several major absorption and development issues, including the integration and absorption of Palestinians who repatriate to the new Palestinian state, those who return to Israel, those who remain in current host countries and those who might resettle in third countries. Housing, physical infrastructure, employment and social service provision issues will loom large in the case of Palestine, and especially given the inevitable wind-down of UNRWA in the eventual aftermath of an agreement. There will also be issues of donor coordination and aid resource mobilization to be considered.

Shaping most of these, however, is the key issue of population flows (see Table 4.1 in this volume for estimates of the current geographic distribution of the Palestinian population).[2] While issues of residency are dealt with in detail in Chapter 4 in this volume, the question is also inextricably linked to development and absorption challenges. This is especially important with regard to repatriation to the Palestinian state, which could involve many tens or hundreds of thousands of people over an extended period of time. Past PA planning exercises, for example, have assumed the arrival of some 100,000 Palestinians per year for the first five years following a peace agreement.[3] There is also likely to be some return of refugees to Israel and some resettlement in third countries. In these latter cases, however, development policies are likely to be much smaller relative to national population and resources, and overwhelmingly determined by the receiving countries with little reference to other actors. The exact number and rate of repatriation is difficult to predict, as it is likely to depend on the nature of an agreement, economic conditions in Palestine (and in host countries), as well as any 'push' factors in the diaspora, for example, political or legal pressures on refugees to leave host countries.

With regard to the first of these factors, negotiators will need to be careful that the 'permanent place of residency' clauses of a refugee agreement do not distort migration flows or patterns through the creation of perverse incentives or through bureaucratic and political bottlenecks.[4] This could well be the case if, for example:

- The parties agreed to immigration quotas for the new state (something that the Palestinian side would be extremely unlikely to agree to in any case).
- Israel retained transitional or permanent control of Palestinian border crossings (a demand that the current Israeli government is likely to make out of security considerations, but which would also be anathema to the Palestinian side).
- A complex system of refugee residential preference were established and administered through some sort of centralized agency (a model suggested in the Geneva Initiative, for example).
- There were substantial but time-limited relocation benefits that accelerated population movements.

In such cases, population flows risks being out-of-synch with the absorptive capacity of the new state, increasing the risk of adverse economic consequences.

Conversely, if interested refugees are relatively free to undertake repatriation on a voluntary basis at a time of their own choosing, and if they are fully informed about conditions within Palestine, it seems likely that the rate of population movement will be closely tied to the employment, investment housing and general economic conditions. Rather than having to apply through some sort of centralized residency determination body, for example, there seems to be little reason why refugees wishing to repatriate to Palestine should not be able to directly acquire the necessary travel and citizenship documents directly from their local Palestinian embassy. Indeed, the legitimacy of the new state will be shaped in part by its ability to address the needs of would-be future citizens. This should be supported by an extensive (and likely donor-funded) information campaign in refugee communities, other forms of local facilitation, and some limited material and logistical assistance to returnees, especially those from major host countries with no contiguous border with the Palestinian state (i.e. Syria and Lebanon).

Refugee Absorption in the Palestinian State

A future Palestinian state will face two main absorption challenges. The first of these will relate to the approximately 1.9 million UNRWA-registered refugees currently living in the West Bank and Gaza, where they comprise almost half of the over 4 million Palestinians resident in the territories. The second relates to Palestinians in the diaspora – refugees or not – who choose to repatriate to the new state of Palestine. With regard to both groups, their needs can and should be primarily addressed within the context of Palestine's overall development strategy, especially given the context of an underlying rate of natural growth (approximately 3 per cent annually, or about 120,000 persons per year) in the territories. On the one hand, this underlying rate of demographic growth poses challenges, especially with regard to limited natural resources. On the other hand, it does point to potential existing capacities in housing, construction and other sectors that might be further strengthened to aid refugee absorption. During peak periods in the years following the 1993 Oslo Agreement, for example, population inflows pushed the net population growth rate as high as 6 per cent in some years, and year-to-year school enrolment increases peaked at 10 per cent in 1996–1997. During 1996–2000, an estimated 15,600 housing units were constructed per year in the West Bank and Gaza.[5]

Existing Refugees in the West Bank and Gaza

Refugees within the West Bank and Gaza are already fully integrated into the social, economic and political fabric of Palestine. Indeed, by most socio-economic indicators their situation is not significantly different from that of non-refugees.

One partial exception to this is the refugee camps, where there will be a need to further transition to 'normal' neighbourhood status. As of January 2012, UNRWA reported some 211,665 refugees residing in 19 refugee camps in the West Bank, and 526,891 refugees residing in eight camps in Gaza. Camp refugees represent about 17 per cent of the current population of the occupied Palestinian territory.[6]

As work by the World Bank has shown, wholesale elimination of the camps is neither socially desirable, nor is it economically feasible given the probable costs involved.[7] Instead, these areas are more likely to undergo a degree of urban redevelopment, involving a certain amount of de-densification and relocation, improvements in access and public space, housing improvements and improvements in public infrastructure. One key challenge in all of this for Palestine will be the question of camp property ownership. Most refugees do not legally own their current homes, even if they may regard them as private property and even engage in real estate transactions. The easiest way to deal with this would be for the state to expropriate or purchase any non-public land upon which the camps are located and then transfer title directly to the current occupants. This process, however, might encounter some equity issues, with some refugee properties clearly worth many times more than others because of their physical location. There will also be a need to integrate urban and semi-urban camps more effectively into nearby municipal infrastructure, and to resolve governance issues (especially in the West Bank).

The new state of Palestine, like other host countries, will also need to eventually assume the burden of providing health, education and other services that were previously provided by UNRWA. This will involve both an institutional element (i.e. incorporating UNRWA services into Palestinian ministries) and fiscal and financial ones (financing services that were previously paid for by the international community). The former task will be facilitated, to some degree, by UNRWA's existing harmonization policy with regard to host country curriculum and salary norms. The latter will pose a major fiscal challenge to the PA, with the current UNRWA general fund budget in the West Bank and Gaza (that is, excluding emergency appeals) totalling some US$319 million in 2012, or around 4 per cent of GDP. These issues are much more fully explored in Chapter 3 on UNRWA in this volume.

Repatriated Refugees

In the case of returnees, the Palestinian state will need to address employment opportunities, housing availability, and the social and physical infrastructure requirements associated with the arrival of tens or hundreds of thousands of new citizens. Overall, work by the World Bank and others has highlighted that there is no meaningful concept of 'absorptive capacity' that can be usefully applied to the West Bank and Gaza, especially under conditions in which population movement is relatively free and hence self-regulating. Given the appropriate political and economic conditions – an end to current Israeli restrictions on the movement of Palestinian goods and people, and sound macro-economic policies; appropriate frameworks to encourage private sector investment; efforts to improve the existing resource base (especially for water); and efficient delivery of public services – it is possible to envisage the absorption of a million or more returnees to the territories. Conversely, given weak policies and poor economic conditions, the territories would struggle to deal with the arrival of a tenth as many persons.

It is particularly important to recognize that, in general, returnees will be a long-term economic asset, not a burden: returnees are workers, investors, taxpayers, and a source of valuable human and social capital. Although in the short term their repatriation requires capital investments in infrastructure and transitional costs for health, education and social services, in the longer-term their economic activity (and the wealth and government revenues that it generates) is likely to cover the marginal cost of their consumption of public goods.

Public income and employment-generation programmes should not be seen as a major component of absorption strategy. Governments are generally quite poor at 'creating' sustainable employment and micro-finance programmes tend not to create new jobs. Instead, both have a limited role as social safety nets for specific, targeted groups. In the case of refugees, job creation is likely to only play a modest and transitional welfare role for otherwise unemployed, involuntary returnees (for example, unskilled workers repatriating from Lebanon). Vocational training might also be important for this group.

In the housing sector, the Palestinian state ought not to attempt to engage in a massive programme of public housing construction for returnees. This was initially envisaged in the 1990s by a few Palestinian planners, some of whom seemed to imagine new towns and cities being constructed strategically along Palestine's borders on the model of Israeli development towns and settlements. However, it is a bad – and untenable – idea, for several reasons.

First, the experience with Palestinian public housing is limited and generally has been poor. Such a system is likely to be highly prone to abuse, mismanagement, cost over-runs, inflexibility and corruption. Indeed, the experience of Israeli immigrant settlement in the 1950s – with its emphasis on development town construction, and its continuing legacies of high unemployment, inadequate housing and infrastructure, political backlash and social bitterness – represents a powerful argument why this is not the best approach.

Second, the provision of public housing to returnees, if coupled with rent or purchase subsidies, would create enormously perverse migration incentives, attracting returnees in numbers wholly disconnected from the economic opportunities in the West Bank and Gaza. It would also create significant equity problems and considerable tension between the returnees who would be eligible for such housing and the current residents (including existing refugees).

Third, such a programme would be far too costly. In its unpublished 2002 study of the 'Absorption of New Residents in the West Bank and Gaza', the World Bank found that the total cost of accommodating returnees in new newly-built housing on public land in the occupied territories varied from US$8,924 to US$13,275 per person, depending on location (including construction costs but excluding the imputed cost of the land itself).[8] If such housing were to be provided for returning refugees and displaced persons, the costs would be astronomical: between US$4.4–6.6 billion for 500,000 returnees, assuming the provision of free public land. Clearly, such outlays are well beyond any amounts of assistance that donors are likely to provide.

Instead, the Palestinian state should consider a range of incentives to encourage 'sweat equity' construction by individual families, investment in real estate construction by contractors and companies, and efforts by municipalities to encourage returnees to settle in their areas (rather than attempting to discourage them as they might become a burden on local infrastructure and services). This might involve such elements as:

- Making public land available for housing purposes at below market rates, whether to contractors for eventual sale or rent, or to qualified individuals undertaking their own construction. Such land would be made available to all, returnees or residents, although income criteria could be developed to limit the largest implicit subsidies to those projects intended for low-income housing or undertaken by low-income families. Affordability targets might also be set, requiring that contractor developments have a certain maximum sale price, or that a certain proportion of low-income housing be built. Increasing the pool of land available for housing in this way should have the added advantage of dampening increases in private land prices during the repatriation period, thus reducing or avoiding the sorts of sharp housing price increases that followed the Oslo Agreement and the establishment of the Palestinian Authority.[9]

- Sites could be made available as serviced lots, with roads, water, sewage access and facilities provided. The funding for this, as well as investments in the required social infrastructure (schools, health facilities, community centres), would be provided by donors. At present, poor infrastructure and the frequent requirement that developers provide feeder infrastructure represents a significant constraint on housing development, pushing prices up.

- Local government units could be provided with incentive grants, proportional to the amount of construction undertaken on public land and the number of returnees attracted. Such grants would be sufficient to cover the cost of providing public infrastructure for new residents and housing, together with a bonus incentive amount intended to make it desirable for local governments to attract new residents.

- Reforms should be undertaken in the local planning, zoning and taxation systems so as to provide a supportive environment for the housing sector. At present, many properties are not properly registered, thus limiting collateral-based lending, slowing transactions, and rendering some purchases potentially insecure. In many cases, municipal zoning regulations are excessively rigid and tend to restrict the supply of land for housing in urban areas.

- Reform is also important in the rental sector, so as to encourage growth of this housing stock. At present, only a very small proportion of Palestinian households reside in rental accommodation. Rent controls, conversion restrictions and existing tax laws do not encourage an expansion of the supply of potential rented accommodation. In absorbing its immigrant flows since the 1990s, Israel has provided landlords with an exemption from existing income tax on rental income. There may also be scope in the Palestinian case for changes in tax rates, the provision of tax credits, or an expansion of investment amounts eligible for tax deductibility, so as to encourage the renting of existing vacant units, conversions, or investment in construction for rental purposes. However, such initiatives would also require suitable reforms of existing rent control laws inherited from Jordan and Egypt. An enlarged rental market would provide a larger array of initial housing choices for returnees, and might lessen or spread out some of the initial demand for housing purchase. However, a strong social bias in favour of privately owned accommodation is likely to continue.

- Housing finance reform is also important. At present, there is only a weak mortgage lending system in the West Bank and Gaza. Instead, purchasers typically use existing savings, family borrowing, remittances, land-swaps and lease-to-own arrangements with developers. Developers have access to some commercial financing, but this is typically short term. As a result, it is common for developers to await initial sales or leases before completing or extending construction projects. Moreover, the absence of larger and longer-term commercial finance means that most developers operate on a relatively small scale. A mortgage/loan guarantee system would increase the flexibility of housing finance. It could also be combined with a voucher scheme for low-income Palestinians and/or involuntary returnees that would allow a buy-down in mortgage rates. Such a scheme of subsidized mortgages – a key element in Israel's immigrant absorption strategy – clearly would require the prior establishment of an effective mortgage system, as well as the establishment of the administrative structures required to determine eligibility, issue vouchers and monitor the programme.

It is important to note the particular needs and vulnerabilities of repatriating refugees whose arrival in the new state is occasioned more by 'push' factors in their host country than by voluntary migration decisions. Palestinians in Lebanon are perhaps most at risk of this in the aftermath of a peace agreement, amid demands from some groups in Lebanon for their rapid departure from the country. Palestinians from Lebanon also tend to have fewer family connections with the West Bank or Gaza, lower levels of education compared to other refugees, and lower amounts of capital resources (although this might be offset by any compensation payments to refugees). Palestinians from Syria might also face pressures from the violence and deprivation of the civil war there pushing them to repatriate. Consequently, there may be a heightened need for low-income housing and other supports for these segments of the returnee population.

Some commentators have assumed that evacuated Israeli settlements in the West Bank and Gaza could provide suitable housing stock for returnees. While this may be true in some cases, simply allocating settlement homes to returnees could be problematic in many respects. First, there may be an inadequate number of homes. Second, settlements may not be conveniently located for Palestinian employment purposes. Third, there may be serious equity issues involved, especially given that most settler housing is relatively luxurious by local Palestinian standards. Why should some returnees acquire ex-settler homes with lawns, air conditioners and even swimming pools, while others acquire nothing at all, and local (and perhaps much poorer) residents remain in their current inferior residences? Finally, there is substantial opportunity for abuse in any programme of using settlements as public housing for returnees, and even a well-run and transparent programme could be subject to politically costly accusations of favouritism in housing allocation.

Given this, it is preferable for the absorption of settler housing stock to be seen in the broader context of a Palestinian national housing strategy, rather than as a refugee specific asset. Most settler homes could be capitalized by selling them at appropriate prices to any interested Palestinian buyer, refugee or non-refugee. The resources thus received by the state could then be used to finance public infrastructure investments, housing finance incentives/subsidies, and other programmes for both returnees and the general population. Equity and transparency would be essential in the design of such a programme.

As noted earlier, one area in which there are absorption constraints (although not limits) is the area of natural resources, and specifically water. This issue needs to be seen as part of an overall regional water problem, due not only to its absolute scarcity which is aggravated by the rapidly growing population, but also due to inefficient pricing, usage and distribution. The repatriation of refugees from nearby countries to a Palestinian state would not increase the total demand on regional water supplies, moreover, but would merely rearrange it.

Refugee Absorption in Israel

In addition to repatriation to a Palestinian state, it is expected that some number of refugees would also return to Israel under a peace agreement. The magnitude of such return is far from clear, however, Palestinian negotiators have, at times, sought numbers well in excess of 100,000, while Israeli negotiators have suggested numbers as low as 5,000 (or even zero).

The integration of returnees to Israel would pose a number of developmental and social challenges. However, the material costs would be much less daunting than those facing Palestine, given Israel's considerably greater economic resources. Moreover, Israel has substantial experience with immigrant absorption that might be adapted to assist the integration of Palestinian returnees. However, other challenges would be substantial, given the Jewish character of the Israeli state and the attendant social and political sensitivities that would be involved. The social challenges would also be heightened in Israel as the restricted return would be allocated to certain demographic groups, such as elderly first generation refugees. The involvement and engagement of Israel's existing Palestinian minority as a partner in the process is likely to be important in implementing effective absorption and integration strategies.

Because of the sensitivity of the issue, Israel is likely to resist any explicit commitments in an agreement regarding the absorption of refugee returnees, beyond simple identification of a quota or process. The Palestinian side, however, would have an interest in, at the very least, monitoring refugee return to ensure that Israel is fully implementing both the spirit and letter of its undertakings in this regard.

Refugee Absorption in Host Countries

As noted earlier, most refugees in Jordan and Syria are integrated into the local economy. Nevertheless, there remain developmental needs and opportunities, especially with regard to low-income refugees in refugee camps. In Lebanon needs are much more severe, given the high proportion of refugees living in camps (50 per cent according to UNRWA) as well as the generally poor housing and infrastructure conditions within those camps. Palestinians in Lebanon also face a number of formal and informal barriers to full force participation, as well as discriminatory laws that prevent them from owning real estate. In all host countries, there might be legal issues regarding non-public ownership of some refugee camp lands, with the original private owner having received little compensation for making the land available after 1948, and possibly wishing to reclaim it in the aftermath of a peace agreement. As in the West Bank and Gaza, there is unlikely to be any wholesale 'decamping' of refugee camp populations to entirely new accommodations, but rather a gradual process of urban renewal involving some degree of de-densification (assisted, perhaps, by significant repatriation flows to Palestine, and a consequent freeing up of land within the camps). The only exception to this might be small and isolated camps – although even here the challenges and complications of wholesale relocation should not be underestimated.

Like Palestine, host countries will also be concerned about the financial costs of providing services that were previously provided by UNRWA. In Jordan, UNRWA expenditures are equivalent to roughly 0.6 per cent of GDP and 1.4 per cent of government expenditures. In Lebanon and Syria, (non-emergency) UNRWA expenditures represent around 0.2 per cent of GDP and 0.5 per cent of government expenditures.[10]

Donors are likely to regard development investments in host countries as part of the 'peace dividend' for host countries, as well as a way of addressing these countries' calls for monetary compensation for having hosted the refugee population. Lebanon will undoubtedly be the most difficult of the cases, not only because of the degree of need, but also because Lebanese society would need to determine whether it was willing to accept the continued residence of some Palestinians in the country, even after a peace agreement was reached. Moreover, of the three major host countries, Lebanon also has the most poorly developed public social infrastructure, and might be least well equipped to address the post-UNRWA health and education needs of former refugees. In Syria it will be impossible to undertake refugee integration or development programmes as long as the civil war continues. Even after the war, Syria will face massive challenges of reconstruction for years to come.

Refugee Absorption in Third Countries

It seems unlikely that refugee resettlement in third countries will be a significant component of any future refugee agreement, certainly not relative to the size of the overall Palestinian refugee population. The integration challenges for refugees may be very large, especially if they are migrating to countries with a very different social, linguistic, cultural and physical context. However, these challenges are likely to be dealt with by pre-existing national systems for refugee resettlement, asylum and immigrant absorption, probably in coordination with UNRWA, UNHCR and IOM.

The Development Implications of Refugee Compensation

Given compensation payments likely to be in the billions or tens of billions of dollars, these amounts would rival and possibly exceed the volume of bilateral development assistance to the parties. Designed well, a compensation regime might prove an important stabilizing element for the broader peace agreement and for the region as a whole. Designed poorly or critically underfunded, however, a compensation regime could instead destabilize both.[11]

Throughout the permanent status negotiations of 2000–01, and in most unofficial and official discussions of refugee compensation since then, there has been a presumption that compensation would certainly be paid to individual refugees (for example, the Israeli position from Camp David through until Taba in 2000–01, as well as the Geneva Initiative), most likely to host countries, and perhaps to the Palestinian state itself (proposed by the PLO in past negotiations, and also noted in analytical work by the Aix Group).[12] The idea of forgoing individual refugee compensation in favour of a lump-sum payment of collective compensation to the Palestinian state has not been given serious consideration in light of the political backlash it is likely to generate among refugees themselves.

One key issue in individual compensation is how payments are made. Do refugees receive compensation in cash, or as a series of vouchers that would enable them to access education, housing or other benefits? While some Israeli scholars have favoured the latter as a way of directing refugee monies towards 'productive' investments,[13] some concern has also been expressed about the possible inflationary effects of a sudden influx of compensation funds into the local economies. Palestinians have generally opposed restricting the ability of refugees to use their compensation payments in this way, however. In this they have found support from the World Bank, which has argued (in an unpublished analysis) that cash provides a useful degree of flexibility, and that individual refugees are likely to be best placed to decide how to use compensation monies to improve their conditions.[14]

The modalities of individual compensation payments would have other effects on the social and economic development of a future Palestine too. Claims-based compensation systems, for example, would tend to reproduce the inequalities of property ownership in 1948 Palestine. Refugees living in camps – who tend to come from the poorest strata of pre-1948 Palestine and tend to have a somewhat larger than average family size – would be substantially disadvantaged compared to those who come from large, landowning families. Those whose families had been non-landowning agricultural labourers or urban workers would suffer in particular. By contrast, a system of per capita payments to all refugees would have considerably fewer regressive effects on economic equality. A system of compensation payments could even be designed that made comparatively more generous payments to the smallest categories of claims, and proportionately less to the largest category – thereby helping to reduce rather than exacerbate Palestinian economic inequality. The modalities of compensation payments might also have significant gendered effects, given both the patterns of legal property ownership and the inheritance laws in the region.[15]

Compensation payments are likely to provide a significant share of the resources available for refugees seeking to repatriate to a Palestinian state, possibly far exceeding the resources allocated by donors to help the new state absorb returnees. In this, Palestinian refugee repatriation would differ significantly from the sorts of repatriation programmes associated with most refugee populations elsewhere in the developing world. In the housing sector, for example, refugees could use cash compensation payments to finance housing construction or to upgrade existing housing. Refugees would also be able to use such capital for business investment or investment in training and higher education. Host countries, including the Palestinian state, would also benefit significantly from compensation payments to refugees within their borders, both through increased fiscal revenues from taxation, and from the multiplier effect of increased expenditures and capital investment in the local economy.

Donor Coordination Mechanisms

Effective implementation of the development components of a refugee agreement would undoubtedly be facilitated through coordination of efforts between donors, host countries, UN and other specialized agencies, NGOs and the refugee stakeholders themselves. What form such coordination might take, however, is a complex question. While the question of how an international mechanism for the refugee issue is more fully discussed in Chapter 2 of this volume, there are nonetheless a number of key dimensions that should also be raised here.

- *Should coordination structures be called for and mandated within the peace agreement, or should they be established later, in the implementation phase?* Several prior negotiating texts – including the Israeli draft Framework Agreement on Permanent Status (2000–01), the Israeli and Palestinian working papers at Taba (2001) and the provisions of the unofficial Geneva Initiative (2003) called for the establishment of an International Commission and International Fund to implement the various aspects of an agreement, including absorption, integration and development. A negotiated agreement could, to an extent, predetermine much of the membership of the Commission, since no country so named by the parties would likely decline the offer. It might, however, prove problematic with regard to countries that were not so named. In general, any donor coordination mechanism should both reflect the way in which donor assistance functions and facilitate it, rather than excessively bureaucratize the process of allocating and disbursing funds. Consequently, an excessively complex mechanism is best avoided.[16]
- *Should there be a single, overall body coordinating donor efforts with regard to refugees?* Such a body would have the significant advantage of a holistic perspective on the challenges and issues arising from absorption, integration and development efforts, especially as developments in one area (such as a host country) might affect another (for example, repatriation to Palestine). It would also reassure host countries that their individual and collective interests are being addressed. On the other hand, what is not clear is the extent to which such 'coordination' could move

beyond the limits of simple information-sharing. Such a body might be marginalized, moreover, by aid coordination structures for the much larger and higher-profile general aid effort in support of the Palestinian state. Given the extent to which developmental good practice would require that Palestinian absorption policy be an integrated part of a broader development strategy, and not a stand-alone effort, the existence of potentially overlapping or even competing 'refugee' and 'Palestinian' aid coordination structures might even prove dysfunctional.

- *Should Israel be a member of refugee aid coordination structures?* Certainly, Israel appears to have an interest in membership in the International Commission, in order to ensure that its interests are taken into account in the highly sensitive issues of refugee population movements and compensation. It is less clear whether Israel has an interest in being a member of aid coordination structures dealing with more mundane and less politicized development issues. Since the establishment of the Palestinian Authority in 1994, Israel has been a member of high-level aid coordination structures for the West Bank and Gaza, in large part because its cooperation was necessary to ensure that development activities could be undertaken in the occupied territories. It has not, however, been a member of lower-level working groups. It has also not served as a member of the UNRWA Advisory Committee. Israel's active presence on a refugee aid coordination body primarily dealing with host countries (Jordan, Syria and Lebanon) could well be problematic from a host country perspective, and needlessly entangle Israel in issues it would prefer to not be involved in.
- *Role of an international (refugee) fund.* As discussed in prior negotiations, an international fund for refugees often serves several purposes: to finance refugee compensation; to provide compensation to host countries; to support refugee return, repatriation and resettlement; and to finance refugee absorption, integration and development programmes. Aspects of this issue have been addressed in Chapter 2 on implementation mechanisms; other aspects will be discussed below under the rubric of donor resource generation. For now, however, it is important to note that some sort of international trust fund for

refugee development would have certain intrinsic coordinating and rationalizing effects, since it would facilitate the central allocation of aid resources in a way that addresses the highest priority needs. On the other hand, it is not clear how much this would appeal to most larger donors, who frequently prefer to have more say (and more political profile) associated with aid investments than a trust fund-type mechanism might allow. Also, unlike most international trust funds, this one would be allocating resources across multiple separate countries, which could add a further element of complication and even political tension to its operations.

Resource Generation

It is difficult to know what the refugee absorption, integration and development costs might be arising from an Israeli–Palestinian peace agreement. Based on data from the World Bank, and assuming a relatively modest programme of limited camp improvements, support for relocation, transitional budget support and some assistance to host countries, one estimate put the cost at between US$8–10 billion in aid over ten years, excluding refugee compensation. In the run-up to Camp David, US officials envisaged an assistance package of some US$20 billion for refugees, providing for compensation, resettlement and rehabilitation/development.[17] The Aix Group, presuming a rather more ambitious set of absorption and development initiatives, estimated the cost at between US$18–33 billion (again, excluding compensation payments).[18] These amounts exclude regular budget support and development assistance to Palestine, which currently stands at almost US$2 billion per year.[19]

Several mechanisms can be envisaged that help raise the necessary level of financial resources:

- A major donor conference would create pressure on donors as well as sending a signal of international support and commitment to the refugees. One would need to be careful, however, to make sure that this didn't result in inflated pledges and unrealistic expectations, as seen in some past donor conferences.
- In addition to its contribution to aid coordination and rationalization, an international fund might also assist with aid

mobilization, since it would facilitate contributions from donors who do not otherwise have a large aid infrastructure in place in the region, and who might find that a trust fund mechanism is a useful way to disburse unspecified support. From an Israeli perspective, a general fund for various aspects of the refugee issue might ease domestic resistance to making compensation payments, since it would allow Israeli officials to partially cloak these in developmental garb. On the other hand, the association of a refugee fund with compensation payments might deter Arab contributions through such a mechanism, since no Arab state would wish to be seen to be relieving Israel of its obligations (in Arab eyes) to compensate the refugees.

- Support for refugee absorption, integration and development projects could be phased over an extended period of time, to reduce the burden in any given year. On the other hand, there is considerable value in front-end loading contributions, so as to ensure that refugees rapidly enjoy substantial tangible benefits associated with the agreement. A draft internal State Department paper on the refugee issue from early 2000, for example, suggested that 'the assistance package must [be] implemented easily and rapidly, with the bulk of assistance provided in the first two years.'[20]

Some care would need to be taken to limit the use of loans and credit within an assistance package, even at concessional rates. While these certainly can make a positive developmental contribution, it would be unfortunate if they saddled the new Palestine with a substantial external debt, or aggravated the existing debt problems of the major host countries.

Care should also be taken to avoid complex financing schemes, such as development shares or bonds. Such schemes are unlikely to be flexible and responsive, and would be open to misunderstanding and confusion from the refugee community.

Conclusion

As this chapter has highlighted, any future negotiated resolution of the Palestinian refugee issue will involve a range of complex repatriation, integration and development challenges. Relatively few of these will be directly addressed in the text of the agreement itself, but rather will be confronted in the implementation phase of the peace process. However, aspects of the agreement – especially with regard to issues of residency and relocation, and also with regard to refugee compensation – will have profound development implications.

It is essential that negotiators understand these linkages. If they fail to do so, they could agree to terms that, while seeming to be politically or legally expedient in the immediate context of negotiations, have unforeseen future social and economic effects. These, in turn, could undercut refugee support, bedevil implementation of the agreement, undermine the new Palestinian state – and ultimately threaten the hoped-for peace itself.

Notes

1. For an overview of this work, see Khalil Nijm, 'Planning in Support of Negotiations: The Refugee Issue', in Rex Brynen and Roula el-Rifai (eds), *Palestinian Refugees: Challenges of Repatriation and Development*, (London and Ottawa: I.B. Tauris and the International Development Research Centre, 2007), online at: www.idrc.ca/en/ev-107711-201-1-DO_TOPIC. html, pp. 121–31.

2. As discussed in Chapter 4 on residency in this volume, it is difficult to be certain of the total number of refugees. UNRWA only deals with refugees in its areas of operation, and so does not register refugees residing in other areas. However, not all refugees registered in an UNRWA area may actually reside there at present – the actual number of Palestinians currently in Lebanon, for example, is generally held to be under 250,000. The BADIL numbers do seek to include refugees who may have never been registered with UNRWA, as well as IDPs and others who have been forcibly displaced. However, they tend to focus on the most generous possible numbers, may double count migrants (for example Jordanian Palestinians working in the Gulf), and hence likely over-report the size of many populations.

3. Nijm, 'Planning in Support of Negotiations: The Refugee Issue', p. 123.

4. The Geneva Initiative, for example, envisaged a centralized Permanent Place of Residency committee that would collect and determine the refugees' residency preferences, a system that was also found in some of the earlier Taba negotiating texts. This would tend to bureaucratize and slow repatriation processes that might otherwise occur with much greater fluidity. Rex Brynen, 'The Geneva Accord and the Palestinian Refugee Issue', unpublished paper, February 2004, online at: www.idrc. ca/uploads/user-S/12075984591geneva_refugees__Brynen_2.pdf

5. Rex Brynen, 'Refugees, Repatriation, and Development: Some Lessons from Recent Work', in Brynen and el-Rifai (eds), *Palestinian Refugees: Challenges of Repatriation and Development*, p. 107.

6. UNRWA, 'UNRWA in Figures', 1 January 2012, online at: www.unrwa. org/userfiles/20120317152850.pdf

7. See Nick Krafft and Ann Elwan, 'Infrastructure Scenarios for Refugees and Displaced Persons', in Brynen and el-Rifai (eds), *Palestinian Refugees: Challenges of Repatriation and Development*, pp. 132–62; and Brynen, 'Refugees, Repatriation, and Development: Some Lessons from Recent Work', in Brynen and el-Rifai (eds), *Palestinian Refugees: Challenges of Repatriation and Development*, pp. 102–20.

8. World Bank, 'Absorption of New Residents in the West Bank and Gaza', unpublished research paper, Washington DC: The World Bank, 2002.

9. There is clearly enough public land to accommodate returning displaced persons in this way, quite apart from private land that would also be built upon. The World Bank's examination of a sample of just five representative urban areas in the West Bank found sufficient land for 106,000–211,000 new residents in these locations, depending on assumptions about housing density. Although more costly, satellite towns could also be developed in new areas, each accommodating 20,000–70,000 residents.

10. Rex Brynen, 'Implementing a (Just) Solution to the Palestinian Refugee Issue: Estimating the Financial Cost', presentation made at the Chatham House workshop on Palestinian refugees, 8 August 2009, online at: www. mcgill.ca/files/icames/refugeecost2.pdf

11. This section draws heavily on the somewhat longer analysis offered in my chapter 'Palestinian Refugee Compensation: Connections and Complexities', in Rex Brynen and Roula el-Rifai (eds), *Compensation to Palestinian Refugees and the Search for Middle East Peace* (London, Pluto, 2012).

12. For details of the Israeli and Palestinian positions on this issue, see Rex Brynen, 'Past as Prelude: Negotiating the Palestinian Refugee Issue', Chatham House Briefing Paper MEP/PR BP 08/01, London: Chatham House, 2008, online at: www.chathamhouse.org/publications/papers/ view/108831. For the work of the Aix Group on the economic aspects of the refugee issue, see Arie Arnon and Saeb Bamya (eds), *Economic Dimensions of a Two-State Agreement between Israel and Palestine*, Aix Group, 2007, online at: www.aixgroup.org/node/118

13. Ruth Klinov, 'Reparations and Rehabilitation of Palestinian Refugees', in Eyal Benvenisti, Chaim Gans and Sari Hanafi (eds), *Israel and the Palestinian Refugees*, (Berlin: Springer, 2007), pp. 323–46.

14. World Bank, 'Assessment of the Absorptive Capacity of the West Bank and Gaza in Integrating Returnees and Associated Costs', unpublished research paper, Washington DC: The World Bank, 2000.

15. On this, see Megan Bradley, 'Gender Dimension of Redress for Palestinian Refugees', in Brynen and el-Rifai (eds), *Compensation to Palestinian Refugees and the Search for Middle East Peace*.

16. The unpublished Geneva Initiative annex on refugees, for example, contains considerable – and probably excessive – detail about how a

proposed Committee for Rehabilitation and Development would operate, guidelines for resource allocation, and so forth.

17. US Department of State, 'Proposed Initiative on Palestinian Displaced Persons and Refugees', unpublished draft, 23 May 2000.

18. Rex Brynen, 'Implementing a (Just) Solution to the Palestinian Refugee Issue: Estimating the Financial Cost'; see also Brynen, 'Refugees, Repatriation, and Development: Some Lessons from Recent Work', in Brynen and el-Rifai (eds), *Palestinian Refugees: Challenges of Repatriation and Development*; and Arie Arnon and Saeb Bamya (eds), *Economic Dimensions of a Two-State Agreement between Israel and Palestine*.

19. As a point of comparison, donors spent some US$15 billion in development assistance and US$25 billion in development assistance in Afghanistan in 2002–2007. In Iraq, donors made available some US$70 billion in development and reconstruction assistance in 2003–2009. World Bank, 'A Palestinian State in Two Years: Institutions for Economic Revival', Economic Monitoring Report to the Ad Hoc Liaison Committee, 22 September 2009, Washington DC: World Bank, 2009, online at: http://siteresources.worldbank.org/INTWESTBANKGAZA/Resources/AHLCSept09WBreportfinal.pdf; Matt Waldman, *Falling Short: Aid Effectiveness in Afghanistan*, (Kabul: Acbar, 2008), online at: http://reliefweb.int/node/260552; Special Inspector General for Iraq Reconstruction, 'Quarterly Report and Semi-Annual Report', January 2010, Washington DC: SIGIR, 2010, online at: www.sigir.mil/files/quarterlyreports/January2010/Report_-_January_2010.pdf

20. US Department of State, 'Proposed Initiative on Palestinian Displaced Persons and Refugees'.

9

Intangible Needs, Moral Acknowledgement and the Palestinian Refugee Issue

Michael Molloy and John Bell,
with Nicole Waintraub and Ian Anderson

Introduction

> Support for violence decreases… when an adversary makes symbolic
> gestures that show recognition of the other's core values. Symbolic
> gestures may then allow and facilitate political negotiations that
> also involve material trade-offs.[1]

The resolution of the Palestinian refugee issue has long been
framed in the West and by Israel as a humanitarian problem
to be resolved through a variety of practical measures. These
include compensation for losses and suffering and the provision of
a range of options, spelled out in the Clinton Parameters, including
return to a new Palestinian state, return to 'swapped' areas, resettlement
in host countries, resettlement in Western countries and return of set
numbers and categories to Israel.

While practical solutions are indeed important to them, the
Palestinians frame the issue, first and foremost, as a matter of rights,
dignity and international law. For their part, Israelis also have concerns

linked to the refugee issue which relate mainly to implications of 'return' on the Jewish nature of Israel and the finality of claims in an end of conflict agreement, especially regarding legal claims related to the refugees.

Both sides have demands related to this issue that are 'intangible' in nature and that go beyond the practical solutions and arrangements. Because of this, it is unlikely that the Palestinian refugee issue can be resolved solely through material compensation and residential solutions. The practical measures mentioned above are insufficient for addressing what we describe here as 'intangible' needs.

The experience of the peace process since Madrid, through the Multilateral Refugee Working Group, the Oslo Process, Camp David, Taba, Annapolis and uncounted Track II encounters suggests that these intangible matters of rights, dignity, identity and legitimacy on both sides will not be pushed aside. The road to resolving the refugee issue runs through, not around, the moral and symbolic or 'intangible' issues.

The Hamas spokesman Ghazi Hamad has said:

> In principle we have no problem with a Palestinian state encompassing all of our lands within the 1967 borders. But let Israel apologize for our tragedy in 1948, and then we can talk about negotiating over our right of return to historic Palestine.[2]

Recently, a senior Israeli official was quoted as saying that if Mr. Abbas accepted – even privately when the two leaders meet alone – an end to the conflict with Israel and its Jewish identity, 'the whole conventional wisdom can change very quickly.'[3]

These statements come from a Hamas official, still dedicated to violent resistance and struggle against Israel and an official in a right-wing Israeli government. Neither is from the peace camp yet their comments go to the heart of the conflict between Israelis and Palestinians and suggest that a satisfaction of the intangible needs of both sides, through acknowledgement, moral or otherwise, will meet the profound emotional needs and calm that dimension of the conflict sufficiently to move the sides much closer to agreement, and to accept practical compromises in implementation.

Indeed, in the case of the Palestinian refugee issue, acknowledgement may be a critical key to moving the refugee question forward and
to opening the door to future discussions on the practical issues. It may
help victims begin to address their victimhood and the actions that led
to their suffering: 'Insofar as moral apologies express acknowledgement of the human dignity and moral worth of victims as well as respect
for victims' feelings of resentment, they can provide reason for an
emotional shift on the part of victims.' In fact, a failure to acknowledge
this dimension of the victims' experience inflicts a 'second wound of
silence' that can preclude any resolution of the conflict.[4]

*The purpose of this chapter is to present a preliminary and introductory
presentation of the intangible dimension of the Palestinian refugee problem
in the hope that this will be given greater consideration and examination
in the future.* It will explore the various facets of the issue, review
past efforts to resolve the refugee issue and how they dealt with this
matter, and outline some options to resolution and their implications.
The chapter is divided into three main sections. The first section
explores the role of narratives of the conflict. The second section
reviews how the refugee issue has been addressed during the many
stages of the peace process, and draws out the occasions when there
has been an attempt to deal with its intangible dimensions. The third
section proposes a range of options from ignoring the intangibles to
addressing them head-on. It explores the latter option in particular
detail, outlining the main elements involved in putting such an
approach into action.

The Role of Narratives

Narratives elucidate how both sides frame their hurt and their denial
of wrongdoing and how they understand the events of history. At the
core of each narrative lie powerful symbolic issues and needs. These
needs will be at the centre of any efforts to address the intangible
dimension of the refugee problem. Each side uses its narrative to
explain, understand and justify the conflict and its victimhood and/
or righteousness. The narrative of the other is rejected as illegitimate.
After a century of conflict, the narratives held by the Israelis and the
Palestinians are as important as the verifiable facts.

The Palestinian Narrative

The Palestinian narrative posits the *Nakba* ('the catastrophe') as the defining moment in the formation of the Palestinian national identity after 1948. This identity is marked by expulsion, suffering and the refugee experience. The Palestinian narrative is that the 700,000 Palestinians who became refugees were forcibly driven from their homes and villages in Mandatory Palestine during the war of 1948 as the result of an expulsion that was deliberately planned and undertaken by pre-independence Zionists and by agents of the State of Israel. The decision made by the Israeli cabinet in June 1948, to bar refugees from returning to their homes, cemented the Palestinians' status as refugees in neighbouring countries and in the West Bank and Gaza. A strong sense of victimhood is part of the Palestinian national identity as a result of these events.

The Israeli Narrative

From the Israeli perspective, while the suffering of the refugees is regrettable, their narrative is that the refugee situation is primarily the consequence of Palestinian and Arab decisions and actions. These include rejection of the UN partition decision and the initiation of hostilities for which Israel bears neither moral nor legal responsibility. Refugees were displaced as a natural consequence of a war thrust on Israel, and Israeli actions were driven by self-defence and constituted an important and justifiable state-building imperative. In parallel, an Israeli sense of victimhood stems from the Jewish people's history of persecution, culminating in the Holocaust that preceded the creation of the State of Israel. This profound sense of victimhood does not easily permit the admission of a wrong against another people. The Israeli narrative has been modified by the Israeli 'New Historians' who have confirmed that many Palestinians who fled were purposely expelled. There remains disagreement and debate inside Israel among the proponents of this view over whether this was the result of a pre-planned organized policy or a consequence of the events of the 1948 war.[5] More recently the debate takes the fact that Israelis drove out Palestinians as a given, but questions whether this was actually reprehensible given the imperative to create a Jewish state.[6]

Intangible Needs Arising From the Palestinian Refugee Issue[7]

Palestinian Needs

In our view, these various formulations are either understandings or mechanisms for dealing with underlying intangible needs that linger today despite the passage of time. These needs can be addressed. For Palestinians, there appear to be three central needs firmly rooted in the refugee experience: the need for recognition of the refugees' 'right of return' (arising out of UN General Assembly Resolution 194), the need to have Israel acknowledge its responsibility for the expulsion of the Palestinians, and the need for Israel to contribute to resolving the plight of the refugees.

Palestinians demand the recognition by Israel of the right of return as a basic principle stemming from a past injustice. This is considered a necessary step towards recognizing and addressing Palestinian refugee suffering during and after the war of 1948.[8] This suffering may be understood in terms of both physical and material loss (land, property and economic development) and intangible loss (identity, dignity and a sense of legitimacy). Palestinians also demand that Israel accepts its responsibility for the creation of the refugee problem, which they view as the direct cause of Palestinian dispossession.

Israeli Needs

For their part, Israelis appear to have three core needs which have links to the refugee issue. First, Israelis require that Palestinians recognize Israel as a Jewish State. This is presented as an existential need that relates to the legitimacy of the state – the fundamental Israeli need for Palestinians and Arabs in general to accept explicitly the Jewish presence in the Middle East within a legitimate nation state. Secondly, Israelis require acknowledgement from the Palestinians that Israel is not entirely responsible for the creation of the refugee problem, as it did not initiate the hostilities in 1948. Third, Israelis require guarantees that a permanent status agreement on refugees will bring an end to all refugee claims against Israel.

Clashing Narratives and Needs

The two sides have great difficulty with each other's narratives and the intangible needs embedded in them. The Palestinians have difficulty recognizing Israel as a Jewish State for numerous reasons, including: 1. recognition could be seen to legitimize the 'catastrophe' that befell the Palestinians; 2. it could have serious implications for other issues, including the disposition of Holy Sites, under negotiation;[9] and 3. it could legitimize and intensify discrimination against fellow Palestinians who are Israeli citizens, as non-Jews in a Jewish state. Furthermore, the right-wing discourse within Israel positions the recognition of the Jewish state as explicitly blocking the right of return. In addition Palestinians are opposed to accepting any responsibility whatsoever for the creation of their own refugee problem. From their perspective, asking them to do so is tantamount to blaming them for their own national tragedy. Palestinians send mixed responses to the Israeli 'end of claims' demand: Palestinian Authority (PA) officials assert that a Palestinian state would have the authority to meet Israeli requirements while refugee advocates stress that the rights to return and compensation are individual rights that cannot be negotiated away.

For their part, Israelis believe that acknowledgement of the right of return, followed by unlimited or unconditional practical implementation, would lead to the end of Israel as a Jewish state. Most Israelis believe there is no morally- or legally-based 'right of return', and offer a legal interpretation of UN General Assembly Resolution 194 that renders it little more than an obsolete, non-binding recommendation. Recognizing the right of return in principle only, with limits on actual return, is also fraught with difficulty for Israelis. It would lead to questions surrounding Israel's role in the creation of the refugee problem, and concerns regarding future legal claims from individuals. Even if the future Palestinian state were to accept limits on return in a peace treaty, Israelis doubt whether the refugees themselves would accept this decision and worry that such an agreement could be undermined in the courts. Even expressing regret for Palestinian refugee suffering is problematic, given the lack of internal consensus surrounding Israel's responsibility for that suffering.

This aspect of the conflict cuts to the core of both sides' sense of victimhood as well as to their original narratives and beliefs: Palestinians believe they have been dealt a historical injustice while Israelis believe a varying combination of: 1. having had no choice but to go to war to defend themselves and create a state for the Jewish people; and 2. having a historical and religious right to the land. The political discourse as presented appears unbridgeable.

Furthermore, there are of course connections between the intangible needs described above and the 'real' world. While the right of return may or may not be something that most Palestinians would plan to exercise, from an Israeli perspective the prospect of large numbers of Palestinians returning to Israel would be very tangible indeed. Acknowledgement, in Palestinian discourse, is presented as a matter of dignity, justice and vindication but it is seen on the Israeli side as opening the door to claims and litigation by Palestinians unsatisfied with whatever compensation and solutions package emerges from the negotiation. The Palestinian insistence on Israeli participation in resolving the refugee issue has intensely practical consequences.

On the other hand, as mentioned above, the Israeli demand for recognition by Palestine as a Jewish state to satisfy Israelis' longing for regional acceptance and legitimacy is feared by the Palestinians as a ploy to block return and a device that could provide the Israelis with justification for degrading the situation of the Israeli Arabs and perhaps even transferring them and the communities they inhabit to the Palestinian state. In this regard, an alternative concept, for example Israel as the *homeland* of the Jewish people, may well provide a less exclusionary formulation. The Israeli requirement for a Palestinian acknowledgement that Israel did not start the war in 1948 is increasingly contested by Palestinian historians. These choose to focus on the roots of the conflict – the arrival of the first Zionist pioneers in the late 1800s. And of course, the Israeli insistence that the peace treaty lead to an end of claims is based on very pragmatic considerations.

There is no doubt that addressing intangible needs will also have implications on tangible and concrete matters, and that the implications of recognition at the intangible level need to be examined in all its complexities and at all levels. However, this linkage can also become an excuse to avoid agreement, and create an irresolvable conundrum on this critical issue.

Examined in this light, there would seem to be little hope for reaching agreement on these matters. Indeed, for the Palestinians the term 'right of return' has become of paramount importance. The right of return provides a bridge between the Palestinian need for moral acknowledgement and their quest for a rights-based solution. Its dual nature complicates the search for resolution. There is little likelihood of Israeli agreement to the actual return of any more than just token numbers but if the issue is seen as a Palestinian intangible need rather than a practical one then there may be more room for accommodation. The 2003 survey of Palestinian refugee attitudes by the Palestinian Center for Policy and Survey Research (PSR) provided an interesting insight. According to the survey conducted in the West Bank, Gaza, Jordan and Lebanon, although only 10 per cent of those surveyed indicated their intent to return, 95 per cent characterized the right of return as a sacred right that could not be abandoned.[10]

While this contradiction may not be resolvable through an insistence on defining and re-understanding the past, it may be advanced through greater understanding of the lingering intangible needs of both sides today that lie behind the discourse. Before investigating this possibility, it is useful to examine how these matters were dealt with during past negotiations.

The Refugee Issue and the Peace Process

Attempts have been made to tackle these issues in the course of the peace process but no agreement has been reached. Over time, there has been some evolution in dealing with the intangible dimension of the refugee question in both official and unofficial negotiations and proposals. The peace process that began in 1991 at the Madrid Peace Conference, followed by the Oslo Accords, initially focused on confidence building, and dealing with borders and security, leaving the most difficult core issues of Jerusalem and the refugees to the end. Yet, if one examines the chronology of the negotiation through Camp David, Taba and beyond, an attempt to bridge the refugee issue can be perceived. In addition, there was an increasing realization of the refugee question's critical role in achieving an end of conflict.

A review of the peace process from a refugee perspective reveals three phases. Phase I, which was marked by the processes launched by the Oslo Accords and the Madrid Peace Conference of 1991, involved the structural development of the general peace process, and a confidence building approach where the refugee issue was mentioned but left to the end of negotiations.

During Phase II, beginning with the Beilin-Abu Mazen Plan, through the Camp David negotiations, and ending with Taba, the refugee issue began to be examined in all its elements, including the intangible dimension. The need to resolve the refugee question began to be understood as necessary for an end of conflict and claims; the most difficult talks revolved around the right of return, its recognition, limits and its consequences. This right is of course embedded in the rights-based approach of Palestinians; however, it also has a significant degree of intangible demand for the Palestinians as a recognition of loss in the past and the right for redress. It is therefore seen as a reflection of the legitimacy of the Palestinian people, their narrative and their historical experience. Agreement on language regarding the right of return has however eluded negotiators.

The idea of a right of return to the Palestinian state, and relatedly, an assertion that a two-state solution implied this, is an important development in the talks of this period. Furthermore, there are many examples from this phase of exploration of some form of acknowledgement by Israel of the suffering of the refugees, if not of responsibility for their plight.

The third phase, which arose out of the second Intifada, produced a sporadic and inconsistent set of proposals. The Arab Peace Initiative focused on principles, the Geneva Accord on practical implementation, and Prime Minister Olmert's statements hinted at acknowledging the intangible dimension. However, although the Geneva Accord is a very comprehensive and detailed document, none of the proposals of this period dealt head-on with the historical issues (acknowledgement) or the right of return, as had been the case during the actual negotiation period of the mid to late 1990s and 2000.

The following is an overview of the major negotiations and proposals related to the peace process between 1991 and today. (It is not exhaustive, but deals with pertinent and major events in the process.) This review provides policymakers with a map of how the issue was dealt with and what proposals were made, in the hope that it might inform future talks. It also provides a chronology of the evolution of positions on the issue. (See Annex 9.B for extracts from the various documents)

The Early Peace Process (1991–94)

The Refugee Working Group: The Refugee Working Group (RWG) was established in January 1992 at the Moscow Conference, which launched a five-track Multilateral Peace Process, following the launch of bilateral talks in Madrid in October 1991. In general, the multilateral tracks were aimed at promoting long-term regional development and security, and focused on environment, water issues, economic development, arms control and regional security, as well as the refugee question.

The RWG was not mandated to deal with core dimensions of the issue – tangible or intangible – and focused instead on the improvement of refugee camp conditions and family reunification. One of its stated parameters was 'supporting the process of achieving a viable and comprehensive solution to the refugee issue,' which could be read to include broader political issues, however, the understanding was that the core of the refugee question was a final status issue to be resolved through bilateral (Israeli–Palestinian) negotiations. The RWG met eight times from 1992–95 and ceased activity following the collapse of the Camp David talks.

The Oslo Accords (September 1993): The Oslo Accords also defined the question of the 1948 refugees as a final status issue to be resolved at the end of the negotiations process. Therefore, this process did not deal with refugees, neither in the text of the Accords nor in the Oslo process of the 1990s. It did, however, provide that persons displaced as a result of the 1967 war should be allowed to return to the West Bank and Gaza during the interim period and established the Quadripartite Committee to work out the modalities.

The Quadripartite Committee: This committee established by the Oslo process, consisting of Israel, Jordan, Egypt and the Palestinians, who first met in 1995 to discuss the procedures for re-admission of those displaced from the West Bank and Gaza in 1967. This forum focused, unsuccessfully, on practical measures only.

Israel–Jordan Peace Treaty (1994): The Treaty of Wadi Araba states that, regarding the refugee question, the case of displaced persons should be dealt with in the Quadripartite Committee and, in the case of other refugees, through the RWG or in bilateral negotiations as part of permanent status negotiations. No mention was made of how the issue, including its intangible aspects, should be dealt with.

Until this stage, the peace process had not begun to focus on the core issues let alone how to resolve them therefore the intangible aspect of the refugee question, one of the most difficult at hand, was not addressed.

Proposals and Negotiations on Core Issues (1995–2001)

Beilin-Abu Mazen Plan (October 1995): Headed by Yossi Beilin and Abu Mazen, these informal talks attempted, among other goals, to create a joint narrative of the events of 1947–48. The refugee clauses of the document that emerged represent the first instance of negotiators from the two sides attempting to come to grips with the intangible issues.

Palestinians reaffirmed the right of return while recognizing that new realities, i.e. Israel, and the demands of peace render its full implementation impracticable. Israelis recognized the 'moral and material' suffering of the refugees as well as the Palestinian refugees' right of return *to the Palestinian state* and their right to compensation and rehabilitation for moral and material losses.

This proposal represents a big step towards the mutual recognition of intangible needs, while placing conditions based on today's realities. There is a strong attempt at reciprocity on core issues between the sides and an awareness of the intangible dimension. The plan deals head-on with the right of return while at the same time defining its limits in practice: return to the Palestinian state but not to Israel, except for family reunification and refugees in specially defined cases.

The last clause of the plan also states that the PLO considers the implementation of the refugee chapter to be a full and final settlement of the refugee issue and that there will be no additional or further claims – an important demand for Israel. This plan was never adopted and, once leaked, was repudiated by some of the authors.

The Core Group Track II Process (July, 1999): A Track II effort on refugees, involving Israelis and Palestinians and led by a Canadian–British team developed a document regarding refugees that fed into the process of formal negotiations a year or two later at Camp David and Taba. Specifically, the document focused on the 'human tragedy' with both parties acknowledging that an end of conflict requires recognition of the suffering inflicted on the peoples of the region and the need to move beyond the past. Importantly, it also states that 'with regard to the Palestinian refugees, the experience of involuntary exile has been central to the Palestinians national narrative.'

Furthermore, it states that both parties recognize and regret that forced displacement does occur in conflict and that it constitutes an unacceptable practice that is in violation of human rights and international law. The Core Group document indicates that the right of return will be primarily achieved through 'voluntary repatriation' to the Palestinian state, and that Israel shall admit a number to be negotiated between Israel and Palestine, but that all applications of admission will be dealt with by Israel on a case-by-case basis.

This document goes some distance to addressing the intangible dimension. It focuses squarely on the tragedy in the past and the need to recognize it and move on. Its use of the term 'both parties' is an attempt at creative ambiguity, however, it presumes a common understanding and symmetry regarding the past that may not exist, and does not sufficiently articulate the experience and needs of each side as they stand today.

Camp David (July 2000): The negotiations at Camp David achieved a measure of agreement on several mechanisms relating to technical questions on refugees, however, no progress was made on acknowledgement and the right of return. Responsibility for the refugee problem was rejected by the Israeli side, despite a willingness to offer private expressions of sorrow for the refugees' plight, but without accepting national Israeli responsibility. Fundamentally, the Camp David talks failed to deal with the refugee issue in depth. Since the Israeli side refused to acknowledge responsibility for the creation of the refugee problem in 1947–49, there could be no discussion of related issues of moral acknowledgement and other intangibles.

The Clinton Parameters (December 2000): The Clinton Parameters contain conclusions arrived at by President Clinton after Camp David regarding the major issues which comprise the Israeli–Palestinian conflict.[11] The President noted that the differences over the resolution of the refugee problem are, to quote from the document, 'more relating to formulations and less to what will happen on a practical level.' This speaks of the importance of framing solutions which move forward to satisfy the intangible needs of the parties. More specifically, regarding intangibles, he stated his belief that 'Israel is prepared to acknowledge the moral and material suffering caused to the Palestinian people as a result of the 1948 war and the need to assist the international community in addressing the problem.' He further stated that this could only occur if there was an agreement that Israel would remain a predominantly Jewish state in the context of a two-state solution, and that this step would not override Israel's sovereign prerogatives.

The document suggests two formulations of recognition of the right of return:

- Both sides recognize the right of Palestinian refugees to return to 'historic Palestine'; or
- Both sides recognize the right of Palestinian refugees to return to their homeland.

The Parameters then make a clear and unequivocal link between the two-state solution and the right of return:

> The solution will have to be consistent with the two-state approach – the state of Palestine as the homeland of the Palestinian people and the state of Israel as the homeland of the Jewish people. ... Under the two-state solution, the guiding principle should be that the Palestinian state should be the focal point for the Palestinians who choose to return to the area without ruling out that Israel will accept some of these refugees.[12]

As with the Beilin-Abu Mazen Plan, the Clinton Parameters hinge on recognizing clearly the needs of both sides, including the right of return, while mitigating and conditioning this recognition with today's realities. There was no agreement reached by the two parties on this document, however, it is widely recognized today as a powerful point of reference for resolving the core issues.

Taba (January 2001): What has been presented in the media regarding discussions on refugees in Taba is based on third-party reports and separate Israeli and Palestinian position papers. These suggest that the negotiations at Taba represent some important breakthroughs on the Palestinian refugee issue.

The Palestinian paper (see Annex 9.B) seeks Israeli acknowledgement of 'its moral and legal responsibility for the forced displacement and dispossession' of the Palestinians. It reiterates the traditional position regarding recognition of the right of return according to international law, and places the responsibility for the resolution of the problem squarely on Israel. Interestingly, there is an emphasis on the status of the Palestinian refugees in Lebanon and the resolution of their situation as a priority.

Participants acknowledged discussing the issue's historical facts, and developing a 'willingness to respect and examine the conflicting... narratives without necessarily accepting them in full.'[13] This resulted in the Palestinian delegation believing that a 'conceptual understanding' had been reached regarding Israel's responsibility for the Palestinian refugee problem.[14] The parties attempted, and abandoned, efforts to focus on the narrative, finding the issue too divisive, and preferring instead to build a sense of common purpose and forward momentum by switching to technical and mechanism issues. Despite significant progress on the issues of compensation, resettlement and technical matters, ultimately no progress was achieved on the issues of acknowledgement, right of return and recognition.[15] Without having this intangible need addressed, the Palestinian delegation was unwilling to conclude the practical issues under consideration.

The Israeli Response Paper (see Annex 9.B) 'solemnly expresses sorrow' for the refugee tragedy and a readiness to actively end their plight, including a reflection on the historical events that created the problem, without accepting responsibility. It also refers to the refugees' 'wish to return' and that it will be implemented 'in a manner consistent with the existence of the State of Israel as the homeland for Jewish people, and the establishment of the State of Palestine as the homeland of the Palestinian people'. The Israeli response reviewed the five Clinton solutions and offered a 'capped to an agreed limit of XX refugees, and with priority being accorded to those Palestinian refugees currently resident in Lebanon'.

Indeed, the Taba documents do provide significant language regarding acknowledgement of a historical trauma, however, the Israeli language on the right of return is vague, and a step further away from previous discussions. It is also important to realize that the positions put forward by the Israelis at Taba were never officially sanctioned, nor did they represent the views of the full Israeli negotiation team. Nevertheless, Taba does represent the most comprehensive and detailed official discussions of the refugee issue to date, including to a considerable degree, the intangible element.

Proposals During the 2000s

The Arab Peace Initiative (March 2003): The significance of the Arab Peace Initiative (API) regarding the refugee question is due to its call for a 'just resolution of the refugee issue to be *agreed upon* in accordance with UN General Assembly Resolution 194' which leaves the door open for a negotiated agreement that takes into account both Israeli and Palestinian interests, while embedding the issue in international resolutions.[16] The API serves as an important set of principles, however, since its introduction in 2002, the initiative has only been discussed sporadically and has failed to gain significant political traction. Despite its conditional approach, and an acknowledgement by the Arabs that the refugee solution must be 'agreed upon', i.e. negotiated, the refugee clause continues to be the most problematic for Israelis. More detail regarding the meaning of this clause will be required in order to begin further discussions.

The Geneva Accord (December 2003): The Geneva Accord was an unofficial 'Track Two' initiative by individual Israelis and Palestinians, and not any form of official negotiation. It includes provisions for 'commemoration of the refugee experience' as well as an entire section on 'Reconciliation Programs' i.e. to address issues of narratives. However, it avoided the issue of Israeli responsibility for the refugee problem, opting instead to focus on the practical solutions for improving the lives of refugees and creating mechanisms to resolve other practical issues in the event of peace. The Accord also suggested mechanisms through which the parties could address their conflicting historical narratives towards enhancing a common understanding of the past, i.e. it encourages the processes required rather than the actual formulations regarding these issues. It also skirts the question of the right of return, and instead simply refers to the API and UN Security Council Resolution 242, as the basis for resolving the issue.

There is no Israeli statement acknowledging the history, trauma or the plight of the refugees. In some ways, the Geneva Accord represents a step backwards from previous discussions in terms of the intangible question. Instead, it offers a highly practical approach that focuses on 'informed choice' on the part of the refugees.

Annapolis (November 2007): The Annapolis meeting involving regional and international heads of state and government produced an interesting statement from the Israeli Prime Minister Ehud Olmert who, addressing President Abbas, stated: 'your people, too, have suffered for many years; and there are some who still suffer … in neglect, alienation, bitterness, and a deep, unrelenting sense of humiliation.' While stopping short of acknowledging Israel's role in the refugee experience, these comments could be construed as progress towards moral acknowledgement, as few – if any – such statements had been made publicly by senior Israel leaders before.

The evolution of the process over the last two decades reveals that while no agreement has been reached, the talks and proposals have tended towards a recognition that the issue of acknowledgement of the trauma of the past as well as the right of return in some form needs to be part of an end of conflict. Similarly, proposals reflect that Palestinian concerns should also take into consideration the existence today and nature of the State of Israel.

Why Failure?

There are many factors that have played into the failure of negotiations between Israelis and Palestinians. With regard to the refugee issue, the intangible dynamics of the conflict and the existential questions of identity, combined with chronic levels of distrust, present a large burden to negotiators. The issue is therefore either ignored or deferred. As a result, over time, both sides have become accustomed to their profound intangible needs being unmet, and despair of any other possible outcome. This state of chronic distrust and talks based on trade-offs, rather than gestures and understandings, stand in the way of alternatives that might have a better chance of success.

Relatedly, the political will and courageous leadership required to deal with these kinds of issues are uncommon. The political risks involved, including reactions from more radical groups against leaders, are considerable. Few political leaders are capable of perceiving the value of recognizing the other side's intangible needs or are ready to go beyond the political obstacles and face the inevitable reactions within their own societies. Recognition by leaders on both sides that dealing with these issues will take both populations and the peace-making process to new and constructive terrain, has been absent so far.

However, in this chapter, we would like to focus on another cause of failure which relates to the very nature of the negotiations. Our research and discussions, which we have had with negotiators, indicate that violent opposition to compromise over issues people consider sacred actually increases when material incentives to compromise are offered. 'Support for violence decreases ... when an adversary makes symbolic gestures that show recognition of other's core values.'[17] Negotiations between Israelis and Palestinians tend to be 'hard-nosed', seeking zero-sum victories and shying away from such approaches. 'Classic' or traditional negotiations and bartering may be well-developed political habits but they may not be appropriate methods of navigating intangible needs rooted in the sensitive aspects of any people's existence. The intangible needs may have been viewed either as interests to be traded for tangible concerns, or as items to be traded against each other. However, neither side can trade them away as 'interests' and both reject any compromise on what are in fact the pillars of their identities and of their understanding of their own histories.

Implications: Both sides remain deeply concerned about the legal and material implications of any recognition of the others intangible needs. Israelis fear that such recognition will not eliminate the risk of further claims; and Palestinians see no reason why they should be required to define the nature of the state of Israel, and are concerned about the implications for Palestinians inside Israel and for the right of return. Negotiations regarding these issues become instantly politicized with questions regarding material and legal implications, i.e. intangibles are rapidly linked in the minds of people on both sides with tangible implications. Furthermore, the discourse is hobbled by reflex reactions to terms such as 'the right of return' or 'the Jewish state'.

Above all, the difficulty is precisely because of how painfully the issues resonate in both societies. The question is whether, despite the obstacles, negotiators and leaders can look to new approaches to resolve this matter and achieve a lasting end of conflict.

Possible Options

The options for dealing (or not) with the intangible barriers to resolving the refugee issue need to be considered in conjunction with the practical proposals presented in the other chapters of this volume.

These two aspects of negotiations will impact on each other and with the solutions proposed for other final status issues. It is not unreasonable to assume that generous offers to refugees in terms of compensation and personal choices could impact on what will be required in terms of acknowledgement, apology and the right of return.

Avoiding the Intangible Needs of Both Sides

After the end of conflicts such as those experienced in Lebanon and Mozambique, the intangible aspect of the problem was ignored in the development of a solution. Avoidance of dealing with intangibles is most often a result of the apparent difficulty of identifying the intangible dimension, crafting a suitable solution, and certainly being ready to acknowledge the needs of a former enemy.

These factors, plus the lack of experience among policymakers in dealing with such matters, could lead some to surmise that addressing the Palestinians' needs regarding acknowledgement and the right of return and the Israeli demand for recognition of the Jewish state are simply too difficult and best ignored.

It is possible that an exceptionally generous package of compensation combined with real and attractive choices for the refugees regarding where and under what conditions they will ultimately reside, reinforced by heavy international involvement in meeting the material needs of the refugees, the new Palestinian state and the host countries (Jordan, Syria and Lebanon) and the security needs of Israel, would make it possible to conclude an agreement. Certainly, dealing with concrete needs and differences has the advantage of being more manageable in the negotiation process and more likely to provide a clear deal. Whether a durable deal between Israel and Palestine can be reached without directly dealing with the long-held Palestinian demand for a rights-based solution and acknowledgement of their plight, and with the Israeli demand for regional acceptance and legitimacy, is open to question.

Attending to Intangibles after Agreement

In South Africa, truth and reconciliation commissions were set up after a political agreement had been achieved. This process was intended to attend to the intangible claims and the history of conflict and suffering once a deal was complete and all sides knew peace was at hand.

This approach has the virtue of providing for a healing process that is not bound to the negotiations time-frame. It has the advantage of being implemented on the basis of an existing peace agreement and the calm established thereafter. In the case of the refugee issue, an environment where the compensation and personal solutions arrangements are rolling out and people can see the results and positive changes in their lives, would ease the task of, for example, a joint commission charged with examining the historical record, promoting reconciliation and creating monuments, ceremonies and the like to acknowledge the past and permit people to move on.

This approach may be useful in the case of the Israeli–Palestinian conflict given the large gap of understanding of narratives between the sides, as well as the amount of time likely to be required for the public on both sides to come to terms with the history and the needs of the other.

Furthermore, the long duration of the peace process in the Middle East has nevertheless engendered a large cadre of knowledgeable and experienced peace-builders and members of civil society who can be tapped in the future to lead and implement a reconciliation process. Again, this approach does not attend to the possible need for intangibles to be directly part of the political solution to the problem, i.e. there may be no deal without addressing the intangible factors.

Diluted Responses

It may very well be that, for political reasons, each side in a conflict might only be able to provide a diluted or weak form of response to the intangible need of the other. Between Israelis and Palestinians, this may be formulated as an Israeli response that recognizes Palestinian suffering in general, and provides an acknowledgement that the creation of Israel had dire consequences for the Palestinians without articulating an Israeli role or responsibility, nor an apology. Likewise, Palestinians may simply, for example, recognize the presence of the Jews in Israel, without recognizing Israel as homeland of the Jewish people or specifically as a Jewish state.

It may be useful at this point to draw an important distinction between acknowledgement – as used here – and apology. Acknowledgement by the state is a process of recognition of past wrongs and the effects of those wrongs. It may be carried out through a number of mechanisms including, but not limited to: public statements, commemorative ceremonies and erecting of monuments. An official apology, in contrast, consists of a statement on the part of government admitting that the state has committed a wrong accompanied by an expression of regret. To be sure, acknowledgement and apology are often part of the same process; it is nevertheless important to establish that the two can exist separately. (Examples of official acknowledgements and apologies can be found in Annex 9.A).

Whether such partial responses are useful or counterproductive is a necessary question to be asked. It may well be that a statement that does not address the need of the other sufficiently, or which is viewed as an attempt to avoid responsibility or recognition of legitimacy, might result in more damage than good. In other words, it may very well be that a diluted response to the question of intangibles might create further antagonism: all will hinge on whether the language used does attend sufficiently to the need of the other side and on how the other elements of both the refugee agreement and the other final status issue are perceived by both sides. As with the two preceding options, the perceived generosity of the compensation and personal solutions packages and the support offered by the international community to Palestine and the host countries in managing the transition to peace and end of the refugee issue will be critical.

These three options are real and possible roads that negotiators may take given the difficulties experienced in the past in dealing with these issues in the Israeli–Palestinian conflict, and the ongoing intransigence of both sides in recognizing the needs of the other. They may very well be valid approaches if this conflict is not being perpetuated due to intangible needs not being met, i.e. if it is simply a question of states, borders and security arrangements, or if an agreement without intangibles can withstand the backlash sufficiently to permit a longer-term reconciliation process to deliver its benefits.

The Fourth Option: Tackling the Intangibles Head-on

An approach that departs from past experience and that yet may prove useful is to treat intangible needs as the baseline for successful political negotiations, rather than deferring them until they become a last-minute crisis in the negotiations.

It might be useful to explore the recognition of symbolic or intangible elements of both sides' needs as the basis for discussions before entering too deeply into the political negotiations. If the two sides and the mediator can map out these needs, painful though it may be, they can form an idea of the kinds of gestures and statements that will need to be produced at the end of the negotiation process. These can then be put aside and revisited once the practical elements of the peace agreement have been resolved.

This is difficult business, but if the Israelis know that, for example, an acknowledgement of Israel as the homeland of the Jewish people is waiting at the end of the process and the Palestinians can see how acknowledgement of their suffering and of the right of return will be in some way satisfied at the end as well, then a great deal of the tension and uncertainty will be removed from the rest of the process.

Practically, this baseline means the following: if Israelis can recognize the natural Palestinian need for redress of past wrongs, suffering and displacement, from that might evolve an acknowledgement of the trauma of the Palestinian people and Palestinian refugees in particular, and of the suffering since 1948 as well as possibly the right of return *as a principle*. In parallel, if the Palestinians can recognize the Israelis' need for legitimacy and belonging in the region, from that, a recognition of a Jewish homeland in the Middle East might evolve.

It is also possible that this early baseline recognition might calm the sides sufficiently to permit less draconian demands at the practical level, i.e. once this is achieved, Israelis might be more ready to recognize the right of return in principle and, Palestinians will have less need for the practical implementation of the right of return. The extent to which these intangible issues have often thwarted progress in previous negotiations is instructive. There is reason to expect that the further the two sides are willing to go in accommodating each other's symbolic or intangible needs, the easier it will be to resolve practical and material issues.

Furthermore, language is critical in this regard and formulations still matter. Possible solutions may lie in language such as:

- An Israeli acknowledgement of, or an apology for, the suffering from the events of 1948;
- A Palestinian recognition of Israel as the homeland of the Jewish people.

These terms are not the same as the right of return or recognition of a Jewish state. Furthermore, these suggested formulations, buttressed by practical solutions, may have the virtue of being both sufficient in meeting the intangible needs and being politically achievable by avoiding the political reflexes that have mustered around the terms 'right of return' and 'Jewish state'.

It is important to understand that while the 'intangibles' need to be explored at the start of the process, they can only be deployed once the package as a whole has been agreed. If Israel meets the symbolic and practical needs of the Palestinians on the refugee file, its image in the eyes of the Arabs will be transformed, permitting it to become an acceptable member of the Middle East family of nations. If the Palestinians acknowledge Israel as homeland of the Jewish people, it will send a powerful message that would go far to reducing Israeli fears of the right of return. Dealing with the two sets of intangible needs in tandem provides both sides with the confidence to move forward positively.

Managing the intangible dimension by itself in the context of negotiations must be recognized as providing direct benefits for both sides, instead of being a Pandora's Box and an excuse for the pursuit or avoidance of material claims. The value of the acknowledgement is in the very effect of achieving a readiness to compromise and create breakthroughs by demonstrating respect of this kind to the other side by recognizing its core values. The need to deal differently between meeting intangible needs (in themselves) and negotiating practical interests is critical to the success of this approach and hinges on the recognition that this step has a direct benefit in itself: it meets a core need for each side and permits them to move towards peace.

Conclusions and Implications for Negotiations

This chapter has attempted to outline the intangible barriers that have prevented Palestinians and Israelis from reaching an accommodation on the complex Palestinian refugee issue. Its purpose is primarily to elucidate this issue in the interest of advancing a complex but untapped approach to the resolution of the conflict. The idea presented here is that behind the discourses and the narratives are actual needs on each side – emotional, symbolic and sacred – that, if left unmet, could propagate conflict and that, if met, might open a new road and methodology of conflict resolution.

Specifically, the Palestinian need for recognition of their trauma and their national tragedy, through acknowledgement, and the Israeli need for a sense of legitimacy and belonging in the Middle East through recognition of Israel as the homeland of the Jewish people are intangible dimensions of the conflict that stand in the way of a complete and sustainable resolution.

Successfully managing these intangible dimensions of a conflict remains a challenge however, and may also require new approaches and new criteria in the process of negotiations. There are several preliminary lessons that may be offered for future negotiators and interested parties on how to deal with these critical elements:

1. Powerful intangible requirements exist on both sides and in a sense precede and often even motivate more concrete political issues. These unmet demands do not permit compromise unless they are directly satisfied. Making an inventory of them may help the positive evolution of negotiations.

2. With the exception of Taba, where an effort to tackle the intangibles was abandoned when it was found to be too difficult, bypassing the intangible issues that divide Palestinians and Israelis has been the dominant and unsuccessful approach since the creation of the Palestinian refugee problem. Delving into these issues will be painful but there is no reason to believe that future efforts could not succeed if a new approach is tried.

3. While intangible needs and tangible solutions are intertwined, efforts to address historic injuries and present fears through practical measures alone will do more harm than good. Intangible needs must be dealt with for their own sake as a critical human need of each group. They can also be viewed as a baseline of recognition between the sides that reduce the tensions, begin to rebuild trust

and facilitate the remainder of the negotiation process. *Therefore, counterintuitively, they need to be dealt with first, not last.*

4. The dominant Israeli and Western approach which has emphasized concentrating on compensation and practical arrangements (return, local integration in the host countries and third country resettlement) has not succeeded because it ignores what is most important to the refugees themselves – acknowledgement of the harm done to them and recognition of their right to return.

The dominant Palestinian and Arab approach which emphasizes the refugees' and Palestinian rights under international law has not succeeded because it glosses over the impact that full implementation of these rights would have on the Israelis and their understanding of their history. The interpretation of international law put forward by the Palestinian side was itself contested.

5. It is important to avoid the trap of implying that the intangible needs of each side are either equivalent or more or less important. There is no way to assign value or weight to a people's longings, grievances, fears or aspirations. It is sufficient to acknowledge their importance to the people concerned.

Beyond these possible lessons for negotiations, at the end of the day, Israelis need to recognize the Palestinian need for redress of past wrongs and suffering, loss and displacement. From that an acknowledgement of the Palestinian tragedy of 1948 and perhaps recognition of the right of return in principle might evolve. In parallel, Palestinians need to recognize Israelis' need for legitimacy and belonging in the Middle East. From that, a recognition of the need for a Jewish homeland might evolve.

These actions are not identical to recognizing a Jewish state and the right of return – issues that appear to be in direct contradiction and that are unlikely to result in agreement. Instead, the approach proposed above might achieve an acceptable level of satisfaction for each side without any threat to their narrative. As such, they could greatly facilitate an end of conflict and an agreement.

Despite the propensities of both sides, this issue will not go away. Given that the refugee issue comprises such sensitive aspects of the Palestinian people's existence, including their identity, humanity and legitimacy, persistent lack of resolution will continue to exacerbate the obstacles leading to the resolution of both the refugee issue and the larger conflict. Dealing with this matter in new and innovative ways that have not been attempted may unlock apparently intractable positions, permitting an advancement towards peace that today seems illusory.

ANNEX 9.A
Case Examples of Public Acknowledgement and Apology

US Acknowledgement of Japanese Americans Interned During World War II and Japanese Acknowledgement of the Experience of the Korean Comfort Women

The case of the victims of Japanese internment camps in the United States during World War II provides an example of the successful use of moral acknowledgement in conjunction with material amends. After significant and mounting political pressure, the US Congress passed the Civil Liberties Act of 1988. The Act provided for US$1.2 billion in compensation to the families that had been interned, and, most significantly, a simultaneous presidential apology to be made to each of the victims individually. While the events of the internment were not contested, for the most part, many still framed the internment as a measure of means of protection for Japanese Americans from their neighbours. The contents of the apology acknowledged, unequivocally, the fact that the wartime practices were wrong and unjust.[18] This dimension was equally important as material compensation; in fact, it is precisely this combination of elements that categorizes the Japanese American case as a successful example of moral acknowledgement combined with reparation.

In the case of the Korean comfort women, acknowledgement of the injustice that had occurred was, arguably, all the more important because historically the position of the Japanese government was that no transgression had occurred. In order to proceed with moral reparation, it was necessary to first establish an account of what had transpired. This required difficult transactions between the state, advocacy groups and the general public. In this case, the process of addressing the intangible needs had to precede the material compensation in order to be perceived as acceptable by victims and advocates.[19] Unfortunately, no such process was undertaken to achieve moral reparation. Instead, the formal action by the Japanese government was to establish the Asian Women's Fund in support of comfort women with no specific acknowledgement of Japan's role in the problem. The fact that the Fund was designed to meet the socio-economic (material) needs of victimized women was overshadowed by the sense, among the victims, that the government was evading responsibility. Ultimately, many women refused the payments and the issue remains unresolved.[20]

It is difficult – if at all possible – to draw useful and justifiable comparisons between various cases where it concerns moral acknowledgement and reparation. Such cases do, however, serve to introduce points of analytical and practical significance when considering the applicability of moral acknowledgement in general. Indeed, the case of the Palestinian refugees, like all examples, has unique dimensions that require a specific analysis and understanding of the political history.

Government of Canada Apology to Japanese Canadians Interned During World War II

'I know that I speak for Members on all sides of the House today in offering to Japanese Canadians the formal and sincere apology of this Parliament for those past injustices against them, against their families, and against their heritage, and our solemn commitment and undertaking to Canadians of every origin that such violations will never again in this country be countenanced or repeated [...] No amount of money can right the wrong, undo the harm and heal the wounds.'

US Government Apology to the Japanese Americans Interned During World War II

'I offer sincere apology to you for the actions that unfairly denied Japanese Americans and their families' fundamental liberties during World War II. In passing the Civil Liberties Act of 1988, we acknowledged the wrongs of the past and offered redress to those who endured such grave injustice. In retrospect, we understand that the nation's actions were rooted deeply in racial prejudice, wartime hysteria, and a lack of political leadership.'

Government of Australia Apology to the Aborigines

'Today we honour the Indigenous peoples of this land, the oldest continuing cultures in human history. We reflect on their past mistreatment. We reflect in particular on the mistreatment of those who were stolen generations – this blemished chapter in our nation's history. The time has now come for the nation to turn a new page in Australia's history by righting the wrongs of the past and so moving forward with confidence to the future. We apologise for the laws and policies of successive Parliaments and governments that have inflicted profound grief, suffering and loss on these our fellow Australians. We apologise especially for the removal of Aboriginal and Torres Strait Islander children from their families, their communities and their country […] We today take this first step by acknowledging the past and laying claim to a future that embraces all Australians.'

British Apology for the Events of 'Bloody Sunday'

'The Secretary of State for Northern Ireland is publishing the report of the Saville inquiry – the tribunal set up by the previous government to investigate the tragic events of 30 January 1972, a day more commonly known as Bloody Sunday. We have acted in good faith by publishing the tribunal's findings as soon as possible after the general election. Mr Speaker, I am deeply patriotic. I never want to believe anything bad about our country. I never want to call into question the behaviour of our soldiers and our army, who I believe to be the finest in the world. And I have seen for myself the very difficult and dangerous circumstances in which we ask our soldiers to serve. But the conclusions of this report are absolutely clear. There is no doubt, there is nothing equivocal, there are no ambiguities. What happened on Bloody Sunday was both unjustified and unjustifiable. It was wrong … Some members of our armed forces acted wrongly. The government is ultimately responsible for the conduct of the armed forces and for that, on behalf of the government, indeed, on behalf of our country, I am deeply sorry.'

Government of Canada Apology for the Head Tax Imposed on Chinese Immigrants

'Mr Speaker, I rise today to formally turn the page on an unfortunate period in Canada's past. One during which a group of people – who only sought to build a better life – was repeatedly and deliberately singled out for unjust treatment. I speak, of course, of the head tax that was imposed on Chinese immigrants to this country, as well as the other restrictive measures that followed. Beginning with the Chinese Immigration Act of 1885, a head tax of $50 was imposed on Chinese newcomers in an attempt to deter immigration. Not content with the tax's effect, the government subsequently raised the amount to $100 in 1900, and then to $500 – the equivalent of two years' wages – in 1903. This tax remained in place until 1923, when the government amended the Chinese Immigration Act and effectively banned most Chinese immigrants until 1947 ... The Government of Canada recognizes the stigma and exclusion experienced by the Chinese as a result. We acknowledge the high cost of the head tax meant many family members were left behind in China, never to be reunited, or that families lived apart and, in some cases, in poverty, for many years. We also recognize that our failure to truly acknowledge these historical injustices has led many in the community from seeing themselves as fully Canadian. Therefore, Mr Speaker, on behalf of all Canadians and the Government of Canada, we offer a full apology to Chinese Canadians for the head tax and express our deepest sorrow for the subsequent exclusion of Chinese immigrants.'

Government of Canada Apology to the Students of Indian Residential Schools

'To the approximately 80,000 living former students, and all family members and communities, the Government of Canada now recognizes that it was wrong to forcibly remove children from their homes and we apologize for having done this. We now recognize that it was wrong to separate children from rich and vibrant cultures and traditions, that it created a void in many lives and communities, and we apologize for having done this. We now recognize that, in separating children from their families, we undermined the ability of many to adequately parent their own children and sowed the seeds for generations to follow, and we apologize for having done this. We now recognize that, far too often, these institutions gave rise to abuse or neglect and were inadequately controlled, and we apologize for failing to protect you. Not only did you suffer these abuses as children, but as you became parents, you were powerless to protect your own children from suffering the same experience, and for this we are sorry.'

ANNEX 9.B
Excerpts from Documents Pertaining to the Palestinian Refugee Issue and its Attendant Intangible Issues

Beilin-Abu Mazin[21]

Article VII: Palestinian Refugees

1. Whereas the Palestinian side considers that the right of the Palestinian refugees to return to their homes is enshrined in international law and natural justice, it recognizes that the prerequisites of the new era of peace and coexistence, as well as the realities that have been created on the ground since 1948, have rendered the implementation of this right impracticable. The Palestinian side, thus, declares its readiness to accept and implement policies and measures that will ensure, insofar as this is possible, the welfare and well-being of these refugees.

2. Whereas the Israeli side acknowledges the moral and material suffering caused to the Palestinian people as a result of the war of 1947–1949. It further acknowledges the Palestinian refugees' right of return to the Palestinian state and their right to compensation and rehabilitation for moral and material losses.

3. The parties agree on the establishment of an International Commission for Palestinian Refugees (hereinafter 'the ICPR') for the final settlement of all aspects of the refugee issue as follows:

… The ICPR shall define the criteria for compensation accounting for:

(1) Moral loss; …

4. The ICPR shall be guided by the following principles in dealing with the 'refugees of 1948' and their descendants as defined in Annex Four to the Final Status Agreement:

a. Each refugee family shall be entitled to compensation for moral loss to a sum of money to be agreed upon by the ICPR …

5. The State of Israel undertakes to participate actively in implementing the program for the resolution of the refugee problem. Israel will

continue to enable family reunification and will absorb Palestinian refugees in special defined cases, to be agreed upon with the ICPR....

7. The PLO considers the implementation of the above a full and final settlement of the refugee issue in all its dimensions. It further undertakes that no additional claims or demands arising from this issue will be made upon the full implementation of this Framework Agreement.

The Core Group Track II Exercise

Extract from *Resolving the Refugee Issue: A Discussion Paper,* 1999.

6.0 Recognizing the Human Tragedy

6.1 Both parties agree that it will be difficult to bring the broader Arab–Israeli conflict to a close without a declarative recognition of the suffering inflicted during the conflict and acceptance of the need for the peoples of the region to move beyond the painful legacies of the past. The parties also acknowledge that, with regard to the Palestinian refugees, the experience of involuntary exile has been central to the Palestinian national narrative.

6.2 Therefore, both parties recognize, and profoundly regret, that forced displacement of civilian populations occurred during the conflict. The parties agree that forced displacement of civilian populations in times of conflict constitutes an unacceptable practice, in violation of both human rights and international law.

6.3 Furthermore, both parties accept their joint responsibility to resolve the refugee issue.

6.4 The parties understand the importance of encouraging Palestinian–Israeli reconciliation through joint historical research, educational initiatives, and other measures.

7.0 Conclusiveness

7.1 The two sides consider the section on Palestinian refugees in the permanent status agreement to be a full and final settlement of the refugee issue in all its aspects. No additional claims or demands arising from this issue will be made by either party upon the full implementation of the permanent status agreement.

Israeli Camp David Position[22]

Article 6: Refugees

71. 'The parties are cognizant of the suffering caused to individuals and communities during and following the 1948 war. Israel further recognizes the urgent need for a humane, just, and realistic settlement of the plight of the Palestinian Refugees within the context of terminating the Israeli–Palestinian conflict.'

73. The termination of the Palestinian refugee problem shall incorporate possible return to the State of Palestine, integration within Host Countries and immigration to other third countries.

74. In light of the new era of peace, the Palestinian Party recognizes that the Right of Return of Palestinian refugees shall apply solely to the State of Palestine. Israel recognizes the right of Palestinian refugees to return to the State of Palestine.

75. Israel shall, as a matter of its sovereign discretion, facilitate a phased entry of (XX) Palestinian Refugees to its territory on humanitarian grounds. These refugees shall be reunited with their families in their present place of residence in Israeli, accept Israeli citizenship and waive their legal status as refugees.

90. [...]. The State of Palestine shall view the implementation of this program as a final settlement of its national claim in this respect.

Clinton Parameters[23]

Refugees

I sense that the differences are more relating to formulations and less to what will happen on a practical level.

I believe that Israel is prepared to acknowledge the moral and material suffering caused to the Palestinian people as a result of the 1948 war and the need to assist the international community in addressing the problem.

The fundamental gap is on how to handle the concept of the right of return. I know the history of the issue and how hard it will be for the Palestinian leadership to appear to be abandoning the principle.

The Israeli side could not accept any reference to a right of return that would imply a right to immigrate to Israel in defiance of Israel's sovereign policies and admission or that would threaten the Jewish character of the state.

Any solution must address both needs

The solution will have to be consistent with the two-state approach – the state of Palestine as the homeland of the Palestinian people and the state of Israel as the homeland of the Jewish people.

Under the two-state solution, the guiding principle should be that the Palestinian state should be the focal point for the Palestinians who choose to return to the area without ruling out that Israel will accept some of these refugees.

I believe that we need to adopt a formulation on the right of return that will make clear that there is no specific right of return to Israel itself but that does not negate the aspiration of the Palestinian people to return to the area.

I propose two alternatives:

Both sides recognize the right of Palestinian refugees to return to 'historic Palestine' or
Both sides recognize the right of Palestinian refugees to return to their homeland.

The agreement will define the implementation of this general right in a way that is consistent with the two-state solution. It would list the five possible homes for the refugees:

- The State of Palestine;
- Areas in Israel being transferred to Palestine in the land swap;
- Rehabilitation in host country;
- Resettlement in third country;
- Admission to Israel.

In listing these options, the agreement will make clear that the return to the West Bank, Gaza Strip and area acquired in the land swap would be a right to all Palestinian refugees, while rehabilitation in host countries, resettlement in third countries and absorption into Israel will depend upon the policies of those countries.

Israel could indicate in the agreement that it intends to establish a policy so that some of the refugees would be absorbed into Israel consistent with Israeli sovereign decision.

I believe that priority should be given to the refugee population in Lebanon.

The parties would agree that this implements Resolution 194.

Palestinian Proposal on Palestinian Refugees at Taba[24]

Moral Responsibility

2. Israel recognizes its moral and legal responsibility for the forced displacement and dispossession of the Palestinian civilian population during the 1948 war and for preventing the refugees from returning to their homes in accordance with United Nations General Assembly Resolution 194.

3. Israel shall bear responsibility for the resolution of the refugee problem.

Right of Return

5. a. In accordance with United Nations General Assembly Resolution 194 (III), all refugees who wish to return to their homes in Israel and live at peace with their neighbors have the right to do so. The right of every refugee to return shall be exercised in accordance with the modalities set out in the Agreement.

End of Claims

60. The full implementation of this Article shall constitute a complete resolution of the refugee problem and shall end all claims emanating from that problem.

61. The right of each refugee in accordance with United Nations General Assembly Resolution 194 shall not be prejudiced until the refugee has exercised his right of return and received compensation under this Article or until the refugee has, based on his voluntary choice, received compensation and settled somewhere else.

Israeli Response to Palestinian Proposal

Narrative

2. The State of Israel solemnly expresses its sorrow for the tragedy of the Palestinian refugees, their suffering and losses, and will be an

active partner in ending this terrible chapter that was opened 53 years ago, contributing its part to the attainment of a comprehensive and fair solution to the Palestinian refugee problem.

3. For all those parties directly or indirectly responsible for the creation of the status of Palestinian refugeeism, as well as those for whom a just and stable peace in the region is an imperative, it is incumbent to take upon themselves responsibility to assist in resolving the Palestinian refugee problem of 1948.

4. Despite accepting the UNGAR 181 of November 1947, the emergent State of Israel became embroiled in the war and bloodshed of 1948–49, that led to victims and suffering on both sides, including the displacement and dispossession of the Palestinian civilian population who became refugees. These refugees spent decades without dignity, citizenship and property ever since.

5. Consequently, the solution to the refugee issue must address the needs and aspirations of the refugees, while accounting for the realities since the 1948–49 war. Thus, the wish to return shall be implemented in a manner consistent with the existence of the State of Israel as the homeland for Jewish people, and the establishment of the State of Palestine as the homeland of the Palestinian people.

6. A just settlement of the refugee problem in accordance with UNSCR 242 must lead to the implementation of UNGAR 194 (Palestinian Position).

7. Since 1948, the Palestinian yearning has been enshrined in the twin principles of the 'Right of Return' and the establishment of an independent Palestinian State deriving the basis from International Law. The realization of the aspirations of the Palestinian people, as recognized in this agreement, includes the exercise of their right to self-determination and a comprehensive and just solution for the Palestinian refugees, based on UNGAR 194, providing for their return and guaranteeing the future welfare and well-being of the refugees, thereby addressing the refugee problem in all its aspects.

8. Regarding return, repatriation and relocation, each refugee may apply to one of the following programs, thus fulfilling the relevant clause of UNGAR 194:

> a. To Israel – capped to an agreed limit of XX refugees, and with priority being accorded to those Palestinian refugees currently

resident in Lebanon. The State of Israel notes its moral commitment to the swift resolution of the plight of the refugee population of the Sabra and Shatila camps.

b. To Israeli swapped territory. For this purpose, the infrastructure shall be prepared for the absorption of refugees in the sovereign areas of the State of Israel that shall be turned over to Palestinian sovereignty in the context of an overall development program.

c. To the State of Palestine: the Palestinian refugees may exercise their return in an unrestricted manner to the State of Palestine, as the homeland of the Palestinian people, in accordance with its sovereign laws and legislation.

d. Rehabilitation within existing Host Countries. Where this option is exercised the rehabilitation shall be immediate and extensive.

e. Relocation to third countries: voluntary relocation to third countries expressing the willingness and capacity to absorb Palestinian refugees.

End of Claims

16. The Parties agree that the above constitutes a complete and final implementation of Article 11 of UNGAR 194 of 11th December 1948, and consider the implementation of the agreed programs and measures as detailed above constitute a full, final and irrevocable settlement of the Palestinian refugee issue in all its dimensions. No additional claims or demands arising from this issue shall be made by either Party. With the implementation of these articles there shall be no individuals qualified for the status of a Palestinian Refugee.

Moratino's Paper on the Taba Talks

3. Refugees

3.1 Narrative

The Israeli side put forward a suggested joint narrative for the tragedy of the Palestinian refugees. The Palestinian side discussed the proposed narrative and there was much progress, although no agreement was reached in an attempt to develop a historical narrative in the general text.

3.2 Return, Repatriation and Relocation and Rehabilitation

Both sides engaged in a discussion of the practicalities of resolving the refugee issue. The Palestinian side reiterated that the Palestinian refugees should have the right of return to their homes in accordance with the interpretation of UNGAR 194. The Israeli side expressed its understanding that the wish to return as per wording of UNGAR 194 shall be implemented within the framework of one of the following programmes:

A. Return and repatriation
1. to Israel
2. to Israel swapped territory
3. to the Palestine state.

B. Rehabilitation and relocation
1. Rehabilitation in host country.
2. Relocation to third country.

3.7 End of Claims

The issue of the end of claims was discussed, and it was suggested that the implementation of the agreement shall constitute a complete and final implementation of UNGAR 194 and therefore ends all claims.

The Arab Peace Initiative

… 2. Further calls upon Israel to affirm:
… b. Achievement of a just solution to the Palestinian Refugee problem to be agreed upon in accordance with UN General Assembly Resolution 194.

The Geneva Accord

Significance of the Refugee Problem

The Parties recognize that, in the context of two independent states, Palestine and Israel, living side by side in peace, an agreed resolution of the refugee problem is necessary for achieving a just, comprehensive and lasting peace between them.

Such a resolution will also be central to stability building and development in the region. UNGAR 194, UNSC Resolution 242, and the Arab Peace Initiative.

The Parties recognize that UNGAR 194, UNSC Resolution 242, and the Arab Peace Initiative (Article 2.ii.) concerning the rights of the Palestinian refugees represent the basis for resolving the refugee issue, and agree that these rights are fulfilled according to Article 7 of this Agreement.

End of Claims

This agreement provides for the permanent and complete resolution of the Palestinian refugee problem. No claims may be raised except for those related to the implementation of this agreement.

Reconciliation Programmes

The Parties will encourage and promote the development of cooperation between their relevant institutions and civil societies in creating forums for exchanging historical narratives and enhancing mutual understanding regarding the past.

The Parties shall encourage and facilitate exchanges in order to disseminate a richer appreciation of these respective narratives, in the fields of formal and informal education, by providing conditions for direct contacts between schools, educational institutions and civil society.

The Parties may consider cross-community cultural programs in order to promote the goals of conciliation in relation to their respective histories. These programs may include developing appropriate ways of commemorating those villages and communities that existed prior to 1949.

Notes

1. Scott Atran and Robert Axelrod, 'Reframing Sacred Values', *Negotiation Journal*, vol. 24, no. 3 (2008), p. 224.
2. Interview with Ghazi Hamad on June 20, 2006, as quoted in Jeremy Ginges, Scott Atran, Douglas Medin, and Khalil Shikaki, 'Sacred bounds on rational resolution of violent political conflict', *PNAS*, vol. 104, no. 18, p. 7359.

3. Ethan Bronner, 'Crude outlines of a Palestinian State emerging in West Bank on eve of talks', *Pittsburgh Post-Gazette*, 31 August 2010, online at: www.post-gazette.com/pg/10243/1083864-82.stm

4. Trudy Govier and Wilhelm Verwoerd, 'Taking Wrongs Seriously: A Qualified Defence of Public Apologies', *Saskatchewan Law Review*, vol. 65 (2002), p. 141.

5. For an analysis of post-'New Historian' trends see Ilan Pappe, 'The 1948 Historiography of Israel', *Journal of Palestinian Studies*, vol. 34, no. 1 (2009).

6. Ilan Pappe, 'The Vicissitudes of the 1948 Historiography of Israel', *Journal of Palestine Studies*, Vol, XXXIX no. 1 (Autumn 2009), pp. 6–23.

7. This section draws on extensive interviews with Israeli and Palestinian retired officials and academics.

8. Rami Khouri, 'Moral Compensation Between Israelis and Palestinians', USIP Special Report, Washington, DC: USIP, forthcoming, p. 7.

9. Ibid., p. 8.

10. Palestinian Center for Policy and Survey Research, 'Result of PSR Refugees Poll in the West Bank/Gaza Strip, Jordan and Lebanon on Refugees' Preferences and Behavior in a Palestinian–Israeli Permanent Refugee Agreement', January–June 2003, Press Release, 18 July 2003, online at: www.pcpsr.org/survey/polls/2003/refugeesjune03.html

11. 'The Clinton Parameters', online at: www.peacelobby.org/clinton_parameters.htm

12. Ibid.,'Refugees' section.

13. Khouri, 'Moral Compensation Between Israelis and Palestinians', p. 19.

14. Akiva Eldar, 'The Refugee Problem at Taba (Interviews with Yossi Beilin and Nabil Sha'ath)', *Palestine–Israel Journal*, vol. 9, no. 2 (2002), p. 21.

15. Rex Brynen, 'Past as Prelude: Negotiating the Palestinian Refugee Issue', Chatham House Briefing Paper MEP/PR BP 08/01, London: Chatham House, 2008, online at: www.chathamhouse.org/publications/papers/view/108831, p. 5.

16. Khouri, 'Moral Compensation Between Israelis and Palestinians', p. 23.

17. Scott Atran and Robert Axelrod, 'Reframing Sacred Values', *Negotiation Journal* 24, 3 (July 2008), p. 223.

18. Michael R. Marrus, *Official Apologies and the Quest for Historic Justice*, (Toronto: Munk Centre for International Studies, University of Toronto, 2006), p. 9; Shahira Samy, 'Would Sorry Repair My Loss? Why Palestinian Refugees Should Seek an Apology for Their Displacement', *International Journal of Human Rights*, vol. 14, no. 3, 2010, p. 7.

19. Samy, 'Would Sorry Repair My Loss?', p. 7.

20. Ibid., p. 5.

21. The Beilin-Abu Mazen Plan, online at: www.jewishvirtuallibrary.org/jsource/Peace/beilinmazen.html

22. Gilead Sher, *The Israeli–Palestinian Peace Negotiations, 1999–2000: Within Reach*, (London: Routledge, 2005), pp. 247–9.

23. The Clinton Parameters, online at: www.peacelobby.org/clinton_parameters.htm

24. Palestinian Proposal on Palestinian Refugees. The Taba Summit, online at: www.mideastweb.org/taba.htm

10

Managing Refugee Expectations

Khalil Shikaki

Introduction: Defining the Context

The purpose of this chapter is to address the issue of refugee expectations in the context of a comprehensive peace agreement between Israel and the Palestinians. Three relevant core features of this peace agreement are assumed: it leads to the creation of a Palestinian state in the West Bank and the Gaza Strip; it imposes serious constraints on the ability of refugees to return to their homes and property inside Israel, and it closes the refugees' file and ends all claims by providing compensation and allowing refugees the choice between three options: unrestricted return to the Palestinian state or so-called 'swapped' areas inside Israel that would later become part of the Palestinian state, somewhat restricted ability to stay in host countries, or a much more restricted access to third countries. These elements meet both Israel's needs to maintain a Jewish character and end future Palestinian claims, and Palestinian post-1967 needs to have a state and end occupation. But therein lies the problem: many refugees will find this agreement unacceptable, some will reject it, and a few will use force to prevent its implementation. Many advocates of refugees' rights and political groups opposed to the peace agreement will frame the refugee solution as a sell-out, treason and abandonment of historic proportion of their 1948 rights. They will call upon refugees to resist the implementation of the agreement by all means and will advance a narrative of refugees' abandonment.

The ideal context for the following discussion is one in which the Palestinians are unified in the West Bank and the Gaza Strip and where the Palestinian state is established in both areas. Hamas might oppose the agreement but will refrain from using violence to prevent its implementation. Indeed, if the agreement was accepted by a majority of Palestinians, presumably in a referendum, Hamas, while still opposed to the agreement, might accept its legitimacy. However, it is conceivable that a peace agreement might be reached by the PLO and Israel at a time when Palestinians are divided and Hamas is still in control of the Gaza Strip. Although highly unlikely, it is even conceivable that a Palestinian state might be established in the West Bank while Hamas continues to control the Gaza Strip. In this case, Hamas will prevent the implementation of the agreement, including the refugee solution, in the areas it controls.

In addressing refugee expectations, the goal of this chapter is not to find ways to make refugees more willing to swallow a bad agreement or to make a bad agreement look pretty. Rather, the objective is to highlight tensions, disillusionments and potential conflicts that might threaten the future of the peace agreement, and to suggest ways of reducing them. To avoid the worst possible implication of the suboptimal nature of the refugee component of the comprehensive peace agreement, ways need to be found to make that peace agreement itself, and the Palestinian state it creates, viable and legitimate while reducing as much as possible refugees' motivation to resort to violence or boycott the implementation of the refugee solution. The centrality of the relationship between state viability and the legitimacy of the permanent Palestinian–Israeli agreement should not be underestimated. An agreement that lacks legitimacy in the eyes of the majority of Palestinians, most of whom are refugees, will make the state illegitimate in the eyes of its citizens. The greater the legitimacy of the peace agreement, the more likely it will be to create a legitimate and viable state, and the more likely the refugee solution will also be seen as legitimate. But finding ways to make the non-refugee components of the comprehensive agreement more legitimate is a topic beyond the limits of this chapter. Instead, the focus here is on addressing the refugee component and its process of implementation.

Moreover, postponing the negotiations of the refugee problem while reaching an agreement on all other issues is *not* an option. Comprehensive surveys on various scenarios and options for a permanent status agreement conducted by the Palestinian Center for Policy and Survey Research (PSR) and the Hebrew University throughout 2008 clearly indicate that no conceivable solution to the refugee problem will ever receive simultaneous support from both Israelis and Palestinians, and that the only way to resolve the refugee problem is to embed its suboptimal solution in a comprehensive package. Both Israelis and Palestinians will reject the refugee component of the package, but they will nonetheless accept the package. The implication is clear: postponing the refugee issue would make it impossible to end the conflict and more difficult to implement or sustain the partial agreement; refugees would be condemned to living in limbo forever. Solving all non-refugee issues while leaving the wounds of refugees open is not likely to lead to the disappearance of the issue; instead it might only create conditions for short-term volatility and long-term strategic destabilization.

But helping to ease the process, and indeed the pain that will come with an agreement that aims at ending the refugeehood of millions of Palestinians in a comprehensive peace agreement, is not an easy task. Conflicts of expectations, between what is and what should be, between the refugees' definition of historical justice and the solution's relative justice, are bound to emerge in any likely peace agreement. Ways need to be found to reduce these conflicts and thus ease the pain of a refugee settlement. The task of this chapter is to highlight the ways that could advance this goal. In doing so, we start by identifying the most critical expectations of refugees in the context of a peace agreement.

Refugees' Expectations: Defining the Problem

In the *Nakba*, or catastrophe, 1948 refugees lost: 1. a national home; 2. property and livelihood; and 3. psychological well-being. Overnight they became stateless, impoverished, humiliated and endured great pain and suffering. They saw themselves as victims; indeed, from this moment on, victimhood, along with justice, would become the two dominant themes in Palestinian and refugee discourse. Any future solution to the refugee problem and process to implement it must manage refugee expectations of how these three losses and the mindset of victimhood will be addressed and compensated. The key elements of the refugee solution must therefore address: 1. the statelessness issue (return to Israel, repatriation to Palestinian state, citizenship in other countries, etc.); 2. the property/livelihood issue (compensation, restitution, socio-economic integration, etc.); and 3. the pain and suffering issue (the recognition of suffering and narrative of victimhood, apology, reconciliation and other psychological well-being matters).

While most refugees carry passports, mostly issued by the Palestinian Authority and Jordan, uncertainty about the future of their citizenship remains high; indeed nothing in the future is taken for granted, not even residency rights, as refugees share the concern of most other Palestinians that they can be easily evicted from their homes, have their land confiscated and have their families sent into exile. Moreover, many, like those living in Lebanon, Syria, Egypt and Iraq carry only travel documents that are accepted by very few countries, even for travel. Without a state of their own, questions about national identity and self-determination keeps refugees in perpetual limbo. Refugees expect any peace agreement to resolve this core problem as they expect it to provide permanent citizenship and residency, recognized national identity, and a valid and internationally-recognized passport. When considering the future, the overwhelming majority of refugees want a Palestinian passport, indeed citizenship, even if they choose to live outside the state of Palestine or maintain other citizenships and passports. By contrast, almost no one seeks an Israeli citizenship or passport, even if some may wish to return to their homes and property. Most refugees living in Jordan highly value their Jordanian citizenship and passport, and will find it extremely difficult to give it up.

A future peace agreement must first and foremost assure refugees of the end of their statelessness. The message should be that they will acquire/maintain their national identity, citizenship, permanent residency and passport but without losing any related rights or privileges which they currently enjoy in host countries. The design, and perhaps more importantly the implementation, of a resolution of the following three elements of the negotiations is likely to affect this refugee expectation: return to Israel, repatriation to the Palestinian state, and absorption in host and third countries. These are both tangibles and intangibles; they are related to the legitimacy of the narrative, identity and citizenship, and rehabilitation and resettlement.

The second refugee expectation is related to property and livelihood. Aside from the intangible elements – the nostalgia and longing for homes and neighbourhoods and the folklore related to the 'good' life and the economic well-being before the *Nakba*, symbolized in preserving their old keys and memories – possessions left behind symbolize assets and indicate lost wealth. Expectations range from repossession of property, to compensation estimates about its current value, compensation about huge losses suffered as a result of inability to benefit from property and other aspects of livelihood throughout the past decades since the *Nakba*, and the consequent impoverishment. Refugees associate their extreme poverty with their refugee status due to loss of property, no matter how meager its value really was, and expect the end of refugeehood to bring about a significant improvement in their living conditions and financial status.

Compensation terms of the refugee solution must be seen as fair by the majority of refugees; the implementation process must be simple and quick. If the value of compensation for lost property and forced impoverishment does not seem to deliver as expected, the tendency of many refugees will be to seek restitution, even if it is not offered to them as an option, and even if they do not wish to live in Israel or gain its citizenship, and indeed even if their property has been destroyed or otherwise no longer exists. Moreover, if the actual process of compensation in its legalistic and practical dimensions seems too inefficient, slow, demeaning or otherwise cumbersome, some refugees will forgo compensation altogether in favour of maintaining the purity of narrative and nostalgia, and in order to ensure that there is no end to claims.

The third refugee expectation relates mostly to intangibles: how to heal the psychological pain and suffering and overcome an overwhelming sense of historic injustice; how to deal with the anger, indeed the rage, which simmers deep inside most refugees; and how to help refugees overcome their deep sense of victimhood. Most refugees are willing to accept reconciliation with Israel. But before they are ready for it, refugees expect their tormentors, defined mostly as Israelis, to acknowledge their great suffering, the catastrophe that befell them, to admit the narrative of forced expulsion, to accept responsibility for creating the refugee problem, and to express sorrow and regret for what they did. Psychologically well-adjusted refugees make it easier to deal with all other issues of the refugee problem.

In designing and implementing a refugee solution, these intangibles must not be ignored. A concept of psychological 'well-being', one that pays attention to the unique conditions of Palestinian prolonged refugeehood and statelessness, must be developed and operationalized.

But before we examine ways to address these issues and reduce the likely conflict of expectations, we examine the ways to make the process of refugee negotiations more legitimate.

The Process Must Be Seen as Legitimate

It goes without saying that no refugee solution is likely to be seen by refugees as 'fair' until the peace agreement in which it is embedded is endorsed by a majority of Palestinians. The Palestinian public, including refugees, must know what it gains in return for concessions it makes in the refugee issue. Leadership must articulate and defend the message of trade-offs and relative gains. But this is not enough. Refugees are likely to resent the idea that for the 'common good', they, the ones who have suffered the most since the *Nakba*, should now be asked for more, to bear the burden of a peace settlement. It is therefore important that the content of the refugee solution itself contributes to its own legitimacy. Moreover, for refugees to accept the outcome of negotiations as legitimate, they must see the process that led to that outcome as legitimate. In this context, legitimacy requires not only acceptable content, but also acceptable terms of reference, acceptable negotiators, and highlighted consultation with representatives of refugees throughout the process.

Terms of Reference

Refugees expect the process of negotiations to be anchored in international law. While this expectation can be easily met, after all the Jordanian–Israeli peace accords recognized that the principles of international law should be applied to the eventual resolution of the refugee issue, the real issue here is the 'right of return'. For Palestinian refugees, the best terms of reference are those embodied in UN General Assembly Resolution No. 194; negotiations ignoring this resolution would be seen as failing to meet the basic test of international legitimacy. Refugees understand this resolution to provide for the right to choose between return to their homes and property or accept compensation.

It is vital for the Palestinians that the Israelis recognize this UN resolution as a basis for negotiations, as accordingly an agreed solution, if one emerges, would give the refugees the choice of return to Israel and/or of accepting compensation and returning to the Palestinian state, or to search for another place for residence. Surveys among Palestinians indicate that the overwhelming majority consider the right of return as sacred. Palestinians also believe that neither the PLO nor the Palestinian state can revoke the right of the individual refugee to return, and therefore without an Israeli recognition of this right, the struggle over this issue will continue. Any negotiations not based on Resolution 194 or one that does not recognize the right of return would lack legitimacy in the eyes of all Palestinians, refugees and non-refugees alike.

But refugees fully understand that when the 'right' is provided for, it will not be unequivocal. It is precisely here that the battle over meaning will be won or lost. So far, the language that has been debated by negotiators revolved around three formulations: the 'international law' language used in the Jordanian–Israeli peace treaty, the 'right of return to historic Palestine or to homeland' in the Clinton Parameters, 'based on 194' in the Geneva Initiative, and finally, an agreed solution which constitutes 'an implementation of 194' in both the Geneva Initiative and the Clinton Parameters. Israel has agreed in the past on accepting thousands of returning refugees within a context of 'family unification'. Palestinian negotiators will consider this as sufficient evidence to support their claim that negotiations will be based on the right to choose, but Israeli and American negotiators will deny that such 'right' applies to sovereign Israel and that 'family unification' is a sovereign Israeli decision. An effective Palestinian opposition will find it easy to present the official Palestinian claims as false. For the Palestinian negotiators to have a chance to win this battle over meaning, they will have to make the choice as real as possible: refugees could be asked, in writing, to make the choice.

But shifting the burden of choice onto the shoulders of refugees, while effective in gaining legitimacy, might again be challenged by an effective opposition. The opposition will argue that the 'return' is not real as it will not allow refugees to return to their homes and properties or even to the areas from where they originally came. It is in this context that negotiators can present 'family unification' as the means for the return to their original villages and towns. Ultimately however, this is the weakest element in any strategy aiming to manage refugee expectations and is one that could present the greatest threat to the peace process as it might seriously jeopardize absorption efforts, as refugee disillusionment with the peace agreement could lead to the creation of a highly unstable political and security environment.

Acceptable Negotiators

The second issue related to the legitimacy of the process is the selection of negotiators: who should speak in the name of refugees? In PSR's 2003 special refugee surveys, respondents were asked about the side they would choose to represent them in negotiations over the refugee problem. As Table 10.1 shows, the overwhelming majority of refugees in Lebanon and the West Bank and Gaza Strip (WBGS) chose the PLO (86 per cent in Lebanon and 73 per cent in the WBGS). But in Jordan, only 40 per cent chose the PLO while 28 per cent selected the government of Jordan and 16 per cent did not express an opinion. In principle, the current negotiators – the PLO negotiators – do indeed have more legitimacy than any other. However, it would be wise to consider widening the list of participants, not only to meet the expectations of refugees regarding this issue, but also to meet their expectations regarding other issues, such as resettlement and compensation.

Table 10.1   Negotiators Acceptable to Refugees

Who do you want to represent you and your interests in the negotiations on refugees?

	WBGS %	Jordan %	Lebanon %
1. Palestine Liberation Organization	72.7	40.0	86.3
2. United Nations	8.7	9.5	4.8
3. Lebanese/ Jordanian Government	–	28.0	1.0
4. Other (specify ____)	13.9	6.3	3.8
5. No opinion/ Do not know	4.7	16.4	4.1

Source: Palestinian Center for Policy and Survey Research (PSR) refugee surveys.

This is especially applicable to Jordan, which has considered the refugees to be Jordanian citizens. Given the fact that the overwhelming majority of refugees in Jordan do not wish to renounce the rights and privileges they currently enjoy in Jordan, the direct involvement of that country in the negotiations can only add to its legitimacy. Similarly, if they were not consulted, other host countries could refuse to cooperate in the process of implementation of the refugee agreement, including the possible absorption of refugees even temporarily regardless of the nature of the solution that could be achieved by the PLO and Israel. But it is highly unlikely that countries such as Syria and Lebanon would be willing to participate in such negotiations in the absence of an existing channel of negotiations between these countries and Israel. Moreover, the PLO might in fact fear the involvement of these countries, who might feel less compelled to entertain compromises and therefore exercise veto power over negotiations.

The involvement of third countries, those who might be willing to absorb refugees or to contribute to the compensation packages, might also be useful in ensuring a smooth implementation process. In the absence of major international donors from the negotiations, Israel might wish to lay the responsibility of gathering the funds necessary for payment of compensation upon the shoulders of the international community. Israel might also wish to link compensation to Palestinian refugees to similar compensation from Arab countries to Jewish immigrants who left after the establishment of the Jewish state. In the absence of clarity on this issue, Israel might seek to delay its payment or impede the process of compensation to Palestinian refugees. Inviting interested Arab countries allows Israel to raise and resolve this issue directly with them.

Consultation with Representatives of Refugees

Consultation with refugees inside and outside the WBGS is a source of power and legitimacy. Refugees should be consulted early in the process while negotiations are underway and later when implementation starts. It is particularly critical that they participate in designing the messages to refugees to structure their motivation before the unveiling of the agreement and later during implementation. If a referendum were selected as the means to ratify the peace agreement, it would be preferable: 1. to present the public with the whole agreement, not only the refugees' component; 2. to ask all Palestinians, refugees and non-refugees; and 3. to include as many diaspora refugees as possible, particularly those living in Jordan. A vote on the refugee component alone is most likely to produce a majority rejection from most, and restricting the vote to refugees will alienate non-refugees who will be asked to share the burden of absorption. It is possible, however, that a referendum might only be feasible in the WBGS. In this case, it would be useful to separate and highlight the vote of the refugees in the WBGS, as this might contribute to neutralizing attacks from refugees in host countries who do not participate. In any case, separating the vote of refugees helps to provide legitimacy to the process of resettlement in the Palestinian state.

Contents of a Solution

A solution that does not provide for a form of recognition of the right of return is almost certainly going to be rejected by most refugees. The Clinton Parameters came as close as possible to an agreement that slightly more than half of the refugees might accept. The language includes recognition of the 'right of return' to 'historic Palestine' or to the 'homeland'. But it makes it abundantly clear that only a small number would be allowed to return to Israel while providing refugees with compensation and other alternatives. Although the Clinton formula did not sufficiently highlight the matter of compensation, it is believed that right of return should always be paired with the right to compensation. PSR's research does not support the view that linking the two issues would be counter-productive. The formulation, in Table 10.2, was presented to refugees in Lebanon, Jordan and the WBGS in PSR's 2003 surveys.

A majority of refugees in the three areas expressed the belief that Israel would reject the proposed solution to the refugee problem, most likely because the solution presented to respondents explicitly stated that Israel would have to accept Resolution 194 or the right of return. This should be taken as an indication that the refugees think that an explicit Israeli acceptance of 194 or the right of return is not realistic. But a majority of 55 per cent in Jordan, 63 per cent in Palestine and 67 per cent in Lebanon believed the PLO would accept the solution. This finding clearly indicates that the refugees expect the

Table 10.2 Terms of Agreement

The agreement stipulates the establishment of a Palestinian state in the West Bank and Gaza Strip, and Israeli recognition of UN Resolution 194 or the right of return. But the two sides would agree on the return of a small number of refugees to Israel in accordance with a timetable that extends for several years. Each refugee family will be able to choose one of the following options:

1. Return to Israel in accordance with an annual quota and become an Israeli citizen;

2. Stay in the Palestinian state that will be established in the West Bank and Gaza Strip and receive a fair compensation for the property taken over by Israel and for other losses and suffering;

3. Receive Palestinian citizenship and return to designated areas inside Israel that would be swapped later on with Palestinian areas as part of a territorial exchange and receive compensation;

4. Receive fair compensation for the property, losses and suffering, and stay in the host country receiving its citizenship or Palestinian citizenship;

5. Receive fair compensation for the property, losses and suffering, and immigrate to a European country or the USA, Australia or Canada, and obtain the citizenship of that country or Palestinian citizenship.

Source: Palestinian Center for Policy and Survey Research (PSR) refugee surveys.

PLO to show flexibility regarding the actual return of refugees to their homes and property inside Israel. However, respondents were split in their evaluation of the likely response of the majority of the refugees with the WBGS refugees split right in the middle, Jordan's refugees leaning towards acceptance and Lebanon's refugees leaning towards rejection. When asked how they themselves felt about the proposal, the respondents in Palestine and Lebanon were divided into two equal groups, rejecting or accepting it, while in Jordan it was accepted by 50 per cent and rejected by only 37 per cent, with the rest expressing no opinion. When asked how they would react to a Palestinian–Israeli agreement embracing the proposal, the overwhelming majority tended to approve such an agreement, even if most felt that they would do so for the lack of a better alternative. But a small percentage (15 per cent in WBGS, 9 per cent in Lebanon and 8 per cent in Jordan) said that they would not only oppose such solution, but would also resist it.

In 2008, three other versions of a refugee solution were presented to refugees in the West Bank and the Gaza Strip (see Table 10.3). Findings of five surveys conducted during that year, as well as findings of focus groups, highlighted three important elements in refugee expectations: that the recognition of the right of return was unequivocal; concern about the size of actual return to Israel; and concern for the framing of return. The explicit recognition of the right of return 'to homeland in historic Palestine' makes a difference by adding 10 per cent more public support –as in version 1 compared with version 2 which is less explicit and recognizes only the right of return to 'homeland'. The framing of return as 'family unification' did not significantly alter support. The number used, 150,000, was seen as substantial even though it only represents less than 3 per cent of the total number of refugees. In versions 1 and 2, which received majority support, return to Israel was framed as 'family unification' and the numbers were identical. The third version, in which support dropped considerably to about 40 per cent, made no direct reference to the right of return although the agreement was based on UN Resolution 194, no numbers for returning refugees were provided, but return to Israel was identified as 'return'.

Table 10.3 Three Versions of a Refugee Solution

Version 1: Palestinian refugees will have the right of return to their homeland in historic Palestine, the Palestinian state will settle all refugees wishing to live in it, and Israel would allow the return of about 150,000 as part of a programme of family unification and will compensate all others. The two sides will agree that this implements UN Resolution 194. [*PSR survey*, March 2008, supported by 63%]

Version 2: Palestinian refugees will have the right of return to their homeland whereby the Palestinian state will settle all refugees wishing to live in it, Israel will allow the return of about 150,000 as part of a programme of family unification, and all others will be compensated. The two sides will agree that this implements UN Resolution 194. [*PSR survey*, June 2008, supported by 54%]

Version 3: Both sides agree that the solution will be based on UN Resolutions 194 and 242 and on the Arab Peace Initiative. The refugees will be given five choices for permanent residency. These are: the Palestinian state and the Israeli areas transferred to the Palestinian state in the territorial exchange mentioned above; no restrictions would be imposed on refugee return to these two areas. Residency in the other three areas (in host countries, third countries and Israel) would be subject to the decision of the states in those areas. The number of refugees returning to Israel will be based on the average number of refugees admitted to third countries like Australia, Canada, Europe and others. All refugees will be entitled to compensation for their 'refugeehood' and loss of properties. [*summarized from the Geneva Initiative*] [*PSR survey*, June 2008, supported by 41%]

Source: PSR refugee surveys.

Another important element related to content that is likely to shape expectations has to do with process management. To gain greater legitimacy, a refugee solution must ensure that the management of the process of implementation is easy, immediate and predictable. All parties to the agreement must be fully ready for implementation. They must know what they are supposed to do; perhaps all should be armed with an 'operational manual', a kind of 'resettlement/compensation for dummies'.

Finally, contents must strike a balance between all four elements of refugee interests: the personal and the national, the tangible and the intangible. Table 10.4 shows a matrix identifying these various elements that must be addressed.

Table 10.4 Four Elements of Refugees' Interests

		Personal v. National Aspects	
		Personal	National
Tangibles v. Intangibles	Intangible	• right of return/right to choose • narrative • apology • recognition of suffering	• legitimacy of peace agreement • nature of the trade-offs • cost of ending of conflict and claims • total number of returnees to Israel
	Tangible	• residency • citizenship • personal and family compensation: how much and when? • how easy/fast the process moves	• state compensation • resettlement programmes • role of international actors, UNRWA • future of refugee camps

Source: PSR refugee surveys.

Statehood, Identity and Absorption

Self-determination in a state affirms national identity, grants citizenship and helps in the absorption and integration process. Refugees will probably demand the right to choose the means that best addresses their political national aspirations and needs. While the refugee solution is likely to allow a small number to return to Israel, it will probably allow unlimited return to the Palestinian state and swapped areas inside Israel that later become part of Palestine. Refugees are also likely to be offered to stay in some host countries and to seek citizenship and permanent residency in other countries. While they do not expect or want Israeli citizenship, they do expect the agreement to give them the right to citizenship in the Palestinian state, even if they choose to reside elsewhere. While they do not expect all host countries to grant them the option of permanent residency and citizenship, they do expect the agreement to protect their *current* political and civil rights in host countries if they choose, and were allowed, to remain there. While some degree of uncertainty remains, most refugees are sure that Lebanon will not allow refugees to resettle in that country. But most do believe that Jordan will indeed allow them, since they are considered citizens under the law, to remain in that country and to maintain their current rights. If reality, in the case of Jordan, turns out to be different, the refugees in that country are likely to react very negatively which would lead to further complications in the implementation of the refugees' resettlement.

In this context, even if the limits on return to Israel are severe, survey research conducted among refugees by PSR indicates that these limitations will not pose a formidable problem in meeting refugees' need for statehood. PSR's 2003 findings showed that only 10 per cent of all refugees in the four areas covered by the surveys chose return to Israel as a first choice. However, for psychological reasons, many refugees might choose to go to 'swapped areas' inside Israel, Israeli areas that are transferred to the Palestinian state as part of a territorial exchange. In PSR's 2003 surveys, almost a quarter of the respondents chose this option as their first choice. However, when we asked them to select a location inside the Palestinian state for permanent residency, none of those opting to go to the swapped areas selected to stay permanently in those areas. Perhaps the selection of this option represents the best of all worlds for the refugees: exercising the right of return to the 1948 land and reside in, and become a citizen of, the Palestinian state.

Any limits on return to the Palestinian state will pose serious difficulties particularly for those who currently do not have other citizenship. Ideally, meeting refugees' expectations would be enhanced if the refugee solution explicitly offers the option of Palestinian citizenship, a passport and permanent residency to all refugees, regardless of where they currently live or where they would like to live in the future. In this context, it is essential however that refugees receive assurances that such an offer would in no way take away any rights they currently enjoy in host countries such as their passport, residency, right to vote, right to own property and others. Since some family members might decide to stay in host countries while others might decide to go elsewhere, returnees might want to maintain socio-economic ties with the host country in which they lived before return. Moreover, since Palestine might not be a highly attractive option for some refugees, having the option of returning to the host country reduces the risks for refugees opting to live in the Palestinian state.

As indicated earlier, a limited number of refugees will implement their right to return to the homeland by actually returning to Israel. Less than 10 per cent of refugees have been born in areas within the green line; and whereas many might feel nostalgia for their place of birth, many of their offspring would probably prefer to practise their right of self-determination within a Palestinian state despite their profound bonds to the lands and possessions of their forefathers. Moreover, the notion of 'return' which exists in the minds of refugees is an idealistic one – almost spiritual. The notion that the return could be to the state of Israel is alien to their way of thinking and it is difficult for them to conceive of any return that does not live up to their ideal and nostalgic expectations. It is not only about the change in the name, from Palestine to Israel, but just as importantly, it is about the hostility towards and the alienation from the culture, society and politics of the new place that they would be returning to. Most do not imagine themselves returning to Israel, but rather to Palestine – as in the Palestine that existed in 1948 of which the new state of Palestine is an integral part. The findings of PSR's 2003 refugee surveys help us to further understand the refugees' motivation regarding statehood, citizenship, passports and permanent residency. The survey's findings highlight the role of four factors as the driving forces that motivate the behaviour of the refugees when confronting the choice between returning to Israel, living in the Palestinian state, staying in host countries and going elsewhere to third countries.

First, the findings clearly show the significance of national identity in determining the respondents' choices. In this regard it is important to remind ourselves of the radical transformation of the Palestinian national movement's aims since the mid-1970s, whereby the main aim of liberating Palestine was exchanged for that of establishing an independent Palestinian state. For most refugees, attaining self-determination and national identity in an independent *Palestinian* state has become an important national-psychological need. The degree of the refugees' attachment to and perception of Palestinian national identity was found to correlate with the decision by the majority of refugees in choosing to exercise the right to return in the Palestinian state. Needless to say, what facilitated the decision for the majority of the Palestinian refugees in seeking to live in a Palestinian state is the fact that their national identity could still be embodied in a part of the historic homeland; they can be on the land and with the people of Palestine. Table 10.5 shows the great identification of refugees in the West Bank and Gaza Strip and Lebanon with their Palestinian identity.

Table 10.5   Refugees' National Identity Preferences

If you have to choose one of the following descriptions of yourself, which one would you choose?

	WBGS %	Lebanon %	Jordan %
1. I am a Palestinian	76.0	89.0	29.0
2. I am a refugee	11.0	2.0	3.0
3. I am (Jordanian/Lebanese) of Palestinian origin	NA	1.0	46.0
4. I am an Arab	13.0	8.0	22.0

And what if the choice is between the following descriptions only, which one would you choose?

1. I am a Palestinian	80.8	93.2	27.7
2. I am a Jordanian/ Lebanese from Palestinian origin	NA	5.5	52.6
3. I am a refugee	18.1	0.0	13.9
4. No opinion/ Don't know	1.1	1.4	5.8

Source: PSR refugee surveys.

Second, the findings also show the strength of the refugees' perception of the nature of their relationship with the host countries. Most refugees might not want to put their right to return to Israel into practice since they would have to uproot themselves and start over after so many years, especially since this might require them to relinquish any benefits they may have attained. This is applicable not only to refugees in the WBGS, but it is also applicable to the Palestinian refugees in Jordan, particularly those who left the refugee camps and integrated within the civil and political life in that country. The perception of relative equality enjoyed by refugees in Jordan (compared to those in Lebanon) increased the percentage of those selecting Jordan as the place where they would permanently reside (33 per cent) as a first choice while only a small minority (10 per cent) opted to stay in Lebanon as a first choice. If one adds to those percentages those who did not select any of the other options as their first choice (16 per cent in Jordan and 17 per cent in Lebanon) the picture that emerges is one in which about half of Jordan's refugees wanting to remain in Jordan, while a little over a quarter of Lebanon's refugees wanting to stay in that country.

Third, refugees were also motivated by family considerations with the location of family members and relatives influencing their choices. Refugees with relatives in Israel, for example, are more likely to choose to live in Israel than those without. Similarly, refugees with relatives in third countries are more likely to contemplate the idea of immigration to those third countries. Lebanon in particular is a good example: PSR results showed the significance of family links leading to the highest percentage of demand on immigration to third countries as a first choice (9 per cent compared to 1 per cent in the WBGS and 2 per cent in Jordan) as well as the demand to live in Israel (23 per cent compared to 5 per cent in Jordan and 13 per cent in the WBGS) – reflecting the extent to which refugees in Lebanon have large numbers of relatives both in Israel and scattered in the diaspora.

Finally, refugee choices were dependent on socio-economic considerations (place of residence, income, property ownership, etc.). The findings show that the percentage of those who opt to stay in host countries increases among refugees living outside refugee camps and that the percentage of those wishing to go to the Palestinian state increases among those with lower- and middle-income levels. Moreover, those who own homes and land in their current place of residence tend to want to stay in those places. Indeed, as Table 10.5 shows, greater socio-economic integration of refugees in Jordan created a greater attachment to their Jordanian/Arab identity and less to their Palestinian identity.

After more than 60 years of displacement, refugees who were mostly peasants in 1948 are no longer peasants. They are educated and live in urban areas. Returning to the villages where they had come from is not the likely option they would choose. Moreover, it is not certain that whole groups of refugees would be able to return to the same villages and towns that they had to leave, either because they have been destroyed or because they have become part of the surrounding Israeli environment. On the other hand, whole communities could be returned to new habitats within the Palestinian state, whereby the Palestinian refugee would not feel uprooted once again, even when putting the right of return into practice. Other research conducted among Palestinian refugees indicates that refugees will behave as a collective, will want to move as groups of families and extended families, and will form their opinions based on messages coming from the heads of those families and groups. Messages from other sources of authority will compete against those emanating from more localized sources. These are likely to include statements of relevant state and non-state actors such as the PA, Fateh, Hamas, Jordan, Egypt, Syria and others.

As indicated earlier, PSR's 2003 surveys showed that about half of the refugees expect a majority of refugees to accept a solution that allows unlimited return to the Palestinian state but a limited return to Israel. A survey conducted in the WBGS by the Palestinian Central Bureau of Statistics (PCBS) showed that only 19 per cent of the Palestinians in these areas expect refugees to return to Israel. Even those refugees selecting Israel as their first choice for return expressed strong opposition to being forced to obtain Israeli citizenship. Given the small number of refugees wishing to immigrate to third countries, the real challenges in managing refugee expectations are going to be those related to repatriation to the Palestinian state.

Integration Into and Repatriation to Palestine

Palestinian statehood is the issue that most represents the link between the refugee solution and the larger peace agreement. This link affirms the belief that the two-state solution provides a means of ending refugee displacement. When asked if they would like to play a role in building the Palestinian state, the percentage of those wishing to do so was very high among refugees in the WBGS (84 per cent) diminishing to 61 per cent in Lebanon and to 52 per cent in Jordan (see Table 10.6). The relatively low percentage in Jordan indicates concerns among refugees about the potential threats to their status in that country. As indicated earlier, when directly asked to choose a 'first choice' from among several options, three-quarters of the WBGS refugees selected integration into the Palestinian state (or swapped areas) and 9 per cent did not select any option. In other words, a total of 85 per cent selected to stay in the Palestinian state. Among Jordan's refugees, 37 per cent selected the Palestinian state or swapped areas. Forty per cent of Lebanon's refugees selected the same.

Will conditions in the Palestinian state, once it is established, allow a smooth process of absorption and repatriation? Answers to this question are not clear. In fact, this matter has received little public attention from Palestinian planners and policymakers in order to protect the Palestinian position at the negotiating table. This state of affairs indicates that the future of refugee absorption is being sacrificed in order to avoid sending a signal of compromise. But closed lips on this matter today could undermine future ability to deal effectively with the demographic and planning challenges posed by the need to absorb hundreds of thousands of residing and returning refugees in the first ten years of the life of the state.

According to data from (PCBS), the Palestinian fertility rate is high, reaching 6.06 (7.41 in the Gaza Strip and 5.44 in the West Bank). While PCBS figures show that the rate is declining, they also show that the population of the West Bank and Gaza Strip is young, with 46.5 per cent aged under 15 years and the median age of the population at 16. It is estimated that the total population is now 4 million and that it will exceed 5 million by 2015. The demand for basic services will continue to rise at a time when the existing infrastructure and service delivery will be grossly inadequate. Moreover, housing density is already high, with an average of 6.4 persons per unit.

Most Palestinians are refugees and most of the Palestinian refugees live outside the boundaries of historical Palestine (which is now Israel and the West Bank and the Gaza Strip), especially in Jordan, Syria and Lebanon. In the West Bank and the Gaza Strip, the future areas

Table 10.6   Refugee Attachment to the Palestinian State

After the creation of a Palestinian state and the settlement of the refugee problem, do you want to play a role in building this state and shaping its political and socio-economic future?

	WBGS %	Jordan %	Lebanon %
1. Yes	84.0	52.4	61.2
2. No	13.6	29.9	28.3
3. No opinion/Do not know	2.3	17.8	10.5

Percentage of refugees who selected state of Palestine or swapped areas as their first choice:

	WBGS	Jordan	Lebanon	Total (% of total population in the three areas)
1. Stay in the Palestinian state that will be established in the West Bank and Gaza Strip and receive a fair compensation for the property taken over by Israel and for other losses and suffering	38.0	27.0	19.0	31.0
2. Receive Palestinian citizenship and return to designated areas inside Israel that would be swapped later on with Palestinian areas as part of a territorial exchange and receive any deserved compensation	37.0	10.0	21.0	23.0
3. Refuse all options	9.0	16.0	17.0	13.0

Source: PSR refugee surveys.

of the Palestinian state, refugees represent about 40 per cent of the total population. The Palestinian state will be required not only to absorb the refugees already living inside the West Bank and the Gaza Strip, but also to absorb close to one million returning refugees over a period of ten years. These returning refugees will come mostly from Lebanon, Syria and Jordan. The injection of such a large number of people, who are most likely to be poor, less educated and less healthy, will dramatically increase demands for service delivery and heighten existing difficulties and tensions.

Most refugees believe that the Palestinian state will have the capacity to absorb 1 million or more returning refugees. Table 10.7 shows that while a majority of Lebanon's refugees believe that the WBGS is unable to absorb refugees from other countries, the percentage drops to 27 per cent in the WBGS and 26 per cent in Jordan. In other words, refugees do indeed expect the state to absorb them. Failure of the state to meet refugee expectation regarding absorption will constitute a shock comparable to one of the chapters of their *Nakba*. Failure of the state and the international community to anticipate the likely problems and difficulties could destroy any chance for a sustainable Palestinian state and peace-building.

Table 10.7   Refugees' Perception of the Capacity of the Palestinian State to Absorb Refugees

After the creation of a Palestinian state and the settlement of the refugee problem, do you think that the West Bank and Gaza Strip can absorb the return of hundreds of thousands, or even millions, of refugees from the Diaspora/outside, in addition to the refugee population they have now?

	WBGS %	Jordan %	Lebanon %
1. They can absorb the refugee population they have now, in addition to a half million refugees from the Diaspora/outside	18.6	12.6	7.1
2. They can absorb the refugee population they have now, in addition to one million refugees from the Diaspora/outside	15.5	12.1	4.9
3. They can absorb the refugee population they have now, in addition to several millions of refugees from the Diaspora	30.3	25.9	6.5
4. The West Bank and Gaza Strip cannot absorb any refugee from the Diaspora	26.6	25.8	56.7
5. No opinion/Do not know	8.9	23.6	24.8

Source: PSR refugee surveys.

PSR research into refugee absorption in the state of Palestine in a manner that would enhance the capacity to meet refugee expectations led to the following conclusions regarding planning considerations:

1. Absorption should be planned as an integral part of a comprehensive plan for development and demographic changes in the Palestinian state. Absorption needs must be considered in every aspect of the larger plan, such as land use, housing and job creation. Absorption solutions and modalities should, for example, help in addressing the causes of current migration from the West Bank and the Gaza

Strip, the socio-economic disparities, particularly between the West Bank and the Gaza Strip, and the long-term structural impact of the Israeli occupation policies on the different sectors of the Palestinian economy.

2. The solution to the refugee problem should be seen as part of the larger context of the peace process. Other issues of final status negotiations, such as borders, settlements and Jerusalem are likely to have a significant impact on the absorption process. The impact could be directly related to practical issues of resources (such as land and water), population distribution (such as the location of the capital, territorial contiguity and main transportation systems) and size of compensation. But it could also be related to the more serious, but indirect, issue of the legitimacy of the absorption process if the public perceives the final status agreement as illegitimate.

3. The process of absorption should be viewed as part of state building. Returning refugees will have needs and expectations that must be met. But they will also bring resources and capacities that should be channelled to assist in building public institutions and economy.

4. The role of the state in implementing projects related to absorption should be limited. The private sector is more efficient in meeting the needs of absorption once the state has provided an enabling environment. Reliance on market forces and the private sector will ensure the voluntary nature of the absorption process away from the dictates of central planning, which might be unable to respond to the changing needs and preferences of the refugees.

In addition to planning considerations, refugee absorption will confront policymakers with various policy challenges and options related to governance and strategic planning, time and size of return, housing and infrastructure, future of UNRWA and others. Failure to meet these likely challenges could undermine the legitimacy of the Palestine state. PSR research has focused on six areas of policy making:

Strengthening Palestinian Capacity in the Areas of Governance, Strategic Planning and Infrastructure

The Palestinian Authority should invest more in strengthening institution building in the areas of governance and strategic planning.

The Ministry of Planning should lead the process by working closely with other public institutions. A legal framework should be proposed and submitted to the PLC. An absorption agency should be created and authorized to prepare plans which stipulate the roles and functions of other institutions, such as the ministries of local government, national economy and interior, during the process of absorption.

For the Palestinian state to be more successful in absorbing its refugees, it must encourage greater political participation. PSR refugee surveys found that refugees took a great interest in participating in the socio-political life of their state. The absence of good governance could play a negative role in the absorption process. Weak public institutions will fail to deliver vital services and exacerbate other likely socio-political tensions. Moreover, slow economic growth, caused by corruption and a weak legal and judicial framework, could reduce per capita income.

Yet, it is clear that the task of absorption might be tremendous and thus might overwhelm the capacity of the state's public institutions at a critical time. Public institutions in the new Palestinian state might lack the capacity to respond to rapidly increasing demands made on them by the refugees. If so, such difficulties might create impulses towards authoritarianism. It is essential therefore that the PA strives now to strengthen its public institutions and consolidate democratic practices before it is too late. Moreover, political and security reforms and anti-corruption measures taken today, could strengthen the credibility of the state in the eyes of refugees.

Options for Managing the Time and Size of Return

The Palestinian state must make refugee absorption its top priority and it must therefore have an open immigration policy. The best policy is one that helps the Palestinian state build its own capacity while allowing a free and relatively unhindered movement of refugees. A policy that aims at forcing or encouraging immediate and large-scale return could cause shocks to existing capacities as it would impose severe demands on housing, job creation and social services. On the other hand, a policy that seeks to impose severe limits on return could increase refugee dissatisfaction. Voluntary return is likely to be sensitive to the prevailing socio-economic and political conditions and therefore will pose fewer absorption challenges. If the Palestinian state lose management control over the time and size of return, due to overriding political considerations, such as demands from host countries and expected response of refugees, it could risk its own collapse. To avoid becoming a failed state, Palestine may need to set flexible annual quota limits and encourage refugees to stay for a longer period or, if possible, permanently, in host countries.

Refugee surveys conducted by PSR during the first half of 2003 indicate, as Table 10.8 shows, that refugees in Jordan prefer a gradual process of repatriation while refugees in Lebanon prefer, for obvious reasons, immediate and mass repatriation. Plans for temporary arrangements should therefore be considered in the case of the refugees from Lebanon. To encourage refugees to stay for longer periods in host countries, steps such as the issuance of Palestinian passports to refugees even before they return to the state should be considered. PSR's refugee surveys indicate that an overwhelming majority of refugees in Lebanon (90 per cent) prefer to hold Palestinian citizenship, even if they also obtain the citizenship of the host country.

Table 10.8   Refugees' Preferences Regarding the Size of Return

After the settlement of the Palestinian question and the refugee problem, some people propose the immediate and simultaneous return of hundreds of thousands of refugees, even a million, from the Diaspora/outside the Palestinian state; whereas some believe that the absorption process should be gradual, and only tens of thousands of refugees should return to the Palestinian state gradually. What's your opinion?

	WBGS %	Jordan %	Lebanon %
1. I prefer the simultaneous return of hundreds of thousands [of refugees]	35.3	35.0	57.6
2. I prefer the gradual return of tens of thousands [of refugees]	60.2	50.9	25.6
3. Other (specify _____)	3.2	1.6	1.1
4. No opinion/Do not know	1.3	12.4	15.6

Source: PSR refugee surveys.

Options for Housing

As potential returnees ponder the question of repatriation to the Palestinian state, some of the critical questions they are likely to ask themselves will revolve around the cost and ease of relocation. To help them make up their minds, the Palestinian state should outline its own baskets of incentives so that they would know what to expect. For returnees, housing is likely to be a major concern. This will also apply to resident West Bank and Gaza Strip refugees who might want to find better housing outside of their refugee camps or simply to renovate their existing homes inside or outside the camps. For refugees who have their own housing, finding jobs or starting businesses might be their most important concern. To meet all these expectations, one option the state might consider is to offer refugees four different baskets of incentives: relocation support, down-payment support, renovation support and business grants. Those incentives are not substitutes for refugees' personal compensation, instead they represent additional support while personal compensation is being negotiated or disbursed.

The various baskets are designed to serve the needs of returning and resident refugees equally. Each refugee family would be able to benefit from any two programmes of those. For example, a returning family might receive US$10,000 for the first few months after arrival to cover relocation costs and once it settles or finds a house or a plot of land it wants to buy, it can also receive another US$10,000 to use as a down payment or as a business grant. A resident refugee family might receive US$10,000 for a down-payment and another US$10,000 for renovation or for investment as a business grant.

A five-year programme aiming at assisting more than 500,000 returnees and a similar number of resident refugees might cost about US$5 billion, that is, US$1 billion per year. The first basket of assistance, for relocation, would offer US$10,000 per family of five for the first 12 months after arrival. The returning family seeking residency in Palestine could use this amount to cover transportation, rent and other relocation and emergency needs. Some 20,000 families, or 100,000 persons, could benefit directly from this package. The programme would run for five years with an annual cost of US$200 million. The second basket, for down payment assistance, would offer US$10,000 per family of five to pay for apartments or plots of land for those returnees wishing to buy an apartment or a plot of land. A total of 20,000 families of returnees and another 20,000 families of resident refugees would benefit annually from this programme. This programme would run for five years with an annual cost of US$400 million. The third basket, for renovation assistance, would offer US$10,000 per family to pay for renovation of existing homes inside and outside refugee camps for those interested in staying where they are. About 20,000 families of resident refugees would benefit annually from this programme. This programme too would run for five years, with an annual cost of US$200 million. The fourth basket, for business grants, would offer US$10,000 per family to pay for the start-up or expansion cost for business ventures, mostly for middle-class refugees. A total of 20,000 families of resident and returning refugees would benefit annually from this programme. It would run for five years at an annual cost of US$200 million.

Building separate towns and neighbourhoods for returning refugees should be avoided as it might lead to an increase in social tension between the local and repatriated populations. Population mix should be left to market forces. PSR refugee surveys indicate that little risk would be involved if the state allows a free choice of housing location. Such free choice is unlikely to lead to the perpetuation of existing socio-political divisions along the lines of those currently existing in host countries. Refugees are likely to disperse to mixed areas based on market dynamics. In any case, any attempt to compel the refugees to live in specific areas is likely to add to existing tensions. PSR's refugee surveys indicate that only 33 per cent of refugees returning from Lebanon and Jordan prefer to live with existing neighbours. Indeed, only 16 per cent of returning refugees from Jordan and 22 per cent from Lebanon prefer to live in towns built for returning refugees while the rest either prefer to live in existing towns and cities or have no particular preference. Only 8 per cent of refugees currently residing in the West Bank and the Gaza Strip prefer to live in towns built especially for them. In any case, the existing legal system in the Palestinian areas makes it difficult for the state to appropriate private land for public housing.

Evacuated Israeli settlements, if left intact after the Israeli withdrawal from occupied Palestinian territories, could be integrated into populated Palestinian urban and rural centres and used for housing purposes. It is expected that at least 10,000 housing units in several dozen settlements in the West Bank might be evacuated as part of a Palestinian–Israeli permanent status agreement. While these units would not be able to accommodate a large number of residents or returning refugees, their short-term availability makes them ideal for urgent housing needs. Settlement housing need not be restricted to refugees and it might be more cost-effective to make housing units located in settlements available to the general public, in order to avoid the negative association between former settlements and absorbed refugees.

PSR refugee surveys found that many of the refugees in the West Bank and Gaza Strip (44 per cent), Jordan (43 per cent) and Lebanon (52 per cent), who opted to live in the Palestinian state would be willing to live in evacuated settlements. Many, but not a majority, of the refugees in the West Bank and the Gaza Strip (48 per cent), Jordan and Lebanon (36 per cent each) who agreed to take compensation, expressed willingness to own a home or a piece of land in evacuated settlements as part of a compensation package.

Existing refugee camps in the West Bank and the Gaza Strip are currently in a state of disrepair. It is suggested that the PA, within the context of a refugee solution, takes various steps to improve living conditions in those camps. Such improvements should include home renovation, resolution of any problems related to landownership related to refugee camps by giving ownership to the refugees living in those camps, build or rebuild roads, rebuild infrastructure and gradually reduce the population density by allowing the building of new neighbourhoods in areas adjacent to the camps. Some of the baskets identified above could allow resident refugees to renovate their own homes or to use the down-payment package to buy new homes outside the camps. PSR refugee surveys found that 69 per cent of resident refugees would support such a step, even if taken today. Moreover, more than 80 per cent of resident refugees (and 74 per cent of non-refugees) in the West Bank and the Gaza Strip support the expansion and renovation of refugee camps after the establishment of the Palestinian state with the objective of absorbing refugees (see Table 10.9).

Options Regarding UNRWA

UNRWA is the UN agency that has been in charge of providing relief services to Palestinian refugees during the last 60 years. Almost 5 million refugees are now registered with UNRWA and currently

Table 10.9   Refugees' Preferences Regarding the Future of Refugee Camps

After the creation of a Palestinian state and the settlement of the refugee problem, some people propose the dismantlement of camps, others think that they should remain as they are now while others propose the expansion and improvement of camps so that they can accommodate the refugees who wish to stay in the Palestinian state. What's your opinion?

	WBGS refugees %	WBGS non-refugees %
1. Dismantlement	11.6	15.1
2. Keep them as they are now	7.2	9.7
3. Expanding and improving them	80.3	73.6
4. No opinion/Do not know	0.9	1.6

Source: PSR refugee surveys.

receive some kind of social or economic service, mostly health and education. In most camps, refugees still receive basic foodstuffs. It would not be an exaggeration to say that most refugees have developed a dependency problem that will be difficult to eradicate even after the refugee problem is resolved. The Palestinian state will have to gradually assume the functions of UNRWA and must find ways to address the dependency problem.

A majority of the refugees in Jordan and Lebanon believe that UNRWA will not be needed once a Palestinian state is established and the refugee problem is resolved. However, as Table 10.10 shows, a majority of refugees in the West Bank and Gaza Strip believe that UNRWA will have a role to play even after the refugee problem has been resolved. While it might continue to exist in the Palestinian state, UNRWA might shift its focus from relief to absorption and integration. In cooperation with the World Bank, UNDP and other international organizations, UNRWA is well suited to working on emergency plans related to the first phases of absorption by providing a database of demographic and socio-economic information on refugees, and providing technical and logistical support in communication with refugees regarding all facets of return, compensation and rehabilitation. Indeed, during the deliberations of the multilateral talks on refugees in the 1990s, UNRWA was discussed as a possible international organization tasked with preparation for refugee compensation. As the process of absorption progresses, normal UNRWA services should be gradually assumed by the state. Similarly, UNRWA assets should be gradually transferred to the state.

Table 10.10   Refugees' Preferences Regarding the Future of UNRWA

After the creation of a Palestinian state and the settlement of the refugee problem, do you see any need for the continuation of the work done by UNRWA?

	WBGS %	Jordan %	Lebanon %
1. Yes	58.0	25.5	35.7
2. No	38.8	58.8	54.4
3. No opinion/Do not know	3.2	15.7	9.9

Source: PSR refugee surveys.

Options Regarding Economic Policies and Infrastructure

While PSR refugee surveys indicate that many of the returning refugees will be of middle-class background, most will tend to be poor and less educated. Such a return may prove to be a drain on the already scarce resources of the Palestinian economy. This will reduce the ability of the new state to expand its absorptive capacity exactly at a time it is most needed. Limiting the return of the poor, while economically desirable, may not be politically feasible. The state may need to distinguish between the needs of the two groups of returnees, offering a relatively more direct absorption to the poor and an indirect absorption to the middle class. Those lacking capital and skills will find it difficult to integrate without direct state assistance in areas of job creation, housing, health and education. Indirect absorption would be suitable for those returnees with capital and skills, and who need temporary assistance in areas of investment and social services. A basket of business grants, as indicated earlier might be demanded by and be more suitable for this group. It is expected that many returnees will contribute to economic and social development in the new state. The objective of the state should be to make it worthwhile for those returnees to come and permanently stay in Palestine.

Greater efforts should be made to improve the infrastructure in the areas of agriculture, industry, construction and services. With greater Palestinian control over resources, such as land and water, agriculture will present an attractive area of investment if properly encouraged by the state. Greater access to outside markets after Palestinian independence will create greater opportunities for investment requiring state-encouraged investment in many sectors including energy, transportation, communication and the identification of additional industrial areas. Greater demand for housing will dramatically increase the cost of home ownership unless the state dramatically encourages supply. To encourage investment, the state needs to upgrade current services especially in areas of tourism, transportation, communication, banking and insurance, and internal and external trade.

The absorption of tens of thousands annually will dramatically increase demand for social services, particularly education and health. Greater resources should be directed to these two areas from both the state and the private sector.

Options Regarding the Potential Socio-Political Consequences of Refugee Absorption

Returning refugees with family links to the West Bank and Gaza Strip will find it easy to integrate. But those without such links might find it difficult to adapt to new ways and a new environment. The development of a distinct group of refugees seeing itself in conflict with the rest of the population could pose a serious threat to the socio-political stability of the new state. Other potential sources of threat include tensions emerging from political discontent over what some refugees might view as a state abandonment of their rights, anger and resentment of non-refugees as they suddenly become a minority in the new state, and resentment of resident refugees as they see more resources allocated to help returning ones. The process of absorption might therefore become a source of political and social instability at a time when the state capacity to deal with such problems is low.

As indicated earlier, many groups representing refugee interests are likely to frame the refugee solution in negative terms. One of the potential consequences of such framing would be the development of an antagonistic relationship between the state and the majority of refugees. This problem might be exasperated by the resentment of non-refugees over the fact that within a short period of time, they will be transformed from a majority to a minority. Refugees, or *'Laji'een'* living in the West Bank and the Gaza Strip already feel a certain social discrimination directed at them by the *'muwatineen'*, or non-refugees; they are seen as occupying a lower socio-economic status. Some resident refugees might feel humiliation and embarrassment as it turns out that, contrary to all their previous denials, finally they have indeed decided to abandon return and have decided to stay in the West Bank and Gaza Strip among the *muwatineen*. As 'temporary guests', resident refugees have claimed for themselves certain rights and privileges and asked non-refugees to tolerate hardships in order to support refugees' right of return. Many of the non-refugees might feel greater resentment over the fact that the state would be allocating great resources for the sake of absorbing refugees. Moreover, political considerations, particularly pressure from host countries, might force the new state to put greater emphasis on absorbing returning, rather than resident refugees. This is most likely to lead to anger among resident refugees.

One way of decreasing the chances for conflict is to improve governance, strengthen public institutions, and encourage greater political participation – a topic we have already referred to. Another way is to examine the lessons learned from the process of integration of about 100,000 *'aideen'* or returnees in the mid-1990s in the context of the Oslo implementation and the return of the PLO. Another way of decreasing the chances for conflict over allocation of resources is by providing greater international commitment to the process of absorption. Availability of greater international resources would allow for the simultaneous absorption of resident and returning refugees and would reduce the concerns of non-refugees over the cost of absorption.

Compensation and Restitution

While the refugee solution must address political national aspirations, such as statehood and identity, it must also address the second refugee need: to restore a level of decent living conditions and material benefits. Once they are satisfied with the national good, refugees will ask the personal cost-benefit question: in what way will this solution improve material conditions for me and my family? Generations of refugees have been suffering in misery; once an agreement is reached, expectations will rise sky-high for relief and compensation that ensure every family's future material well-being. Failure to meet this need could seriously impair all efforts to close the file and end the conflict, let alone give the future state legitimacy and stability.

Palestinians expect three types of compensation: 1. for movable and immovable possessions; 2. for pain and suffering and loss of opportunities due to their dispossession; and 3. for the Israeli use of the refugee possessions. They will probably demand compensation to be paid in fixed sums as well as according to the value of possessions, and on a collective basis as well as individually. Moreover, Palestinians are likely to demand the option of returning remaining possessions to their rightful owners. Israel will demand that the peace agreement end all claims and close the refugees' file and it will probably seek a Palestinian agreement not to pursue the restitution of Palestinian property inside Israel. In this context, the 'ending of claims' and 'closing of the file' might not be easy as many refugees might not cooperate in the implementation of the agreement, particularly regarding restitution.

Refugees believe that restitution is an essential component of a just solution and will expect the Palestinian state to protect their right to reject compensation and instead seek restitution. Indeed, they will expect the Palestinian state to support their demands for restitution or at least consider the agreement not binding to individuals wishing to pursue litigation at various Palestinian, Israeli and international courts, or at courts of the countries in which they are citizens. However, if the PLO agreed to accept compensation in lieu of restitution and to accept end of claims, the restitution cases which refugees might submit to courts might become weak. Refugees in this case might blame the PLO and the Palestinian state for squandering their property rights. An agreement that allows refugees to take their restitution cases to courts of their choosing strengthens confidence in the process of compensation and reduces conflict of expectations. One way of strengthening the moral case for restitution is by providing long-term leases for current occupants, so that the restitution act would not be seen as a dispossession of Israelis occupants.

Confidence in the compensation process could be strengthened by creating an international mechanism to implement it, one that is bound by the terms of international law. PSR's refugee surveys showed refugees' confidence in the PLO, which stood high when the matter concerned negotiations to resolve the refugee problem, dropped considerably when it came to the management of compensation, probably due to concerns about corruption. As Table 10.11 shows, the largest percentage (42 per cent) in the West Bank and Gaza Strip favoured a joint team from the PLO, the UN and representatives of refugees. But in Lebanon, the largest percentage (45 per cent) favoured the PLO, and in Jordan, the joint team received 28 per cent, the PLO 22 per cent, and the Jordanian government 23 per cent.

Table 10.11 Refugees' Preferences Regarding the Distribution of Compensation

Who do you think should distribute these compensations to refugees?

	WBGS %	Jordan %	Lebanon %
1. PLO	22.4	21.6	45.4
2. United Nations or another international organization	16.6	15.3	27.1
3. Representatives of refugee camps	15.8	9.3	2.3
4. Lebanese/Jordanian Governments	–	22.9	0.3
5. A joint body made up of all the above parties	41.7	27.6	23.2
6. Other (specify _____)	3.5	3.3	1.7

Source: PSR refugee surveys.

Another issue that has the potential of conflict with refugee expectation is related to the balance between individual and collective (state) compensation. Understandably, refugees are likely to seek greater personal compensation even if that comes at the expense of state compensation. The nature of the compensation for the individual, fixed for all or negotiated case-by-case, might also involve conflict of expectations. To expedite the process of compensation, it would be wise to group together the claims of landless refugees and those with a certain minimum of property claims into a single package, to receive a fixed amount per family. It is likely that such a package would address the compensation needs of the overwhelming majority of refugees. Instead of waiting for years and paying considerable amounts of litigation fees to produce documents that might have been lost, this process would allow for almost immediate payment of compensation. It would also mean avoiding the hugely agonizing family disputes over how to address the question of compensation, given the fact that these properties by now have dozens, if not hundreds of owners. Remaining property owners could then utilize a more effective international mechanism given the dramatic reduction in the number of claimants. This would shorten waiting periods and allow for this matter to be closed relatively fast.

The potential conflict with refugee expectation here involves the concerns of some refugees that any large-scale package of a fixed amount would inevitably underestimate the real value of their property. PSR's refugee surveys found slightly more refugees in the West Bank and Gaza Strip and Jordan preferring compensation in the real value of their property rather than a fixed sum per family. As Table 10.12 shows, only Lebanon's refugees preferred the fixed sum. It is highly unlikely that refugees would oppose the fixed package if the benefits of such a process are clearly felt: immediate payment, no documentation necessary, no family consensus required and no litigation costs.

Table 10.12   Refugees' Preferences Regarding the Value of Compensation

If you accept an option that includes equitable compensation for your property and losses in Israel, would you prefer the compensation to be in the real value of the property and losses, or as a flat-sum compensation to be paid to every family expelled in 1948?

	WBGS %	Jordan %	Lebanon %
1. I prefer compensation in the real value of my property	48.4	48.4	19.4
2. I prefer flat-sum compensation to every family expelled in 1948	46.1	41.7	64.3
3. No opinion/ Do not know	5.5	9.8	16.3

Source: PSR refugee surveys.

Finally, potential conflict of expectations is likely to arise regarding the value of compensation. PSR's refugee surveys asked refugees who opted for a modality of residency and return that involved compensation to make their own estimates of what they thought would be paid to each refugee family and what they thought would be a fair compensation. The estimates for a fair compensation were much higher than the estimates of what would actually be paid. For example,

66 per cent in the West Bank and Gaza Strip believed that what would be paid would be US$100,000 or less, while 65 per cent believed that a fair compensation should be between US$100,000 and US$500,000. One way of meeting the expectations of the refugees is by ensuring that the value of their property is not below the current market value of a similar property in the area where they live. When thinking of the value of their property, most refugees assume it to be equivalent to property in the Palestinian state or host country. For example, when asked if they would accept compensation in kind instead of in cash, as Table 10.13 shows, the majority in the three areas covered by the surveys accepted such compensation.

Table 10.13   Refugees' Views Regarding Compensation in Kind

If you are offered compensation in kind (land or houses) instead of cash, would you accept it?

	WBGS %	Jordan %	Lebanon %
1. Yes	72.6	59.6	53.2
2. No	25.1	26.2	37.3
3. No opinion/Do not know	2.3	14.2	9.5

Source: PSR refugee surveys.

Reconciliation and Psychological 'Well-Being'

A third dimension of refugee expectations is moral, revolving around Palestinian rights, Israeli responsibilities and Arab–Jewish reconciliation. These are the three facets of the refugees' psychological 'well-being'. Addressing them in a satisfactory manner can help refugees overcome psychological barriers and allow them to embrace a refugee solution, even one that does not meet the definition of the refugees' conception of justice. They can finally start a new beginning, one in which they can move beyond their sense of victimhood.

The greater the clarity of the Israeli acknowledgement of suffering and responsibility, the faster the process of reconciliation can move. With their desire for moral vindication clearly met, their narrative accepted, and the feeling that their wait for many decades in refugee camps has not been in vain, refugees can now face up to their own responsibility of being part of their own state, helping to build and strengthen it. By contrast, if the agreement is perceived as an insult, lacking empathy or compassion, and one that implies rejection of their narrative and denial of Israeli responsibility, refugees might fall back on their deep sense of victimhood and reassert their demand for absolute justice, which they know they cannot achieve.

The following is the outline of one paragraph in a preamble to the refugee solution that might meet refugee expectations. It starts by acknowledging the fact that refugees lived in Palestine, Israel before it was established, and that since 1948, they had to endure terrible pain and suffering, without a state of their own. This acknowledgement should be followed by Israeli admission of responsibility for what happened that year, perhaps referring to positive trends within Israel concerning this issue, whereby Israeli 'new historians' have rewritten their historical narrative thus clarifying the Israeli responsibility for expelling a part of the refugees. With admission of responsibility, an expression of regret should follow, one that contains an apology for Israel's role in creating the refugee problem. The statement could then affirm the commitment of the two sides to put this behind them and embark on a process of reconciliation, one in which Israel agrees to put up signs in its territories where Palestinian villages once existed and organize visits for refugees wishing to have a look at the places where their parents or grandparents once lived. For those who want more before closing the books, and perhaps to make reconciliation more meaningful, a mechanism along the lines of a 'truth and reconciliation' committee might be established. In this context, a joint committee of Palestinian and Israeli historians might be tasked with writing a joint narrative of the 1948 war and its immediate aftermath.

Messaging

Messages should focus on all three dimensions of the refugee solution: the national aspirations for state and identity but without losing rights and privileges which they currently enjoy in host countries, the material benefits that come with compensation, and the moral/ethical satisfaction that comes from the acknowledgement of suffering and responsibility. They should emphasize the context of a comprehensive package, a permanent settlement and end of conflict, one in which trade-offs are made, sacrifices are offered, and fairness and relative justice is obtained.

In this overall context, the first message of the refugee solution should be one in which refugee victimhood and the search for justice is finally coming to an end, in a context of rights and needs and *in the context of a two-state solution*. The message should stress that the agreement charts a new beginning, one that delivers end of statelessness, compensation and restitution, and compassion and reconciliation.

The second message to refugees should assert the right of refugees, the Palestinian people, to *self-determination in their own state, a Palestinian state,* ending all forms of statelessness and denial of identity, one in which they, the refugees, are automatically citizens or entitled to become citizens. It is critical that this message be accompanied by another one that addresses potential fears that such gains might come at the cost of losing the rights and privileges which they currently enjoy in host countries. Host countries, who should have been involved in, or at least consulted, during negotiations, should be the ones to affirm such assurances, again and again, to refugees.

The third message should highlight the *lack of compatibility in the demand for the fulfilment of self-determination and the quest for Israeli citizenship.* Repatriation should be defined as the return to one's own country of citizenship, Palestinian citizenship. Although the choice is the refugees', the Palestinian state cannot be expected, nonetheless, to encourage its own people, the Palestinian people, to become citizens of another country, the state of Israel.

The fourth message should focus on the critical need of Palestine to be built by its own people: it is the *duty of Palestinian refugees to build their own state*, not the state of Israel. In this context, return to and absorption in Palestine is not *tawteen* (resettlement), a word completely rejected in refugees' public discourse. The use of this word is akin to raising a red flag.

The fifth message should focus on the material benefits, *compensation, as a right granted to refugees by international law*, including UN Resolution 194. There is nothing to be ashamed of in seeking compensation. Moreover, it should be made clear to heads of households, the older generation of refugees, that it is their *duty to compensate their children* and grandchildren for past suffering and ensure their future material well-being so that they can have the best education, the best health care and the best living conditions which compensation money can buy.

The sixth message should focus on reconciliation. Great injustice was done to innocent Palestinians in 1948; *it will never be possible to undo this injustice*. In this context, while it is the responsibility of the Israelis to acknowledge suffering and responsibility, and while it is the right of refugees to return to their homes and lands, Palestinians should also consider the possible consequences of such action. One of the consequences of returning things to where they were in 1948 might be to inflict an incredible injustice on millions of *innocent Israelis who now live there but who played no role in the catastrophe of 1948*. Instead, refugees should be open to reconciliation if and when Israelis seek it.

Finally, messaging should *be consistent and internally coherent* and should avoid sending conflicting messages from the various parties involved: the Palestinians, the Israelis, the host countries, the donors, the third countries, the international agencies, etc. One cannot say the agreement provides for the 'right of return' while another says it does not; one cannot say that refugees have the right to choose from a number of modalities while another gives a different number or denies altogether the principle of the right to choose.

11

A Never-Ending End to Claims[1]

Geoffrey Aronson

Introduction

There is an argument that any agreement that establishes a Palestinian state at peace with Israel would signify 'an end to claims' by all victims in this conflict and would by necessity have to create agreed mechanisms to define, negotiate, resolve and implement solutions to a complex range of outstanding issues, including most notably the Palestinian refugee issue.

For Israel, an end to claims is embraced as part of the demand to close accounts arising from the *Nakba*, including the implementation of United Nations General Assembly Resolution 194.[2] For Palestinians, an end to claims is promoted as a vehicle for realizing Palestinian demands for a just resolution to Palestinian losses – national, personal and territorial – over the last 70 years. Before leaving office, President Bill Clinton presented, in a White House meeting, US parameters for a final status agreement between Israel and the PLO that 'clearly mark[s] the end of the conflict and its implementation put[s] an end to all claims.'[3] The Clinton Parameters spell out an agreement that will mark out an 'end to the conflict', establishing: 1. a Palestinian state at peace with the state of Israel; and 2. an agreed upon framework for the conduct of peaceful relations between the two states.

Closure can have both legal and moral perspectives that are inter-related when it comes to implementing a peace agreement and achieving reconciliation. The moral perspective is dealt with in Chapter

9 of this book, which focuses on the psychological and more intangible aspects of closure. Legal closure, which is achieved when all claims of the Palestinian refugees have been comprehensively resolved through a legally-binding agreement, is addressed elsewhere in a recent paper commissioned by IDRC.[4] That paper argues that the experiences of other claims programmes and the jurisprudence of national and international courts,

> clearly indicate that it is just as impossible as undesirable to devise a 'water-proof' system that will prevent any legal challenges ... A mechanism for Palestinian refugees will have to balance this right against the need to resolve Palestinian refugee claims in a final and binding manner.

This chapter identifies those arenas for claims that a peace treaty will not, and in some respects cannot address, let alone solve, and those claims that the treaty itself may create – with a focus on issues of relevance to Palestinian refugees. It argues that a peace agreement, no matter how detailed and inclusive, will do many things, but it won't, it simply cannot, do everything. Despite the best efforts of well-intentioned diplomats and politicians, it is asking too much of an agreement to anticipate, understand, resolve, or even to create an operational mechanism that will enable resolution of a comprehensive 'end to claims', let alone the intangible, emotional demands for justice and legitimacy. In this vital sense, the value of a peace agreement between Israel and Palestine, if it ever materializes, runs a very real risk of being oversold. Notwithstanding its very real advantages, a peace treaty is less likely to end the conflict and the claims arising out of it, than to inaugurate a new beginning for airing past disputes as well as those disputes created by the agreement itself. The establishment of the State of Palestine, as a result of a peace agreement, enjoying normal relations with the State of Israel, will not so much end the conflict or its competing claims as it will create what is in many respects an entirely new legal, diplomatic and conceptual framework, and with it, an entirely new set of issues confronting both countries and their citizens. A never-ending 'end to claims' can be expected, despite the best efforts of diplomats to preclude this.[5]

This chapter will refer to the experience of peace treaties between Israel and Egypt, and Israel and Jordan. It is noteworthy that neither of the terms 'end of conflict' or 'end of claims' appear in those treaties – yet another example of the extraordinary nature of the conflict between Israelis and Palestinians, as one that 'covers all the aspects of life'.[6]

Defining, Not Limiting an End to Claims

It is safe to expect that upon signature of a peace deal, expectations will be high. In addition to ending the conflict between the Palestinians and Israelis, a prospective peace treaty between Israel and Palestine will be expected to address the demands for recognition – by Israel, of the historic injustice done to Palestinians – and by Palestinians, of the Jewish state of Israel, described in Chapter 9 as the 'intangible needs'.[7]

Both sides have demands related to this issue beyond the practical solutions and arrangements that are 'intangible' or 'emotional' in nature. Because of this, it is unlikely that the Palestinian refugee issue can be resolved solely through material compensation and logistical mechanisms. These practical measures simply do not go far enough towards addressing what we describe here as 'intangible' needs. Elsewhere, these intangibles are described as the '"emotional" demands' of each side.[8]

This expansive vision of an agreement is embraced, if not with the same aspirations, by many Israelis and Palestinians.

In discussions following the November 2007 Annapolis conference, for example, Israel's foreign minister Tzippi Livni observed, 'Just like Jews dreamt of Israel for thousands of years, I don't think that just getting a cheque from the international community [is enough] ... we need to (make it clear) that the (Palestinian) dream (has to change).'[9]

Palestinians too, harbour expansive views of how to address an 'end to claims'. According to a draft document prepared by the Palestinian Negotiations Support Unit (NSU) in July 2010, for example:

Ending any conflict requires settling all claims arising out of it. Reaching a comprehensive and sustainable peace agreement that ends all claims and redress[es] wrongs committed during the conflict is certainly in the best interest of Palestinians and Israelis. Moreover, an end to claims pertains to all permanent status issues and must be comprehensively addressed to conclusively end the conflict.

Palestinian Claims

Palestine and the Palestinian people have suffered and continue to experience severe losses due to Israel's gross violations of international law, which resulted in considerable suffering, profound underdevelopment, and poverty. The PLO seeks redress for the economic loss and damage resulting from the occupation. In addition, the PLO demands reparations for Israel's wrongs, including restitution and full compensation for material and non-material damages resulting from the following breaches of international law:

- Denial of the Palestinian people's right to self-determination under international law;
- Damages caused by the colonial settlement activity, including the Wall, its associated régime and bypass-roads, as well as the property-related damages and unlawful destruction of public and private property;
- Depletion and illegal exploitation of Palestinian natural resources, including depletion and exploitation of, and failure to develop, Palestinian water resources, natural gas resources, and the electromagnetic spectrum;
- Damage to the environment due to Israeli acts and policies, or Israel's failure to implement sufficient protections;
- Losses resulting from Israel's misuse of Palestinian financial resources, including taxes and custom duties, and failure to use such resources for the benefit of the local population;
- Loss of, as well as damage to, Palestinian cultural property, which requires complete and unqualified restitution of all artifacts and other cultural property illegally removed from the occupied Palestinian territories;
- Violations of international human rights and humanitarian law, including collective punishment.

Failure to address the issue of reparations risks rendering any negotiated agreement illegitimate in the eyes of the Palestinian people because it will signal a failure of the process to address past injustices and the rights and concerns of the Palestinian people. Successfully addressing this issue will suggest to Palestinians that negotiations can deliver the justice required for lasting peace.[10]

In contrast to Israelis who perceive 'end of claims' as a limiting device, the NSU argument could reflect Palestinian negotiators' belief that any agreement should not prematurely declare an 'end to claims' but rather is a mechanism to keep open the implementation process until a comprehensive set of issues related to Palestinian demands have been adequately addressed. Yezid Sayigh, in a memo to the NSU on 23 September 1999, argued for a wide-reaching diplomatic effort to anticipate and address future Palestinian claims. He proposed that a peace agreement should also resolve issues that will 'generate renewed disputes and conflicts in future,' such as 'Israeli laws (citizenship and return, land ownership, etc.) that effectively discriminate between Jews and non-Jews (wherever Israeli law applies, including in Israel proper and in the WBGS) ... The status and rights of the Palestinian citizens of Israel should in particular be addressed as part of a Comprehensive Agreement.'[11]

The first article of the draft agreement produced by the Geneva Initiative in 2003, a document authored by Israeli and Palestinian academics, activists, and current and former officials which offered a model of a possible peace agreement, including a detailed section and annex on refugees, more simply – but nonetheless significantly – notes (Article 1) that the very purpose of the Permanent Status Agreement is to:

'End[s] the era of conflict and usher[s] in a new era based on peace, cooperation, and good neighborly relations between the Parties.'

Furthermore, the agreement will also 'settle all the claims of the Parties arising from events occurring prior to its signature. No further claims related to events prior to this Agreement may be raised by either Party.'

Some, however, argue that a treaty should serve a more limited and traditional diplomatic purpose. Peacemaking, it is argued, is first and foremost about making peace – that is, stopping the shooting and defining borders. As Ehud Barak has said 'We [Israel] are here, and they [Palestine] are there.' And as Egyptian President Anwar Sadat declared in a statement that presciently summed up, and limited, Egypt's peacemaking experience with Israel, 'No More War!'

Dov Weisglas, confidant to Prime Minister Ariel Sharon, wrote in 2010 that,

In the Middle Eastern reality, the peace that is available to Israel is a peace between states and governments, not between peoples. Israel's relations with Egypt and Jordan are relations of peace between governments: no tourism, no scientific, cultural, or athletic cooperation, and virtually no economic ties. We enjoy full diplomatic ties, but most important of all – there is security. Complete quiet reigns on the borders that once knew wars that produced thousands of casualties.[12]

Yet even the hard-boiled Weisglas insists that, 'the central goal of peace should be putting an end to past claims and stringent security measurements that will guarantee peace and calm for both Israelis and the Palestinians. "To live and let live".'

In a similar vein, *Ha'aretz* editor Aluf Benn has written that,

Ending the conflict is a lofty goal, but Netanyahu and 'Abbas will not be able to achieve it. Not because they are bad leaders or because they want the conflict to continue, but because its conclusion does not depend on them. No signature can do away with the conflicting narratives of the two peoples, each considering itself the victim and seeing its rival as an unwanted invader. It is impossible to compromise on a national ethos with the stroke of a pen, and there is no chance today of formulating a joint Israeli–Palestinian narrative. If the negotiations focus on who is right and who is wrong, and who was here first, we can forget about them in advance.

The question of narratives must be left to historians, educators and creators of culture. The statesmen must focus on life's practical aspects and agree on the border in the West Bank and East Jerusalem as well as security arrangements that will ensure stability. The border must make clear where Israel ends and Palestine begins; where we are and where they are.[13]

Israelis opposed to an agreement with the PLO argue that a two-state solution will not end Palestinian claims. Former Israeli foreign minister Avigdor Lieberman, for example, argued,

> Let's assume for a moment that we do withdraw to the '67 lines and we do divide Jerusalem. What would happen the day after? Would there be peace? Would there be security? I can assure you that more demands would be made of us, more pressure would be applied and the conflict would not be over. Withdrawing to the 1967 lines would merely move the conflict closer to Tel Aviv. That's all.[14]

In a poll conducted in November 2010, 41 per cent of East Jerusalem Palestinians polled believe that the 'armed struggle' would continue even after an agreement and an end to the conflict is declared. David Pollock, who conducted the poll for Pechter Polls, noted that 'Yes, this is in fact a realistic assessment of the reality. The Palestinians believe that the peace agreement will resolve neither the violent conflict between the people nor the problem of open borders, free access and other issues.'[15]

Understanding an End to Claims in a Broader Context

There are many precedents to reparations movements that extend for decades, such as that of Holocaust survivors, which could be relevant and inform the post-agreement actions of Palestinians and Israelis alike, especially on the Palestinian refugee issue.[16] Issues relating to rights of residency, refugee return, repatriation, compensation and property claims and rights, freedom of movement across borders, legal status, citizenship and the legal presumption of non-discriminatory treatment on these and other matters, will test the commitment of both nations.

The rights of Palestinian citizens of Palestine, including Palestinian refugees, who are interested for whatever reason in interacting with the state of Israel – buying property or businesses, temporary residence, or immigration and family reunion – will have to be addressed by Israel in an entirely new political, security and diplomatic context. No longer stateless or occupied, the interests, obligations and rights of the citizens of Palestine to conduct commerce, travel, petition for a redress of grievances in Israeli and international fora will test not merely the practical implications of an 'end to the conflict', but more broadly Israel's concept of peace, and the Palestinians' readiness to be reconciled with a state in 22 per cent of Mandate Palestine.

Palestinians will also be challenged to address the claims of Israelis – some whom today may be settlers – to live in, buy property and do business in Palestine, and who themselves may not accept the absence of Jewish sovereignty in 'Judea and Samaria'.

The Jordanian Experience

Since the signature of their peace treaty in 1994, Israel and Jordan have preferred not to forcefully address demands for a resolution of claims, despite the creation of legal and diplomatic mechanisms for doing so. Each has sought, in its own way, to be true to legal and treaty norms and requirements, but the experience has not been without controversy or shortcomings. It serves as a cautionary experience for those with high expectations of dramatic, unambiguous advances on the issue of an end to claims in the context of peace.

Jordan's peace treaty with Israel establishes mechanisms for the bilateral treatment of refugee-related issues without reference to a global, final status resolution of the issue. Jordan's unsuccessful experience in winning Israeli recognition of the property claims of Jordanian citizens, however, offers an instructive demonstration of the extent to which the bilateral Israeli–Palestinian negotiating framework on refugees superseded other avenues of negotiation.

In the wake of the treaty, both countries were obliged to remove any legislation that had the effect of discriminating against the nationals of the other country. Jordanian legal prohibitions on land sales to Jews and Israelis fit into this category and subsequent legislation rescinded such restrictions. The Jordanians, for their part, argued that the large body of Israeli legislation relating to lands owned or claimed by Palestinian refugees, now citizens of a state at peace with Israel, had to be amended in a non-discriminatory fashion. The Israeli Knesset legislated an end to the discriminatory treatment of Jordanian nationals, but the effective date of the legislation was 10 November 1994. Any actions before that date, most particularly the seizure of refugee land and property in the decades since Israel's establishment, remained covered by previous legislation.[17]

In response, Marwan Muasher, at that time Jordan's ambassador in Israel, recalled that he 'wrote to Israel, saying that this treatment was a violation of the treaty prohibiting the existence of discriminatory legislation and that a formal reply was expected. We never received one.'[18] In October 1995, Foreign Minister Shimon Peres met with Crown Prince Hassan in Amman, where the issue was raised once again. According to Muasher, 'Peres said, "Please don't push us."' When Jordan raised the issue with the government of Benjamin Netanyahu, Israeli officials 'claimed ignorance'.

Jordan has also been wary of bilateral Israeli–Palestinian diplomatic efforts to establish their peace treaty as the exclusive forum for the settlement of all claims arising from the conflict. 'This *bilateral* declaration will not be binding to Jordan, which will stress that this text only binds the two sides (Israel and the PLO) and will pursue its rights under international law arising from the conflict (mainly the Jordanian State claims).'[19]

Legal and Judicial Norms in Israel

Israeli practice may at times obstruct an 'end to claims'. In other respects, legal precedent may facilitate their resolution.

The Disposition of Absentee Property

As noted in the case of Israel–Jordan relations, one of the standard features in contemporary peace treaties is a mutual pledge to remove discriminatory legislation and similar barriers to normal relations. An existing and dynamic body of Israeli legislation and practice, however, focuses upon the transfer of refugee properties to Israel/Jewish control, proceeding without reference to the possibility of a peace treaty. To the extent that an agreement to end all claims addressing land and ownership issues, '[Israel's] sale or transfer of refugee properties will complicate the return of Palestinian refugee properties currently held by the state of Israel to their owners.'[20]

Israeli legislation has also created extra-treaty legal and legislative precedents in areas other than those relating to absentee property that may be applicable to the resolution of Palestinians claims. Israel has established legal and judicial frameworks that honour the property claims of Jews in annexed areas of East Jerusalem and the West Bank (i.e. Hebron). In doing so, it also establishes a framework for similar treatment of Palestinian property claims in Israel.[21]

Palestinian Israelis – Part of and Apart from an End to Claims

Palestinian citizens of Israel may well be excluded from the terms of an Israel–PLO peace agreement. In particular, they may be excluded from the mechanisms established for the resolution of refugee claims. In the aftermath of an agreement however, a host of issues, many deferred for decades due to the absence of a final status agreement, as well as others addressed in the new context resulting from such an agreement, will arise, including a range of issues relating to the property rights of Palestinian-Israelis generally and internally-displaced refugees in particular. This process will necessarily include a review of existing Israeli legislation that currently regulates such matters. Will this be a process conducted under the sovereign prerogatives of the State of Israel, as Israel insists, or will it be part of the overall 'end of claims' process?

Sha'ul Ari'eli, a former advisor to Ehud Barak on border and settlement issues, writes that:

> the permanent status issues between Israel and the Palestinians, which today are a central and well-founded part of international processes, will immeasurably increase the interest of other countries and international organizations in relations between the state of Israel and its Arab minority.[22]

'This process broaches the need to deal with a large minority of more than a million Arab citizens, who are fighting from within against Israel's Jewish and democratic identity,' argues Haifa University's Dan Scheuftan. 'This will be Israel's major domestic dilemma, in confronting Europe and the United States. If a solution is found for Israel's conflict with the Palestinians and the Arab world, this is the next area where they will attempt to delegitimize the state.'[23]

The community of internally-displaced persons (IDPs) in Israel numbers between 140,000–250,000. Discussions between IDP representatives and the PLO soon after the Declaration of Principles (DOP) was signed in 1993 initially focused on the issue of the presentation of IDP claims within the context of the Oslo process. Said Suhail M. Miari, a member of the executive committee of the Committee of Displaced Persons in Israel recalled that:

> The PLO told us that the issue of negotiations was sensitive. They explained that our situation was better than others – that at least we were still within Palestine. 'You are in a better economic situation,' we were told. 'We will not forget you in the final status talks.' [But] they also said, 'You are Israeli citizens and you have to address your concerns at an Israeli level.'
>
> After Oslo it became clear to us that no one was going to address the [claims] of internal refugees. We said [to the PLO], 'Since you have abandoned us, we will do it our own way, within Israel's legal parameters.'[24]

However, during the Taba talks, the PLO demanded recognition of its claim to represent property claims of Israeli Arabs not covered by the anticipated final status agreement. 'The PLO wanted to claim some responsibility for this,' explained an Israeli diplomat. 'We said no.'[25]

Family Reunification in Israel

Following a peace agreement, will Israel treat Palestinians like citizens of other states, or will expansive security considerations continue to define treatment of Palestinians?

'There is the principled question that we would like to discuss', noted a Palestinian negotiator during the Annapolis talks, 'which is the following: in a permanent status setting, will citizens of Palestine be treated like the citizens of any other state when it comes to family unification or will they be specifically targeted and excluded.'[26] So for example, will arrangements that enable family unification in Israel or Palestine be in line with international standards? To do so would require changes in Israeli law.

Israeli Claims in the Palestinian State

Establishing an agreed upon border in the West Bank between Israel and Palestine will solve an important element of the Israeli settlements issue – including some settlements within sovereign Israeli territory while requiring the evacuation of the remainder (the issue of letting settlers remain under Palestinian sovereignty has however been raised, most recently by Palestinian negotiators during the Annapolis talks). But drawing an agreed border will not end the dream of 'Greater Israel' and associated efforts by some Israelis to lay claim to the West Bank; it will raise entirely new issues of jurisdiction resulting from the agreement itself.

In the context of Israeli claims for extraterritorial rights in Palestine, PLO negotiators insisted that,

It is our position that Palestine will have full sovereignty and jurisdiction over its territory and all persons present on its territory in conformity with international law, just like any other state. Exceptional categories of arrangements deviating from the general norm of full jurisdiction, if at all, must also confirm to the principle of reciprocity.[27]

It was in this context that Palestinian negotiator Muhammad Dahlan had raised the issue of settler arms in discussions with an Israeli delegation led by Gilad Sher on 18 September 2000. A transcript of Dahlan's remarks prepared by the NSU notes 'concerns regarding the arms of the settlers, who will be remaining for a while. Even though they'll be annexed, they'll be in the heart of our territories. And we have had a terrible problem with the settlers.'[28]

Similar concerns about jurisdiction were raised by Palestinians concerning the issues of Israeli Jewish visitors to holy sites located in Palestine, Israeli technicians sent on the basis of mutual agreement to Palestine, and Israelis using Palestinian roads.

'Palestine will be open to Israeli visitors and worshipers; they shall be afforded the freedom of worship in Jewish holy sites,' noted a Palestinian negotiator, 'but this does not warrant granting Israeli citizens' immunity if they commit crimes.'[29]

During these discussions the Israeli team raised four categories of immunities from Palestinian criminal jurisdiction, including: 1. Israeli soldiers on Palestinian territory pursuant to an agreement; 2. Israeli technicians present in Palestine in order to provide services as per arrangements agreed between the two states on certain issues, e.g. electricity; 3. Israeli civilians traversing Palestinian roads as may be designated safe passage; and 4. Israeli worshipers at Jewish holy sites located in Palestine, e.g. Joseph's Tomb in Nablus.[30]

The Dispute over Residual Authority of the PLO

An agreement between Israel and the PLO will set the terms of peace and establish a framework for the conduct of state-to-state relations. What about those issues affecting the Palestinian (Diaspora) community that the PLO considers to be an inseparable part of its representative mandate not covered or anticipated, ignored or beyond the scope of the agreement? On the one hand, it could be expected that the State of Palestine will assume all applicable obligations of the PLO and PA. Subsequent to the creation of a Palestinian state however, would the PLO maintain residual interest/authority in extraterritorial matters? Or would these issues then become the province of another sovereign state, i.e. Palestine? During the Camp David era, the issue was approached by Palestinian negotiators from a different direction. At that time, Palestinians argued for the PLO – as opposed to the State of Palestine – maintaining extraterritorial 'residual authority' for issues affecting diaspora communities that were not addressed in the peace treaty.

During the Taba talks in particular, the PLO, for its part, was striving for Israeli recognition of a post-agreement PLO mandate to represent the interests of Palestinians beyond its borders. 'The question of the state of Palestine representing refugees in Jordan and Syria is for us a red line,' explained an Israeli official who participated in the Taba talks. 'We said, "No way!" Israel will never recognize the political standing of the state of Palestine vis-à-vis Palestinians [outside Palestine].'[31]

In part, Israel was determined to 'protect Jordan from Palestinian irredentist inclinations or unfair division of the compensation package,' inclinations represented, in Israel's view, by the PLO demand for residual responsibility beyond its borders. This demand for residual responsibility was described by one Israeli diplomat not only as the PLO's 'long arm into Jordan', but the organisation's 'short arm into Israel'. That is, Israel was determined not to establish for the PLO any recognized standing among Israel's Palestinian minority, be they refugees or not.

The issue has been raised once again in the context of the PLO's application to the UN in September 2011. In November 2012, the UN General assembly voted to upgrade the PLO status to that of a 'non-member observer state' compared to its previous 'permanent observer' status. The PLO chairman Mahmoud Abbas explained that the PLO would retain residual responsibilities after a UN recognition of statehood.

> The Palestinian Liberation Organization represents all Palestinian people, not only those who live on the Palestinian land and they are estimated to be 4 million people, but also represents all the Palestinians who live everywhere in the world and they are estimated to be 8 million people. This organization will keep working until the case is completely over and solved in all aspects including the issue of the refugees and other issues. Therefore, the organization will remain...[32]

Concerns have nevertheless been raised that UN recognition of statehood might not only precipitate a division of Palestinian representation but might also prejudice outstanding refugee claims by removing them from the debate over statehood.

Host Country Claims – The Jordanian Example

Based upon its actions during the Taba and Annapolis talks, Jordan appears satisfied with a negotiating framework in which the general modalities of a compensation regime will be agreed upon bilaterally – by Israel and the PLO – leaving the details to be negotiated in a wider forum in which they will play a central role. Article 24 of the Israel–Jordan peace treaty also was mentioned by one former senior official as an important mechanism for the resolution of financial claims against Israel.[33] Jordan cannot be seen to be usurping the sovereign prerogatives of the PLO, charged as it is with representing Palestinian interests. In practice, this consideration has meant a Jordanian deferral, however wary, to the PLO.[34]

'After the basic understandings are reached,' explained a very senior Jordanian official, 'the three of us [Israel, Jordan, and the PLO] will sit together' and work out the details.[35]

These basic understandings must in Jordan's view establish a mechanism for the contribution of significant sums to state coffers if only because Jordanians will then feel that they also are sharing in the benefits from a resolution of this issue and will be therefore less likely to oppose the subsequent rehabilitation of and integration of those Palestinians remaining in Jordan. 'The state needs money to close the gap between Palestinians and Jordanians,' explained a Jordanian journalist. 'If there is no money for Jordan it will be a recipe for catastrophe.'[36]

When bilateral diplomacy resumed via the Annapolis discussions, Jordan once again demanded recognition of its standing to represent the claims of Palestinians, including refugees, who are Jordanian citizens. In a 4 September 2008 letter to Israel, the Jordanian foreign minister wrote that Jordan,

> reserves its rights under international law and the 1994 Treaty of Peace in relation to the refugee issue and would not acquiesce to any process or resolution to which it is not a party that would exclude or limit its legal standing and rights relating to the refugee issue, including state rights and individual rights.[37]

Non-refugee-related Claims

Although outside of the scope of this chapter focusing on Palestinian refugees, it is worth mentioning other non-refugee related claims and issues which are likely to arise following a peace agreement. As argued in this chapter, these issues offer a cautionary example to those confident of achieving a 'full and final' settlement of claims arising out of the conflict as well as those new claims that result from such a settlement. These are: *settler compensation*, the precedent for which arose out of Israel's disengagement from the Gaza Strip in 2005 and the ensuing evacuation of approximately 1,500 families from Gaza's 17 settlements, a total population of approximately 7,500. This new class of claimants has been the subject of tortuous and often acrimonious compensation efforts – addressed in a seemingly endless saga of legislative, legal, judicial and public efforts.

Another new class of claimants may be those individual Palestinians who suffered *losses incurred during occupation*, such as land confiscation and land seizure and loss of livelihood, some incurred as a result of the building of the separation barrier in the West Bank to separate Israelis and Palestinians there. Such losses were enumerated by the Palestinians during the Annapolis talks as an integral part of the discussion of an end to claims,[38] while Israel maintained that compensation for such claims is not one of the permanent status issues under the Oslo Declaration of Principles. Finally, *land swaps* or the exchange of territory as part of the demarcation of agreed borders between Israel and Palestine will create new classes of Palestinians and Israelis impacted by an agreement, from whom an entirely new set of claims can be expected.

Conclusion

The yearning for an end to the conflict and a final and complete settlement of outstanding claims is a laudable objective, and one that has inspired the so far unrewarded efforts of peacemakers over many decades. When a treaty of peace between Israel and Palestine is, at long last, signed, a new era in relations will dawn. Implicit and widespread assumptions for 'an end to claims' are most surely misplaced. A territorial division of Palestine and the creation of a Palestinian state in the West Bank and Gaza Strip will create a new playing field upon which continuing debate over nationality and territory will be conducted. Those asserting disadvantage as a consequence of these new arrangements – for claims both old and new – will not rest quietly.

Notes

1. This chapter refers to documents from 'The Palestine Papers', as released in 2010 by Al Jazeera Television. The documents referenced in this paper can be found by using the search function at: thepalestinepapers.com/Services/Search/default.aspx
2. AJPP Document 113, 'Non-Paper: Palestinian Refugee Problem', 23 January 2001; AJPP Document 7, 'Non-Paper: Draft Framework Agreement on Permanent Status', 1 May 2000.

3. AJPP Document 48, 'Meeting with President Clinton', 23 December 2000.
4. See Heike Niebergall and Norbert Wühler (International Organization for Migration), Development of Three 'Technical Options Papers on Aspects of a Just and Comprehensive Solution for Palestinian Refugees', on the subjects of *Inheritance Regimes, Organizational Structures, and Legal Closure*, November 2012, prepared for IDRC.
5. AJPP Document 2831, 'Joint Agreement – Article 15 – End of Conflict and Finality of Claims', 2 July 2008.
6. AJPP Document 38 'Permanent Status Negotiating Session – Saeb Erekat and Gilad Sher', 18 September 2000.
7. See Chapter 9.
8. Weisglas, see, 'Between Governments Not Between Peoples', *Yediot Ahronoth*, 21 September 2010.
9. AJPP Document 2437, 'Minutes from Plenary Session Post-Annapolis', 24 March 2008.
10. 'End of Claims Non-Paper', no attribution, July 2010.
11. AJPP Document 2, 'Yezid Sayigh Memo Re: NSU Negotiating Strategy', 30 September 1999.
12. 'Between Governments Not Between Peoples', *Yediot Ahronoth*, 21 September 2010.
13. *Ha'aretz*, 8 September 2010.
14. *Ma'ariv,* 2 June 2011.
15. 'Feeling at Home – The Palestinians of East Jerusalem: What Do They Really Want?' *Ma'ariv*, 6 May 2011. (Findings from a survey conducted by Pechter Middle East Polls in partnership with the Council on Foreign Relations, 12 January 2011).
16. A group of Israeli Holocaust survivors, who were born in Austria, are working to reopen the symbolic compensation agreement signed by the Austrians a decade ago, and demand: 'Pay us for all the property you robbed from us.' The value of the Jewish property was estimated in the past by Austrian historians at about EUR 15 million, without interest.

    Since the Austrian and American governments signed the symbolic agreement in 2001, Holocaust survivors have filed claims in a total amount of about EUR 1.5 billion (without added interest). However, in the agreement it was determined that Austria would transfer a total of USD 210 million in compensation to the Holocaust survivors and their descendants, and therefore, in most cases, only about 10 per cent of the amount specified in the claim were paid... Eldad Beck, *Yediot Ahronoth*, 15 August 2011.
17. Marwan Muasher, interview, 14 February 2001, 26 August 2011; *Sefer Ha'Hokim (Book of Laws)*, 111. Restatement of the Treaty of Peace between Israel and the Hashemite Kingdom of Jordan, 1995. Paragraph 6 (A). Although whatever is said in the law of property of present absentees from 1950, starting November 10, 1994, there will not be property for a present absentee for this alone: that the person who [claims] a right to it was a citizen or a native of Jordan or was in Jordan after this date (Hebrew). *Ha'tzaot Hok (Suggestions for Law)*, 253. Explanation of Paragraph 6: The

law of property of present absentees, 1950, indicates the legal situation with regard to the property rights of those that were in a situation of war with Israel during the War of Independence. Within the expression of the peace agreement between Israel and Jordan and the relationship that was created in its aftermath, is found that the property rights that were created in Israel will be like those of citizens of other countries, and these properties will not turn into property of present absentees. The status of property that was property of present absentees before the peace treaty will not change.

This paragraph does not deal with the subject of refugees and displaced that the peace treaty deals with specifically (Translated from Hebrew).

18. Ibid.
19. AJPP Document 2854, 'Jordanian comments on Palestinian Agreement Draft – Refugees and Finality', 20 June 2008.
20. 'At least since 2007, the Israel Lands Administration (ILA) has been engaged in the sale of properties belonging to Palestinian refugees. As of June 2009, some 282 tenders had been published by the ILA for the sale of so-called "absentee" properties. In addition, recent legislation passed by the Israeli Knesset on 3 August 2009 will initiate broad land reforms that will have adverse effects on Palestinian refugee property rights. Adalah – the Legal Centre for Arab Minority Rights in Israel has stated that the new law 'will lead to the transfer of title to private owners in real estate properties which were expropriated by the state from the Palestinian Arab population. The law will also lead to privatization of property of some of the lands of destroyed and evacuated Arab villages, as well as many properties belonging to Palestinian refugees, which are currently controlled by the state's Custodian of Absentee Property and the Development Authority.'

'If and when Palestinians seek the restitution of refugee property, it may be expected that Israel will argue that in cases where properties were transferred to third parties restitution is either materially impossible or imposes an undue burden.

The sale of refugee properties constitutes an on-going violation of Palestinian collective and individual rights that causes continuous damage to Palestinian interests, particularly those interests relating to the right to property restitution. AJPP Document 4810, 'NSU Paper: Refugees – Issue Overview and Guidelines', September 2009.

21. The occupation of East Jerusalem created two classes. The Arabs who lost their homes in West Jerusalem in 1948 were not permitted to demand their property back. At most, they could request compensation for the nominal value of their property – which was no more than a mockery. However, Jews who lost their homes in East Jerusalem could receive their property back. They received it even if they had previously received other housing. By law, the custodian general is required to release the property to them. The law bars him from exercising judgment.

The Knesset passed this apartheid law in the euphoric period between the Six-Day War and the Yom Kippur War. The Supreme Court adopted it without reservation. This cooperation explains why the courts did not dare block the dispossession of the Arabs in the Sheikh Jarrah neighbourhood.

The Sephardic Community Committee and the Knesset Israel Committee were given ownership of the compound in Sheikh Jarrah. They demanded rent from the Arab tenants. The tenants refused to pay. The committees sued them and won. In the meantime, they sold the ownership of the compound to a right-wing non-profit organization (NPO). The NPO demanded that the court instruct the eviction of the Arabs. The first eviction was carried out in November 2008. The second eviction was in August 2009. Demolition and eviction orders are pending against more families ... Nahum Barnea, 'Evacuation, Construction, Condemnation', *Yedioth Ahronoth*, 12 November 2010.

22. Sha'ul Ari'eli, Doubi Schwartz and Hadas Tagari. *Injustice and Folly: On the Proposals to Cede Arab Localities from Israel to Palestine*, Floersheimer Institute for Policy Studies, Hebrew University of Jerusalem, 2006.
23. Roni Shaked, 'The Arab Minority is Looking for One Thing: The Destruction of the State', *Yediot Ahronoth*, 15 April 2011.
24. Suhail Miari, interview, 7 November 2001.
25. Interview, 21 November 2001.
26. AJPP Document 3356, 'Minutes from the 8th Meeting of the Joint Legal Committee', 14 August 2008.
27. AJPP Document 2594, 'Talking Points for the Plenary Meeting with the Legal Committee', 20 May 2008.
28. AJPP Document 38 'Permanent Status Negotiating Session – Saeb Erekat and Gilad Sher', 18 September 2000.
29. AJPP Document 2594, 'Talking Points for the Plenary Meeting with the Legal Committee', 20 May 2008.
30. Ibid.
31. Interview, 26 November 2001.
32. *Al-Watan* (Qatar), 28 August 2011.
33. Former Minister of Foreign Affairs of the Hashemite Kingdom of Jordan, Kamel Abu Jabber, interview, 22 September 2001.
34. Former Minister in charge of the Occupied Territories, Marwan Dudin, interview, 23 September 2001.
35. Interview, 22 September 2001.
36. Interview, 23 September 2001.
37. AJPP Document 3263, 'Jordanian Letter to Israel Regarding Refugees', 9 September 2008.
38. 'End of Claims Non-Paper', no attribution, July 2010; AJPP Document 3357, Minutes from the 9th Meeting of the Joint Legal Committee, 22 September 2008.

Notes on Contributors

Ian B. Anderson is a former development officer of the Canadian International Development Agency, who was posted to the Kandahar Provincial Reconstruction Team in Kandahar, Afghanistan (2010–2011). He was an international development fellow of the Aga Khan Foundation in Kulob, Tajikistan (2009–2010), and worked as a research assistant on a number of Track II diplomacy projects focused on the Middle East and South Asia (2007–2009). Ian Anderson now serves as a national security analyst for the Government of Canada.

Geoffrey Aronson is the Director of Research and Publications and is the Editor of the Foundation's bimonthly Report on Israeli Settlement in the Occupied Territories. A journalist and historian who has published widely on international affairs and a former visiting fellow at Georgetown University, he is the author of *Israel, Palestinians and the Intifada: Creating Facts on the West Bank* (Kegan Paul International, 1990) and *From Sideshow to Center Stage: U.S. Policy Toward Egypt, 1946–1956* (Lynne Rienner, 1986).

John Bell is Director of the Middle East and Mediterranean Programme at the Toledo International Centre for Peace in Madrid. He was formerly Middle East Director in Jerusalem for Search for Common Ground, a global conflict resolution organization. He is also a former United Nations and Canadian diplomat who served as a political officer at Canada's embassy in Cairo, a member of Canada's delegation to the Refugee Working Group in the peace process, Political Advisor to the Personal Representative of the Secretary-General of the United Nations for southern Lebanon, advisor to the Canadian Government during the Iraq crisis in 2002–03 and Consultant to the International Crisis Group on developments in Jerusalem. He is also a founding member of the 'Jerusalem Old City Initiative' (University of Windsor), an effort to find creative options for this contentious issue. John Bell also has extensive experience in communications as spokesperson for the Canadian Department of Foreign Affairs and Communications Coordinator for the Signing Conference for the International Treaty to Ban Landmines in Ottawa, 1997.

Liana Brooks-Rubin is a former Deputy Director of the US Department of State's Bureau of Population, Refugees, and Migration in the Office of Assistance to Asia and the Near East (PRM/ANE) where she advised on policy, operations and budget relating to Palestinian, Iraqi, Yemeni, Tibetan, Sri Lankan, Burmese and Lao Hmong refugees, and conflict victims. In recognition of her work on behalf of refugees in the Middle East and Asia, Liana Brooks-Rubin won the prestigious Warren Christopher Award for Outstanding Achievement in Global Affairs in November 2009. During her tenure in PRM, Liana Brooks-Rubin also held the position in Washington of Senior Palestinian Program officer and at the US Consulate in Jerusalem of Acting Regional Refugee Coordinator for Palestinian refugees. Liana Brooks-Rubin holds dual master's degrees in Public Affairs and in Middle Eastern Studies from the University of Texas in Austin.

Rex Brynen is Professor of Political Science at McGill University and coordinator of Palestinian Refugee ResearchNet (www.prrn.org). He is author of *A Very Political Economy: Peacebuilding and Foreign Aid in the West Bank and Gaza* (United States Institute of Peace, 2000) and *Sanctuary and Survival: The PLO in Lebanon* (Continuum International, 1990), co-editor (with Roula El-Rifai) of *Compensation to Palestinian Refugees and the Search for Palestinian–Israeli Peace* (Pluto Press, 2013) and *Palestinian Refugees: Challenges of Repatriation and Development* (I.B. Tauris, 2007), and editor or co-editor of six other books. In addition to his academic work, Prof. Brynen has served as a member of the Canadian Department of Foreign Affairs and International Trade, and as a consultant to the Canadian International Development Agency, the International Development Research Centre, the World Bank, the United Nations and others.

Roula El-Rifai is a Senior Program Specialist with the Governance, Security and Justice Programme Initiative at the International Development Research Centre (IDRC) in Ottawa. She was formerly the Coordinator of IDRC's Middle East Unit. She has worked extensively since 1999 on the Palestinian refugee issue and the Middle East Peace Process, and on governance and reform issues in the Arab world. She is co-editor (with Rex Brynen) of *Compensation to Palestinian Refugees and the Search for Palestinian–Israeli Peace* (Pluto Press, 2013) and *Palestinian Refugees: Challenges of Repatriation and Development* (I.B. Tauris, 2007).

Michael R. Fischbach is professor of history at Randolph-Macon College in Ashland, Virginia, USA. He researches and writes about land and property ownership in the modern Middle East, particularly in connection with Israel/Palestine, Jordan, and the Arab–Israeli conflict. Michael Fischbach is the author of *Jewish Property Claims Against Arab Countries* (Columbia

University Press, 2008); *The Peace Process and Palestinian Refugee Claims: Addressing Claims for Property Compensation and Restitution* (United States Institute of Peace Press, 2006); *Records of Dispossession: Palestinian Refugee Property and the Arab–Israeli Conflict* (Columbia University Press, 2003); and *State, Society, and Land in Jordan* (Brill, 2000).

Michael Molloy is a former official at the Department of Foreign Affairs and International Trade and Citizenship and Immigration Canada with 35 years of experience in international affairs. His involvement in Middle East affairs includes his role as Canada's Ambassador to Jordan (1996–2000), Special Coordinator for the peace process at DFAIT (2000–03) and Advisor to the Canadian delegation to the Refugee Working Group in the multilateral peace process (1993–96). An expert in global refugee affairs, Michael Molloy coordinated the movement of 60,000 Indochinese Refugees to Canada (1979–80) and served as Director General for Refugee Affairs at Immigration Canada (1989–91) and Director General, Citizenship and Immigration Operations, Ontario. (1994–96). He is a Senior Fellow at the University of Ottawa's Graduate School of Public and International Affairs, Co-Director of the Jerusalem Old City Initiative at the University of Windsor and President of the Canadian Immigration Historical Society.

Heike Niebergall works as a Senior Legal Officer in the Land, Property and Reparations Division of the International Organization for Migration (IOM) in Geneva, Switzerland. She provides technical assistance and capacity building services in the area of property restitution and victims' redress to transitional governments and international actors engaged in post-conflict, reconciliation and rehabilitation efforts. She has worked on reparation and transitional justice issues in, amongst other countries, Cambodia, Sierra Leone and Iraq. Prior to IOM, Heike Niebergall was Deputy-Secretary General of the Claims Resolution Tribunal for Dormant Accounts in Switzerland. She studied law at the University of Passau (Germany) and at King's College London (UK) and in 2003 earned an LL.M. in international and comparative law from the George Washington University in Washington DC (USA). She co-edited with Norbert Wühler an IOM publication titled: *Property Restitution and Compensation – Practices and Experiences of Claims Programmes* (2008).

Nadim Shehadi is an Associate Fellow of the Royal Institute of International Affairs, Chatham House, where he directs a programme on the regional dimension of the Palestinian refugee issue in the Middle East Peace Process. He is also a senior member of St Antony's College,

Oxford where he was Director of the Centre for Lebanese Studies from 1986–2005. Mr. Shehadi is a member of the executive board of the Centro de Estudios de Oriente Medio of the Fundación Promoción Social de la Cultura in Madrid. In 2010 he was a visiting fellow at the Aspen Institute in Washington DC and in the summer semester of 2012 he was a visiting scholar at Tufts University. He is also a consultant to several governments and international organizations. Nadim Shehadi was trained as an economist with an interest in the history of economic thought. He has several publications and contributes regularly to the media on Middle Eastern affairs.

Khalil Shikaki is a Professor of Political Science and director of the Palestinian Center for Policy and Survey Research (Ramallah). Since 2005 he has been a senior fellow at the Crown Center for Middle East Studies at Brandeis University. He finished his PhD in Political Science from Columbia University in 1985, and taught at several Palestinian and American universities. Between 1996–99, Dr. Shikaki served as Dean of Scientific Research at al Najah University in Nablus. He spent summer 2002 as a visiting fellow at the Brookings Institution in Washington DC. Since 1993, Dr. Shikaki has conducted more than 200 polls among Palestinians in the West Bank and the Gaza Strip and, since 2000, dozens of joint polls among Palestinians and Israelis. His research has focused on the peace process, Palestinian state building, public opinion, transition to democracy, and the impact of domestic Palestinian politics on the peace process. He is the co-author of the annual report of the *Arab Democracy Index*. His recent publications include 'Coping with the Arab Spring; Palestinian Domestic and Regional Ramifications', *Middle East Brief*, no. 58, Crown Center for Middle East Policy, Brandeis University, December 2011; and *Public Opinion in the Israeli–Palestinian Conflict: The Public Imperative During the Second Intifada*, with Yaacov Shamir, (Indiana University Press, 2010).

Nicole Waintraub is a facilitator and project manager at the University of Ottawa. She facilitates Track II dialogues on Middle East and South Asia issues.

Norbert Wühler is the former Director of Reparation Programmes at the International Organization for Migration (IOM) in Geneva, Switzerland. During his tenure, he was responsible for the implementation of the German Forced Labour Compensation Programme (GFLCP) and the Holocaust Victim Assets Programme (HVAP), and provided expert advice and assistance to claims and restitution commissions and programmes in

Bosnia-Herzegovina, Iraq, Colombia, Nepal and Turkey. Dr. Wühler's other relevant experience includes: Member of the Kosovo Property Claims Commission (KPCC) (since 2007); Chief of the Legal Services Branch, United Nations Compensation Commission (1992–2000); Legal Adviser to the President and Deputy Secretary-General, Iran–United States Claims Tribunal (1983–1991); Member of the Steering Committee on Mass Claims Processes, Permanent Court of Arbitration; and Member of the Advisory Group on Victims Participation and Reparations, International Criminal Court. He co-edited with Heike Niebergall an IOM publication titled: *Property Restitution and Compensation – Practices and Experiences of Claims Programmes* (2008).

Index

Compiled by Sue Carlton

Page numbers followed by 'n' refer to end of chapter notes